From the Library of

MYSTERIES OF GENESIS

Unity Classic Library Series
Offers Timeless Titles of Spiritual Renewal

Every book in this series has earned the "classic" status due to its popularity, durability, and uncompromising quality. Each brings a special viewpoint and understanding of the beliefs and principles of Unity. Each book is a respected addition to any metaphysical collection.

MYSTERIES OF GENESIS

CHARLES FILLMORE

Unity Classic Library

Unity Village, Missouri

"Unity is a link in the great educational movement inaugurated by Jesus Christ; our objective is to discern the Truth in Christianity and prove it. The Truth that we teach is not new, neither do we claim special revelations or discovery of new religious principles. Our purpose is to help and teach humankind to use and prove the eternal Truth taught by the Master."

—Charles Fillmore
Co-founder of Unity

Mysteries of Genesis is a member of the Unity Classic Library.

To place an order, call the Customer Service Department at 1-800-669-0282 or visit us online at *www.unitybooks.org*. For information, write to Unity Books, 1901 NW Blue Parkway, Unity Village, MO 64065-0001.

Sixteenth printing 1998
Second edition 2007, fourth printing 2012

Library of Congress Cataloging-in-Publication Data
Fillmore, Charles, 1854-1948.
    Mysteries of Genesis / Charles Fillmore. — Rev. and enl.
        p. cm.
    Includes bibliographical references and index.
    ISBN 0-87159-219-3
    Softcover: ISBN 0-87159-219-3
            ISBN 978-0-87159-219-4

    1. Bible. O.T. Genesis—Miscellanea. 2. Unity School of Christianity—Doctrines.   I. Title.
BS1235.F47   1998
222'.1106—dc21   97-44069
                                                              CIP

Canada BN 13252 9033 RT

"The Bible is the history of man. In its sixty-six books it describes in allegory, prophecy, epistle, parable, and poem, man's generation, degeneration, and regeneration. It has been preserved and prized beyond all other books because it teaches man how to develop the highest principle of his being, the spirit. As man is a threefold being, spirit, soul, and body, so the Bible is a trinity in unity. It is body as a book of history; soul as a teacher of morals; and spirit as a teacher of the mysteries of being."

Charles Fillmore

CONTENTS

FOREWORD

THE BOOK OF GENESIS is the key to the Bible. In the New Testament it is quoted twenty-seven times literally and thirty-eight times substantially. It tells in a very few words how God first imaged man and the universe and then turned the development over to Jehovah, who has been in a process of manifestation for ages and aeons.

The "Five Books of Moses," of which Genesis is the first, have always been credited to Moses, but that he was the author seems doubtful in the face of the many stories of creation found in the legends and ·hieroglyphs of ancient Egypt, Chaldea, and other nations that are almost identical with those of Genesis. It would thus seem that Moses edited the legends of the ages and compiled them into an allegorical history of creation.

As printed in English translations there is little to reconcile Genesis with creation as revealed by modern geology. It is said that Hugh Miller, the brilliant Scottish geologist, went insane in his efforts to reconcile Genesis with the geological record. However more accurate translations of the Hebrew show that the literal reading of the English is often not warranted by the original text. For example, the English Bible reads, "In the beginning God created the heavens and the earth." Fentons translation renders it thus: "By periods God created that which produced the Suns; then that which produced the Earth." When we realize that God is mind (Spirit-mind), we see that this latter rendition is correct. God creates the ideas that form the things. Here we have the key that unlocks not only the mysteries of Genesis but the whole Bible. God's creations are always spiritual. This includes the spiritual man, called Jehovah, through whom all things, including personal man, Adam, are brought into manifestation.

We ask our readers to dwell on this initial proposition until its truth is established in consciousness, because it is repeated over and over in both the Old and the New Testament. Jesus said, "I speak not from myself: but the Father abiding in me doeth his works." Jesus was here referring both to His personality, the external I, and to the inner spiritual entity that He named the Father, in Genesis called Jehovah.

Hebrew words are composite; they contain a variety of meanings, to be determined by the context. For example the Hebrew word *yom*, translated "day" in the English Bible, means "to be hot"; that is, with reference to the heat of the day as compared with the cool of the night. The word *yom* was also used to represent a period of time, an age.

It will readily be seen that the translator had a rich field of ideas from which to choose and that he could make his text historical or symbolical according to his consciousness. If he thought the original story was a statement of facts his translation would be to that end. The Pharisees of Jesus' time were condemned by Him for teaching the letter of the Scriptures and neglecting the spirit. The same charge can be brought today against those who study the Bible as history rather than as parable and idealistic illustration of the spiritual unfoldment of man.

The Bible veils in its history the march of man from innocence and ignorance to a measure of sophistication and understanding. Over all hovers the divine idea of man, the perfect-man pattern, the Lord, who is a perpetual source of inspiration and power for every man. Those who seek to know this Lord and His manifestation, Jesus Christ, receive a certain spiritual quickening that opens the inner eye of the soul and they see beyond the land of shadows into the world of Spirit.

The truths in this book will be revealed to you through your own spiritual unfoldment. Spiritual things are spiritually discerned. The spiritual revelations that you seem to get from books and teachers already existed as submerged experiences in your own soul. The essential truths have been worked out in this or previous incarnations, and when you were reminded of the buried idea it blazed forth as a light from without. So all that you are or ever will be must come from your own spiritual achievements.

"Seek, and ye shall find; knock, and it shall be opened unto you."

Chapter I

Spiritual Man

GENESIS 1

THE WORD *genesis* means "source" or "origin." It points to new birth and to the perfection of man in the regeneration. The law of generation is undoubtedly one of the mysteries in human consciousness. Men have probed with more or less success nearly every secret of nature, but of the origin of life they know comparatively nothing. In the matter of life we discover that the clues given us by our own experience point to intelligence as well as force. In other words, life falls short of its mission if it is not balanced by intelligence.

Man is constantly seeking to know the origin of both the universe and himself. But nearly all his research of a scientific nature has been on the material plane. As a rule, he has ascribed the beginning to matter, to atoms and cells, but much has eluded his grasp because their action is invisible to the eye of sense. Now we are beginning in the realm of mind a scientific search for the origin of all things. We say "scientific" because the discoveries that come from a right understanding of mind and its potentialities can be arranged in an orderly way and because they prove themselves by the application of their laws.

What is stated in the Book of Genesis in the form of allegory can be reduced to ideas, and these ideas can be worked out by the guidance of mental laws.

9

Thus a right understanding of mind, and especially of Divine Mind, is the one and only logical key to an understanding of the beginnings of man and the universe. In this book we have many symbols explained and their meaning interpreted, so that anyone who sets himself the task can understand and also apply to his own development the rules and laws by which ideas are related to one another and discover how they are incorporated into man's consciousness, thus giving him the key to the unfoldment of the primal ideas implanted in him from the beginning.

It is found that what is true in the creation of the universe (as allegorically stated in Genesis) is equally true in the unfoldment of man's mind and body, because man is the microcosmic copy of the "Grand Man" of the universe.

The Bible is the history of man. In its sixty-six books it describes in allegory, prophecy, epistle, parable, and poem, man's generation, degeneration, and regeneration. It has been preserved and prized beyond all other books because it teaches man how to develop the highest principle of his being, the spirit. As man is a threefold being, spirit, soul, and body, so the Bible is a trinity in unity. It is body as a book of history; soul as a teacher of morals; and spirit as a teacher of the mysteries of being.

The student of history finds the Bible interesting if not wholly accurate; the faithful good man finds in it that which strengthens his righteousness, and the overcomer with Christ finds it to be the greatest of all books as a guide to his spiritual unfoldment. But it must be read in the spirit if the reader is to get the lesson it teaches. The key to its spiritual meaning is that back of every mentioned thing is an idea.

The Bible will be more readily understood if the fact is kept in mind that the words used have both an inner and an outer significance. Studied historically and intellectually, the external only is discerned and the living inner reality is overlooked. In these lessons we shall seek to understand and to reveal the within, and trace the lawful and orderly connection between the within and the without.

Genesis, historically considered, falls into three parts: first, the period from the creation to the Flood; secondly, the period from the Flood to the call of Abraham; and thirdly, the period from the call of Abraham to the death of Joseph.

The 1st chapter describes creation as accomplished in six days, and refers to a seventh day of rest. There is no reason to believe that these days were twenty-four hours in length. "One day is with the Lord as a thousand years, and a thousand years as one day." They simply represent periods of development or degrees of mind unfoldment.

Numbers are used throughout the Bible in connection with faculties or ideas in Divine Mind. There are twelve divine faculties. They are symbolized in the Old Testament by the twelve sons of Jacob and in the New Testament by the twelve apostles of Jesus. All of these have a threefold character: first, as absolute ideas in Divine Mind; secondly, as thoughts, which are ideas in expression but not manifest; and thirdly, as manifestations of thoughts, which we call things. In man this threefold character is known as spirit, soul, and body. Therefore in studying man as the offspring of God it is necessary to distinguish between the facul-

ties as they exist in the body. We find heaven to be the
orderly arrangement of divine ideas within man's true
being. Earth is the outer manifestation of those ideas,
this manifestation being man's body.

In the 1st chapter of Genesis it is the great creative
Mind that is at work. The record portrays just how
divine ideas were brought into expression. As man must
have an idea before he can bring an idea into manifestation, so it is with the creations of God. When a man
builds a house he builds it first in his mind. He has the
idea of a house, he completes the plan in his mind,
and then he works it out in manifestation. Thus God
created the universe. The 1st chapter of Genesis describes the ideal creation.

The 1st chapter shows two parts of the Trinity:
mind, and idea in mind. In the 2d chapter we have the
third part, manifestation. In this illustration all theo-
logical mystery about the Trinity is cleared away, for
we see that it is simply mind, idea in mind, and manifestation of idea. Since man is the offspring of God,
made in the image and likeness of Divine Mind, he
must express himself under the laws of this great
creative Mind. The law of manifestation for man is
the law of thought. God ideates: man thinks. One is the
completion of the other in mind.

The man that God created in His own image and
likeness and pronounced good and very good is spiritual
man. This man is the direct offspring of Divine Mind,
God's idea of perfect man. This is the only-begotten
Son, the Christ, the Lord God, the Jehovah, the I AM.
In the 2d chapter this Jehovah or divine idea of perfect
man forms the manifest man and calls his name Adam.

The whole of the 1st chapter is a supermental statement of the ideas on which evolution is based. Mind projects its ideas into universal substance, and evolution is the manifestation of the ideas thus projected. The whole Genesiac record is an allegory explaining just what takes place in the mind of each individual in his unfoldment from the idea to the manifest. God, the great universal Mind, brought forth an idea, a man, perfect like Himself, and that perfect man is potentially in every individual, working himself into manifestation in compliance with law.

> *Gen. 1:1-5.* In the beginning God created the heavens and the earth. And the earth was waste and void; and darkness was upon the face of the deep: and the Spirit of God moved upon the face of the waters. And God said, Let there be light: and there was light. And God saw the light, that it was good: and God divided the light from the darkness. And God called the light Day, and the darkness he called Night. And there was evening and there was morning, one day.

To understand the creation of the universe by God, we must know something of the character of God. Jesus said, "God is Spirit." The works of God, He said, were done in Him (Jesus) and through Him. "The Father abiding in me doeth his works." That God is an intelligent force always present and always active is the virtual conclusion of all philosophers, thus corroborating the statements of Jesus. God is eternally in His creation and never separate from it. Wherever there is evidence of creative action, there God is.

God is mind, and He created through His word or idea, and this is the universal creative vehicle. It is plainly stated in this 1st chapter of Genesis that "God said." Jesus corroborated this creative power of the word or idea again and again. He said that His words were so powerful that if we let them abide in us we might ask whatsoever we would and it should be done to us.

God is a mind force carrying forward creation under mental law. That law may be known to anyone who will follow the example of Jesus. Jesus said, "Be perfect, as your heavenly Father is perfect." This means that we should strive for the perfection that God is. We are the image and likeness of this great creative Mind, and being in a certain aspect of our mind just like it, we can through mental adjustment attain the same conscious unity that Jesus did.

God creates through the action of His mind, and all things rest on ideas. The idea back of the flower is beauty. The idea back of music is harmony. The idea back of day is light or the dispensation of intelligence.

This whole chapter is a statement of the creative ideas involved in the universe. It deals with involution. Evolution is the working out in manifestation of what mind has involved. Whatever mind commands to be brought forth will be brought forth by and through the law of evolution inherent in being. This applies to the great and the small. In mind there is but one.

The first step in creation is the awakening of man to spiritual consciousness, the dawning of light in his mind, his perception of Truth through the quickening of his spirit. Light is wisdom; and the first day's work is the calling of light or wisdom into expression. Light represents intelligence, and darkness represents undeveloped capacity. Symbolically these are "day" and "night."

The word *God* in this instance stands for Elohim, which is God in His capacity as creative power, including within Himself all the potentalities of being. The "beginning" indicates the first concept of Divine Mind. "Created" means ideated. The "heavens" is the realm of ideas, and the "earth" represents ideas in expression. Heaven is the idea and earth the mental picture. A comparison is found in the activity of our own mind: we have an idea and then think out a plan before we bring it forth.

Ferrar Fenton, the well-known student of Hebrew and Greek, says that the first verse should read: "By periods God created that which produced the Suns; then that which produced the Earth. But the Earth was unorganized and empty; and darkness covered its convulsed surface; but the breath of God vibrated over its fluid face." From this we are to understand that God created not the earth as it appears but that which produced the earth. Elohim, Spirit, creates the spiritual idea, which is afterward made manifest through Jehovah God.

The earthly thought was not yet clear. Harmony of form had not yet come into expression. "The deep" represents the capacity of the earth idea to bring forth. "The face of the deep" represents its intelligence. Understanding has not yet come into expression, and there is no apparent action. "The Spirit of God" or divine intelligence moved upon "the face of the waters." "Waters" here represents unexpressed capacities, the mental element out of which all is produced. Man is conscious of unexpressed capacities within himself, but only as he moves upon mind substance with intelligence are his inherent spiritual qualities molded into forms. "Light" is intelligence, a spiritual quality. It corresponds to understanding and should precede all activity. At the beginning of any of our creating we should declare for light. Our declarations of Truth are instantly fulfilled in Spirit.

James says in his Epistle, "Every good gift and every perfect gift is from above, coming down from the Father of lights." The Evangelist John speaks of "the true light . . . which lighteth every man, coming into the world."

All that emanates from God is good. In the process of bringing forth our ideas we need a certain degree of understanding in order properly to regulate our thoughts. The light must be divided from the darkness, as in Divine Mind the light was separated from the darkness.

"Day" represents the state of mind in which intelligence dominates. "Night" represents the realm of thoughts that are not yet illuminated by the Spirit of God.

> *Gen. 1:6-8.* And God said, Let there be a firmament in the midst of the waters, and let it divide the waters from the waters. And God made the firmament, and divided the waters which were under the firmament from the waters which were above the firmament: and it was so. And God called the firmament Heaven. And there was evening and there was morning, a second day.

The second step in creation is the development of faith or the "firmament." The "waters" represent the unestablished elements of the mind.

The second day's creation is the second movement of Divine Mind. The central idea in this day's creation is ·the establishment of a firmament in the "midst of the waters" dividing the "waters from the waters." "Waters" represent unexpressed possibilities in mind. There must be a "firm" starting point or foundation established. This foundation or "firmament" is faith "moving upon" the unformed capacities of Spirit consciousness. The divine Logos—God as creative power— gives forth the edict "Let there be a firmament." The first step or "day" in creation involves "light" or understanding, and the second step, faith in the knowing quality of mind.

The word is instantly fulfilled in Spirit. "And God made the firmament." This does not refer to the visible realm of forms but to the mental image in Divine Mind, which deals only with ideas. In every mental state we have an "above" and a "below." Above the firmament are the unexpressed capacities ("waters") of the conscious mind resting in faith in Divine Mind. Below the firmament are the unexpressed capacities ("waters") of the subconscious mind.

The word "Heaven" is capitalized in this passage because it relates directly to Divine Mind. Faith ("firmament") established in consciousness is a state of perfect harmony, therefore "Heaven." Another degree of mind unfoldment has been attained. "And there was evening and there was morning, a second day." "Evening" represents completion, and the "morning" following represents activity of ideas.

> *Gen. 1:9-13.* And God said, Let the waters under the heavens be gathered together unto one place, and let the dry land appear: and it was so. And God called the dry land Earth; and the gathering together of the waters called he Seas: and God saw

that it was good. And God said, Let the earth put
forth grass, herbs yielding seed, *and* fruit-trees bearing fruit after their kind, wherein is the seed thereof,
upon the earth: and it was so. And the earth brought
forth grass, herbs yielding seed after their kind,
and trees bearing fruit, wherein is the seed thereof,
after their kind: and God saw that it was good. And
there was evening and there was morning, a third
day.

The third step in creation is the beginning of the
formative activity of the mind called imagination. This
gathers "the waters . . . together unto one place" so
that the "dry land" appears. Then the imagination
begins a great multiplication of forms and shapes in
the mind.

The first day's creation reveals the light or inspiration of Spirit. The second day establishes faith in our
possibilities to bring forth the invisible. The third
day's creation or third movement of Divine Mind
pictures the activity of ideas in mind. This is called
expression. The formative power of mind is the imagination, whose work is here represented by the dry land.
There is much unformed thought in mind ("the heavens") that must be separated from the formed.

In this proclamation "earth" is the mental image
of formed thought and does not refer to the manifest
world. God is Divine Mind and deals directly with
ideas. "Seas" represents the unformed state of mind.
We say that a man is "at sea" when he is in doubt in
his mental processes. In other words he has not established his thoughts in line with the principle involved.
The sea is capable of production, but must come under
the dominion of the imagination.

Divine Mind images its ideas definitely and in

every detail. The idea precedes the fulfillment. "Let there be" represents the perfect confidence necessary to demonstration.

Ideas are productive and bring forth after their kind. They express themselves under the law of divine imagery. The seed is within the thought and is reproduced through thought activity until thought habits are formed. Thoughts become fixed in the earth or formed consciousness. In Divine Mind all is good.

Again a definite degree of mind unfoldment has been attained. Man, in forming his world, goes through the same mental process, working under divine law. Jesus said, "The seed is the word of God."

> *Gen. 1:14-19.* And God said, Let there be lights in the firmament of heaven to divide the day from the night; and let them be for signs, and for seasons, and for days and years: and let them be for lights in the firmament of heaven to give light upon the earth: and it was so. And God made the two great lights; the greater light to rule the day, and the lesser light to rule the night: *he made* the stars also. And God set them in the firmament of heaven to give light upon the earth, and to rule over the day and over the night, and to divide the light from the darkness: and God saw that it was good. And there was evening and there was morning, a fourth day.

The fourth step in creation is the development of the "two great lights," the will and the understanding, or the sun (the spiritual I AM) and the moon (the intellect). These are but reflectors of the true light; for God had said, "Let there be light: and there was light"—before the sun and the moon were created.

The "firmament of heaven" is the consciousness of Truth that has been formulated and established.

In the second day's creation a firmament was established in heaven (realm of divine ideas). This firmament divides the day (illumined consciousness) from the night (unillumined consciousness). Through faith the "lights" are established; that is, understanding begins to unfold. The "signs," "seasons," and "days and years" represent different stages of unfoldment. We gain understanding by degrees.

The "earth" represents the more external processes through which an idea passes, and corresponds to the activity of an idea in mind. In man the "earth" is the body consciousness, which in its real nature is a harmonious expression of ideas established in faith-substance. "And it was so"; that is, an idea from divine consciousness is instantly fulfilled.

The "greater light," in mind, is understanding and the "lesser light" is the will. The greater light rules "the day," that realm of consciousness which has been illumined by Spirit. The lesser light rules "the night," that is, the will; which has no illumination ("light" or "day") but whose office is to execute the demands of understanding. The will does not reason, but in its harmonious relation acts easily and naturally upon the inspiration of Spirit. Divine will expresses itself as the I AM in man.

The "stars" represent man's perceptive faculties, including his ability to perceive weight, size, color, sound, and the like. Through concentrating any of the faculties ("stars") at its focalizing point one may come into an understanding of its action.

Divine Mind first images the idea, then perceives its fulfillment. Man, acting in co-operation with Divine Mind, places himself under this same creative law and thus brings his ideas into manifestation.

The idea is the directing and controlling power. Every idea has a specific function to perform. When our ideas are constructive and harmonious we see that they are good and realize that their power to rule is dominant in consciousness.

"Evening" stands for the fulfillment of an idea and marks another "day" or step or degree of unfoldment in consciousness.

Again referring to Fenton's translation of the 1st chapter of Genesis, "By periods God created that which produced the solar systems; then that which produced the earth," we see that God did not create the worlds directly; He created that which produced or evolved them. Then God said, "Let there be light." The Hebrew word for light is *owr*, meaning "luminosity" either literally or metaphysically. On the fourth day God said, "Let reflectors appear in the expanse of the heavens." Then God made two large "luminaries." The Hebrew word here used to express light is *maowr*, "a luminous body." The author of Genesis made a distinction between the source of light and how it was to be bodily manifested. But both were concepts in Divine Mind.

Our modern dynamos produce luminosity out of the ether equal to sunlight. The earth whirling on its axis generates electricity. Modern scientists are accepting analogy then, holding that bodies in motion generate energy that under certain conditions becomes luminous, and the conclusion is that the primal force that produces light existed before its manifestation through matter. This conclusion is in harmony with the symbolic story of creation as found in Genesis.

Modern critics have questioned the accuracy of Scripture on these points. Robert Ingersoll in his book "Some Mistakes of Moses" calls attention to the creation of light before the sources of light, the sun and the stars, were created, as evidence of the ignorance and inaccuracy of Moses. But scientific research and study of the original Hebrew reveals their harmony.

> *Gen. 1:20-23.* And God said, Let the waters swarm with swarms of living creatures, and let birds fly above the earth in the open firmament of heaven. And God created the great sea-monsters, and every living creature that moveth, wherewith the waters swarmed, after their kind, and every winged bird after its kind: and God saw that it was good. And God blessed them, saying, Be fruitful, and multiply, and fill the waters in the seas, and let birds multiply on the earth. And there was evening and there was morning, a fifth day.

The fifth step in creation is the bringing forth of sensation and discrimination. The "creatures" are thoughts. The "birds . . . in the open firmament of heaven" are ideas approaching spiritual understanding.

"Water" represents the unformed substance of life, always present as a fecundating element in which ideas ("living creatures") increase and multiply, just as the earth produces a crop when sown with seed. The "birds" represent the liberated thoughts or ideas of mind (heavens).

In connection with the body, "water" represents the fluids of the organism. The "sea-monsters" are life ideas that swarm in these fluids. Here is pictured Divine Mind creating the original body idea, as imaged in the 20th verse. In the 2d chapter of Genesis we shall read of the manifestation of this idea. Idea, expression, and manifestation are the steps involved in bringing anything forth under divine law. The stamp of good is placed upon divine ideas and their activity in substance.

In the fifth day's creation ideas of discrimination and judgment are developed. The fishes and fowls represent ideas of life working in mind, but they must be properly related to the unformed (seas) and the formed (earth) worlds of mind. When an individual is well balanced in mind and body, there is an equalizing force flowing in the consciousness, and harmony is in evidence.

Another orderly degree of mind unfoldment is fulfilled. Another step in spiritual growth is worked out in consciousness when the individual enters into the quickening of his judgment and seeks to conform his ideas to those of Divine Mind.

> *Gen. 1:24-31.* And God said, Let the earth bring forth living creatures after their kind, cattle, and creeping things, and beasts of the earth after their kind: and it was so. And God made the beasts of the earth after their kind, and the cattle after their kind, and everything that creepeth upon the ground after its kind: and God saw that it was good. And God said, Let us make man in our image, after our likeness: and let them have dominion over the fish of the sea, and over the birds of the heavens, and over the cattle, and over all the earth, and over every creeping thing that creepeth upon the earth. And God created man in his own image, in the image of God created he him; male and female created he them. And God blessed them: and God said unto them, Be fruitful, and multiply, and replenish the earth, and subdue it; and have dominion

over the fish of the sea, and over the birds of the
heavens, and over every living thing that moveth
upon the earth. And God said, Behold, I have given
you every herb yielding seed, which is upon the face
of all the earth, and every tree, in which is the
fruit of a tree yielding seed; to you it shall be for
food: and to every beast of the earth, and to every
bird of the heavens, and to everything that creepeth
upon the earth, wherein there is life, *I have given
every green herb for food: and it was so.* And God
saw everything that he had made, and behold, it
was very good. And there was evening and there
was morning, the sixth day.

The sixth step in creation is the bringing forth of
ideas after their kind. When man approaches the creative level in his thought, he is getting close to God
in his consciousness, and then the realization that he is
the very image and likeness of his Creator dawns
on him. This is the consciousness in man of Christ.

On the sixth day of creation ideas of life are set
into activity. "Cattle" represent ideas of strength established in substance. "Creeping things" represent ideas
of life that are more subtle in their expression, approaching closer to the realm of sense. They are the
micro-organisms. The "beasts" stand for the free energies of life that relate themselves to sensation. Divine
ideas are always instantly set into activity: "and it
was so."

Underlying all these ideas related to sensation,
which in their original purity are simply ideas of life
functioning in substance, is the divine idea of life.
When life is expressed in divine order it is pronounced
good. What is termed "sense consciousness" in man is
not to be condemned but lifted up to its rightful place.

"As Moses lifted up the serpent in the wilderness, even so must the Son of man be lifted up; that whosoever believeth may in him have eternal life." When the ideas of life are properly related to love and wisdom, man will find in them eternal satisfaction instead of sense pleasure.

Wisdom and love are the two qualities of Being that, communing together, declare, "Let us make man in our image, after our likeness." This is the mental image of man that in Truth we call the Christ. The Christ man has dominion over every idea emanating from Divine Mind.

The creation described in these six days or six "steps" or stages of God-Mind is wholly spiritual and should not be confounded with the manifestation that is described in the succeeding chapters. God is mind, and all His works are created in mind as perfect ideas.

This statement of man's creation, "And God said, Let us make man in our image, after our likeness," has always been a puzzle to people who read the Scriptures literally. The apparent man is so at variance with the description that they cannot reconcile them. Theologians began first to admit that the Garden of Eden story was an allegory, and now they are including the whole of Genesis.

But this is more than an allegory; it is a description of the ideal creation. In their calculations engineers often use mathematical symbols, like the letters x, y, and z, to represent quantities not yet given precise determination but carried along for development at the proper time. Involved in these symbols are ideas that are to be brought out in their proper order and made visible when the engineer's plans are objectified. So man plans in his mind that which he proposes to build. First the idea, then the visible. This is the process through which all creation passes. God makes all things in His mind first, which is involution; then they are made into form and shape, and this is evolution.

In some such way then we can think of man as represented by an *x* in God's plan or calculations. God is carrying man along in His mind as an ideal quantity, the image-and-likeness man of His creation, and His divine plan is dependent for its success on the manifestation by man of this idea. The divine plan is furthered by the constant idealism that keeps man moving forward to higher and higher achievements. The image-and-likeness man pours into "mankind" a perpetual stream of ideas that the individual man arranges as thoughts and forms as substance and life. While this evolutionary process is going on there seem to be two men, one ideal and spiritual and the other intellectual and material, which are united at the consummation, the ideal man, Christ.

When the mind attains an understanding of certain creative facts, of man's creative powers, it has established a directive, intelligent center that harmonizes these two men (ideal and spiritual vs. intellectual and material). This directive center may be named the I AM. It is something more than the human I. Yet when this human I has made union with the image-and-likeness I, the true I AM comes into action, and this is the Christ Jesus, the Son of God, evolved and made visible in creation according to divine law.

God ideated two universal planes of consciousness, "the heavens and the earth." One is the realm of pure ideas, the other of thought forms. God does not create the visible universe directly, as a man makes a concrete pavement, but He creates the ideas that are used by His intelligent "image and likeness" to make the universe. Thus God's creations are always spiritual. Man's creations are both material and spiritual, according to his understanding.

Mental activity in Divine Mind represents two phases: first, conception of the idea; and secondly, expression of the idea. In every idea conceived in mind there is first the quickening spirit of life, followed by the increase of the idea in substance. Wisdom is the "male" or expressive side of Being, while love is the "female" or receptive side of Being. Wisdom is the father quality of God and love is the mother quality. In every idea there exist these two qualities of mind, which unite in order to increase and bring forth under divine law.

Divine Mind blessed the union of wisdom and love and pronounced on them the increase of Spirit. When wisdom and love are unified in the individual consciousness, man is a master of ideas and brings forth under the original creative law.

"Seed" represents fundamental ideas having within themselves reproductive capacity. Every idea is a seed that, sown in the substance of mind, becomes the real food on which man is nourished. Man has access to the seed ideas of Divine Mind, and through prayer and meditation he quickens and appropriates the substance of those ideas, which were originally planted in his I AM by the parent mind.

Provision is made for the sustenance of all the ideas emanating from Divine Mind. The primitive forms of life are fed on "herbs"; they have a sus-

taining force that is food to them, even as the appro-
priation of divine ideas is food to man.

Divine Mind, being All-Good itself, sees only its
own creation as good. As man co-operates more fully
with Divine Mind, imaging only that which is good,
he too beholds his production with the "single" eye,
sees them only as good. The sixth step in creation is
the concentration, in man, of all the ideas of Divine
Mind. Man is given authority and dominion over all
ideas. Thus is completed another step in mind unfoldment.

In the six mental steps or "mind movements,"
called days, Elohim God creates the spiritual universe
and spiritual man. He then rests. He has created the
ideas or patterns of the formed universe that is to follow.

In the next chapter we shall find Jehovah God ex-
ecuting what Elohim God created or ideated. In the
Hebrew the name Jehovah means "I am." We identify
Jehovah as the I AM, the spiritual man, the image and
likeness of Elohim God. But Jehovah, spiritual man,
must be made manifest, so He forms a man called
Adam.

Chapter II

Manifest Man

GENESIS 2

T HE BOOK OF GENESIS gives two accounts of the creation of man, the first that of the creation by Elohim and the second that of the creation by Jehovah. A right understanding of the processes the mind uses in bringing forth its children (ideas) enables us to perfect harmony between these apparently conflicting accounts. The first act of mind is the formation of the idea, and the second is the expression of that idea. Elohim or God-Mind creates a spiritual man, in whom are conceived to be present all the attributes of his source. Next this spiritual man, Jehovah God, God-Mind indentified as I AM, forms man in spiritual substance, in the "dust of the ground."

The unfolding man is God's man, or the divine idea of man in process of construction. The various ideas are being "clothed upon," that is, made manifest. The manifest man is an idea until the Elohim mind in its I AM or Jehovah form begins its process of expression. Then Jehovah God begins to form or clothe the idea man in substance, which process, described symbolically in these Scriptures, has been going on all down the ages.

The manifest man is the man we see, the man we behold with our senses. Manifest man evolves or makes manifest the ideas that exist eternally in Being. The spiritual man is the man we behold in our ideals.

"Ye are a temple of God." Eventually the manifest man
and the ideal man merge into one, as Jesus said: "I in
them, and thou in me, that they may be perfected into
one."

Many have caught sight of the fact that the true
body of Christ is a state of consciousness in man, but
few have gone so far as to realize that this body is a
temple in which the Christ holds religious services at
all times. "Know ye not that ye are a temple of God
and *that* the Spirit of God dwelleth in you." Under
the direction of the Christ, a new body is constructed
by the thinking faculty in man; the materials entering
into this superior structure are spiritual substances, and
the new creation is the temple or body of Spirit. It
breathes an atmosphere and is thrilled with a life
energy more real than that of the manifest man. When
a person has come into the realization of his true
Christ body, he feels the stirring within him of this
body of the indwelling Spirit or Christ. He knows
what Paul meant when he said: "There is a natural
body, there is also a spiritual *body*." "If any man is in
Christ, *he is* a new creature: the old things are passed
away; behold, they are become new."

Jehovah I AM breathes the breath of life into Adam,
who names the animals (the elemental life forms in
which he exists) and becomes cocreator with Jehovah
God in bringing forth his own perfection.

The image-and-likeness man is God's idea of man, a
man spirtually conceived, in whom are implanted the
dominion and power necessary to bring forth the
perfection of his Father, God-Mind. "Ye therefore
shall be perfect, as your heavenly Father is perfect,"
said Jesus.

> *Gen. 2:1-3.* And the heavens and the earth were finished, and all the host of them. And on the seventh day God finished his work which he had made; and he rested on the seventh day from all his work which he had made. And God blessed the seventh day, and hallowed it; because that in it he rested from all his work which God had created and made.

The plans of Divine Mind were finished although there was as yet no outward manifestation. All is finished first in consciousness and mind then rests, in faith, from further mental activity. This "rest" precedes manifestation. The seventh day refers to the mind's realization of fulfillment, its resting in the assurance that all that has been imaged in it will come forth in expression.

To hallow the seventh day is to rest in the stillness, quiet, and peace of the silence of Mind. "Be still, and know that I am God." To hallow means to keep holy. Holiness is resting in the conviction that there is no lack in the absolute law that is the law of God. One creates first in mind by idealizing the desired object and then resting in the assurance that the law of manifestation is being fulfilled. God has finished creating His universe, including man, and is resting in His perfect idea. God rested on the seventh day.

Our Sunday is a symbol of the true Sabbath, a time when men turn away from business and the pleasures of the senses to seek a day of quiet and holy rest. The great Sabbath, the rest of God, is for all who will enter it.

It is the state of mind in which we rest from outer work, cease daily occupation, and give ourselves up to meditation or the study of things spiritual. The Sabbath

also symbolizes an attitude of mind in which we relax
the outer consciousness, let go of all thought about
material things, about the affairs of daily life, and enter
into the stillness of the consciousness and begin to
think of God and His law. This Sabbath is kept any
time we enter into spiritual consciousness and rest
from thoughts about temporal things. Then we let go
of the external observance of days, because every
day is a Sabbath on which we retire into Spirit and
worship God.

> *Gen. 2:4-8.* These are the generations of the
> heavens and of the earth when they were created, in
> the day that Jehovah God made earth and heaven.
> And no plant of the field was yet in the earth, and
> no herb of the field had yet sprung up; for Jehovah
> God had not caused it to rain upon the earth: and
> there was not a man to till the ground; but there
> went up a mist from the earth, and watered the
> whole face of the ground. And Jehovah God formed
> man of the dust of the ground, and breathed into his
> nostrils the breath of life; and man became a living
> soul. And Jehovah God planted a garden eastward,
> in Eden; and there he put the man whom he had
> formed.

Jehovah (I AM) in the Hebrew is written *Yahweh.*
Yah is the masculine and *weh* the feminine. The word
is made up of masculine and feminine elements and
represents the joining together of wisdom and love as a
procreating nucleus. This is the Jehovah God who made
the visible man, the man of self-consciousness. God
manifest in substance is the Jesus Christ man. Elohim,
universal Mind, *creates,* but Jehovah God *forms.* Being is without beginning or ending. Universal Mind
imaged itself in all that it created, and all its ideas

are contained in the divine-idea man, which is Jehovah
or the Christ. Jesus Christ is that perfection made
manifest in man. Spiritual creating is ideation in Truth.
The ideas of Divine Mind are contained potentially in
substance, but until these ideas are consciously recognized by Jehovah God, the divine-idea man, they are
not wholly manifest. All things exist as ideas, but
these ideas are manifested only as spiritual man, becomes conscious of them. The "rain" represents the
descent of potential ideas into substance. Spiritual
man, in whom all the ideas of Divine Mind are imaged,
is not yet manifest in substance. "There was not a man
to till the ground."

The "face" represents the outward aspect, while
"ground" stands for formed substance, the product of
related ideas. When man begins to focus his mind on a
purpose, there appears at first to be a "mist" or lack
of clear understanding between the earth consciousness and the spiritual mind. But this "mist" has its
place in the divine economy, for it "waters" or softens
the divine radiance.

"Dust" represents the radiant earth or substance.
When spiritual man (I AM) enters into this "dust
of the ground" (substance) and makes use of the
God ideas inherent in him, he brings forth the ideal
body in its elemental perfection. The real body of
man is not material but is of the nature of the universal-
dust body, which is the divine-substance body. Therefore the perfect image-and-likeness man is perfect in
body as well as in mind. We should remember that the
first Adam was perfect as an idea in his elemental soul
and body. "Howbeit that is not first which is spiritual,
but that which is natural; then that which is spiritual."

Spiritually, "nostrils" represents openness to the inspirations of mind. The "breath" is the inner life flow that pulsates through the soul. The breathing of the manifest man corresponds to the inspiration of the spiritual man. When any man is inspired with high ideas, he breathes "into his nostrils the breath of life." Spiritual inspiration quickens man to the awareness that he is a "living soul." The soul is the sum total of consciousness and its great goal is a consciousness of eternal life. Through his I AM or Jehovah God man enters into his soul realm and rebreathes into it the true ideas of Being until these ideas quicken his consciousness to a response that harmonizes it with the underlying Christ principles. Man, spiritually identified, is Jehovah God, co-operating with Elohim God, divine principle, developing a spiritual being, the Christ man, to the consciousness of his divinity. "I speak not from myself: but the Father abiding in me doeth his works."

The Garden of Eden represents a region of being in which are provided all primal ideas for the production of the beautiful. As described in Genesis it represents allegorically the elemental life and intelligence placed at the disposal of man, through which he is to evolve a soul and body.

The Garden of Eden also represents allegorically the elemental forces named by scientists as composing the invisible, etheric universe that Jesus referred to as the "kingdom of the heavens" and "Paradise." It also comprehends the activity of those forces in man's soul and body that, when quickened and regenerated, make him a master of all creation. "The kingdom of God is within you." "East" represents the within as "west" represents the without. Jesus also said, "Ye who have followed me, in the regeneration when the Son of man shall sit on the throne of his glory, ye also shall sit upon twelve thrones, judging the twelve tribes of Israel." In our analysis of the Garden of Eden we consider it as a concentration, in man, of all the ideas of God concerned in the process of unfolding man's soul and body. When man is expressing the ideas of Divine Mind, bringing forth the qualities of Being in divine order, he dwells in Eden, a state of bliss, in a harmonious, productive consciousness containing all possibilities of growth.

> *Gen. 2:9.* And out of the ground made Jehovah God to grow every tree that is pleasant to the sight, and good for food; the tree of life also in the midst of the garden, and the tree of the knowledge of good and evil.

"Ground" represents formed substance: ideas of Truth of which man is conscious. The "tree" is the substance that connects mind and body, earth and heaven, represented physically by the nerves. The "tree that is pleasant to the sight" represents the pleasure derived from ascending and descending currents of life over the nerves. The substance of spiritual thought is the "food" that is good. The "tree of life also in the midst of the garden" represents the absolute-life principle established in man's consciousness by Divine Mind, the very center of his being. The roots of the "tree of life" are centered in the solar-plexus region, and they are symbolized in the physical organism by the nerves of that plexus.

The "tree of the knowledge of good and evil" represents the sympathetic nervous system whose fruit is sensation. When man controls his feelings and emotions his sensations are harmonized and all his functions are supplied with nerve energy. But when man gives way to the pleasure sensation he consumes or "eats" of that energy and robs his body of its essential nerve food. Thus excessive sense pleasure and the pain that follows are designated as "good and evil."

> *Gen. 2:10-14.* And a river went out of Eden to water the garden; and from thence it was parted, and became four heads. The name of the first is Pishon: that is it which compasseth the whole land of Havilah, where there is gold; and the gold of that land is good: there is bdellium and the onyx stone. And the name of the second river is Gihon: the same is it that compasseth the whole land of Cush. And the name of the third river is Hiddekel: that is it which goeth in front of Assyria. And the fourth river is the Euphrates.

"River" symbolizes the activity of life in the trees or the current of life in the organism (garden). The "head" of the river represents its directive power.

The name *Pishon* is variously defined as "fully diffused," "real existence," "perfect substantiality," "being, carried to its highest degree." Spiritually interpreted, this definition is descriptive of Spirit at work in man's consciousness, Spirit diffusing its ideas of intelligence and light into man's soul. However this work of Spirit is not confined to man's body or to the earth but is everywhere present. It is the activity of divine ideas in their fullness.

The river Pishon is described as encompassing "the whole land of Havilah." Havilah represents the struggle of elemental life, virtue born of trial, travail, or suffering. There is gold in this land and also precious stones, which means that it is the realm of reality. In other words, we have locked up in our elemental body all the treasures of Spirit. All the precious things of life for which we have been looking are in our body, and it is through the inflow of this mighty spiritual Pishon that these precious ideas are released. But there is a struggle or, as Jesus said, "tribulation" between the spiritual and the natural.

The name *Gihon* means variously "formative movement," "a bursting forth," "whirlpool," "rapid stream." This river represents the deific breath of God inspiring man and at the same time purifying his blood in the lungs. Job said that "there is a spirit in man" and that "the breath of the Almighty giveth them understanding." The river Gihon "compasseth the whole land of Cush." The name *Cush* means "firelike," "darkness," "impurity"; and the passage refers to the blood-purifying process of the breath. God is breathing His breath through man's being, cleansing the blood stream, and filling his whole being with spiritual inspiration.

The name *Hiddekel* means "universal generative fluid," "rapid stream," "rapid spiritual influx." The river Hiddekel symbolizes the spiritual nerve fluid that God is propelling throughout man's whole being continually, as the electromagnetic center of every physically expressed atom and cell, the very elixir of life. This wonderful stream of nerve fluid finds its way over all the many nerves in man's body, giving him the invigorating, steadying power of the Holy Spirit.

Assyria represents the psychic realm or the soul. The nerve fluid, the most attenuated and volatile fluid of the body, breaks into flares at the ends of the

nerves, giving rise to various kinds of psychical and
mental action, forming character or soul. The mind
uses the nerve flares to express its ideas.

The name of the fourth river, *Euphrates,* means
"fructifying" or "that which is the fructifying cause."
Metaphysically it represents the blood stream. The
circulatory system receives and distributes the nutrients
contained in the food we eat. The blood stream is
charged with the food substance for bone, muscle, brain,
teeth, and hair. Every part of the organism is supplied
with substance through this wonderful river Euphrates.

> *Gen. 2:15-17.* And Jehovah God took the man,
> and put him into the garden of Eden to dress it
> and to keep it. And Jehovah God commanded the
> man, saying, Of every tree of the garden thou
> mayest freely eat: but of the tree of the knowledge
> of good and evil, thou shalt not eat of it: for in the
> day that thou eatest thereof thou shalt surely die.

The Garden of Eden symbolizes the omnipresent,
unseen realm out of which comes the visible universe.
Modern science has named it the cosmic ether. It cannot
be described in human language, because it transcends
all the comparisons of earth. Jesus said that the "mysteries" of the kingdom were revealed to those who were
spiritually awake but to others must be told in parables.

The human body with its psychical and spiritual
attributes comprises a miniature Garden of Eden, and
when man develops spiritual insight and in thought,
word, and act voluntarily operates in accord with the
divine law, then rulership, authority, and dominion
become his in both mind and body. "The kingdom of
God is within you."

Jehovah God, the active representative of Divine

Mind in man, places man in the Garden of Eden to "dress it and to keep it." Man dresses and keeps this garden by developing, in his consciousness, the original, pure ideas imparted by Divine Mind. As man establishes ideas of Truth he calls into manifestation his spiritual body imaged in substance by Divine Mind.

"Tree" represents the connecting link between the formed substance (earth) and the formless (heaven). To "eat" is to appropriate the substance of ideas through thinking about them. "Evil" represents error thought combinations; that part of consciousness which has lost sight of true principles and through sensation becomes enamored of the thing formed. Form has its place in creation, but it is subject to the creative idea that begets it. The activity of an idea in man's mind produces sensation. To become involved in the sensation of an idea to the exclusion of control is to eat of the "tree of the knowledge of good and evil" and die to all consciousness of the original idea.

Materiality as the obverse of spirituality was set up when man became involved in thoughts of the external, in sensation, and lost sight of the true creative idea. Because of this, man gradually became separated from the realm of divine ideas; in other words, from God. Death is the result of this separation from God. Jesus restored the broken life current between God and man and so became the "Saviour" for those who follow Him.

Gen. 2:18-25. And Jehovah God said, It is not good that the man should be alone; I will make him a help mate for him. And out of the ground Jehovah God formed every beast of the field, and every bird of the heavens; and brought them unto the man to see what he would call them: and whatsoever the man

called every living creature, that was the name thereof. And the man gave names to all cattle, and to the
birds of the heavens, and to every beast of the field;
but for man there was not found a help meet for
him. And Jehovah God caused a deep sleep to fall
upon the man, and he slept; and he took one of his
ribs, and closed up the flesh instead thereof: and
the rib, which Jehovah God had taken from the man,
made he a woman, and brought her unto the man.
And the man said, This is now bone of my bones,
and flesh of my flesh: she shall be called Woman,
because she was taken out of Man. Therefore shall a
man leave his father and his mother, and shall cleave
unto his wife: and they shall be one flesh. And they
were both naked, the man and his wife, and were
not ashamed.

Man must have avenues through which to express
himself. These avenues are the "help meet" designed by
Jehovah God. Man represents wisdom. It is not good for
wisdom to act alone; it must be joined with love if harmony is to be brought forth. Both the soul and the
body are helpmeets to man (spirit), avenues through
which he expresses the ideas of Mind.

It is on the soul or substance side of consciousness
that ideas are "identified," that is, "named." Whatever
we recognize a thing to be, that it becomes to us because of the naming power vested in man (wisdom).
"Every beast of the field" and the "cattle" represent
ideas of strength, power, vitality, and life. These ideas
must be recognized by the I AM before they can be
formed. "The birds of the heavens" represent free
thoughts and the interchange between the subconscious
and the conscious activities of mind. Man has power
to name all ideas that are presented to his conscious
mind, whether they come from within or without.

Wisdom, the masculine phase of man, needs a helpmeet or balance. Love in the soul (woman) has not yet been developed and established in substance.

A limited concept of Jehovah God caused a deep sleep (mesmeric state) to fall on the man (Adam). Nowhere in Scripture is there any record to show that Adam was ever fully awakened; and he (man) is still partly in this dreamlike state of consciousness. In this state he creates a world of his own and peoples it with ideas corresponding to his own sleep-benumbed consciousness.

Paul said, "As in Adam all die [fall asleep, lose spiritual consciousness], so also in Christ shall all be made alive [awaken from coma or lethargy into the awareness of Spirit life]."

Awakening cannot be associated with dying. The idea that man awakens to spiritual or any kind of consciousness immediately after "death," whether in heaven, hell, purgatory, or elsewhere, is opposed to Truth. His awakening must take place here, during the time of "life," at least while he is partially awake and before he sinks into that deeper sleep or coma that we call death.

The Scripture admonishes us: "Awake, thou that sleepest, and arise from the dead [the mortal dream of life], and Christ [Truth] shall shine upon thee." David, sensing this, said, "I shall be satisfied, when I awake, with *beholding* thy form."

The soul is here coming into the positive development of divine love (the woman). Love is the passive quality of mind and must become active through man's volition, before it can be brought forth; and man must enter into the passive side of Being and cease from outer mental activity. This state is symbolized by "deep sleep"; the outer consciousness is quiet, allowing the spiritual to express itself fully.

Man evolves, attains consciousness in mind and body, as he becomes aware of the divine ideas implanted in his being. In this chapter Adam "names"—calls to consciousness in life's activities—the beasts of the field and the birds of the heavens (animal and intellectual realms). Then in moments of meditation, when the outer mind is still, he makes contact with the subconscious.

The Hebrew word from which "rib" is translated means "curved surface," not specifically one of Adam's ribs; rather, the curves of beauty innate in Adam. The development of Eve is a refining process that helps man to bring forth his divine feminine nature. The rib or bone that became woman is symbolical of the very substantial character of the love that she represents.

Adam is the objective and Eve the subjective in primal man, both in the same body. As man evolves Eve becomes objective. "This is now bone of my bones, and flesh of my flesh: she shall be called Woman, because she was taken out of Man."

If the ego or will that is man has adhered to the guiding light of Spiritual faithfully and has carried out in its work the plans that are ideated in wisdom, it has created a harmonious consciousness. The original Adam in Eden is symbolical of such a consciousness.

The "deep sleep" into which the intellect is plunged when true love is experienced still prevails in human relations. Love is the great mystery of life. The spiritually wise see love as the force that enfolds with mathematical precision the galaxies in space as well as the tiniest atom. Science names it gravity.

Chapter III

The Fall of Man

GENESIS 3, 4, and 5

ACCORDING to the Bible, "the word of God" is the power that created the world, as stated in Hebrews:

"By faith we understand that the worlds have been framed by the word of God, so that what is seen hath not been made out of things which appear."

The 1st chapter of John explains that "the Word" was in the beginning with God and was God and that through the Word all things were made. So it is not true to say that the Bible is "the creative Word" of God. The Christ in Jesus is the creative Word. Spiritual man is the Word of God, and the Bible bears "witness of the word of God." As Jesus taught: "Ye search the scriptures because ye think that in them ye have eternal life; and these are they which bear witness of me; and ye will not come to me, that ye may have life."

Man fell because he did not keep his mind on the source of life. He departed from spiritual consciousness and saw both good and evil. If he had held to the one good, good is the only thing that he could have manifested.

The Word of God is the living, creative force that is man's spiritual mind. As Jesus said to those Jews who searched the Scriptures for eternal life: "Ye have not his word abiding in you."

Those who search the Scriptures and think that through them they will get life are, according to Jesus, ignoring the omnipresent creative word and separating themselves from its perfect manifestation, man.

Man is falling just to the extent that he is ignoring the living Word in himself. Man must keep affirming the living Word; then he will have the transformed body.

Jesus Christ is the Word demonstrated as perfect man, and through Him we are saved from the fall. In these words we find an epitome of both the law and the gospel.

The Bible is at the same time the simplest and the greatest of all books. It is great because it deals with great matters in simple ways. It eliminates the transient, unnecessary temporalities and goes direct to the gist of the subject.

We have not understood the depth and height of these simple allegories and symbols sprinkled all through the Bible. They are condensed explanations, stripped of minor details, of the great underlying laws of existence. A mortal description of creation would make time a necessary element, but the author of Genesis is not caught in this trap of mortality. "In the beginning God created."

Time is a human invention and acts as a barrier to a broader conception of creative processes. All attempts to find a date for the beginning of man are futile. Years are associated with events, and when the events are past the years go with them. States of mind make events, and new states of mind are constantly being formed; consequently every moment is the beginning

of a new creation to the individual. It is of no practical
value to a man to know that the world has journeyed
around the sun six thousand or six million years since
it was formed. The important thing is to know where
man stands in relation to the creative law. The Bible
puts history before us as if we were part of every event,
which we are. The one Mind is moving in its realm
of ideas "over all, and through all, and in all."

The allegory of the Garden of Eden, of the man
and the woman and the serpent, represents the development of ideas in individual consciousness, not the
development of a planetary system. The latter is the
narrow conclusion of the casual observer. Creation is
the evolution of ideas in mind. Creation is the development of individuality; hence the one object of all
creative processes is the making of man.

In the development of individuality the factors described in the allegory are active in every one of us
at this moment, and the creating is going on right
now. The reason why God created man potentially perfect and then set him the task of proving it is found
in the mysterious process called self-identification.
Man makes himself after the pattern designed by the
Great Architect. In proving his ability to carry out the
divine plan he proves himself perfect.

As we study mind we find that every thought tends
to find expression; that the formless and the formed go
hand in hand; that you cannot have an idea in your
mind without its immediately taking form as a mental
picture, which in due course is clothed upon with
substance and life, "a local habitation and a name."

Three fundamental factors are at the basis of all
manifestation, namely intelligence, life, and substance.

Divine intelligence reveals perfect ideas as the basis of existence. Any conception other than this is "eating" or appropriating thoughts that seem both good and evil. This conception of opposites leads to all kinds of inharmonies. It is the "serpent," "more subtle than any beast of the field," that suggests this to man. The serpent represents life, in which is vibration, color, sound, in fact all sensation. Sense consciousness is another name for the serpent. The word *sensation,* either written or spoken, suggests the sinuous movement and warning hiss of the serpent. The life idea is manifest in the sinuous shape of the mighty lightning chain darting from sky to earth as well as in the subtle sensations that sweep through the soul.

The soul (Eve) is attracted by this realm of sensation and is psychologized by its promises of pleasure. It is a "delight to the eyes," is "good for food," is to be desired to make one wise. When we indulge any of the sensations of the flesh for the mere pleasure that accompanies the indulgence, we are following the delusive suggestions of the serpent instead of listening to the word of God. Pain, disease, and finally death always result from such ignorant trangression of the divine daw.

Life is a fundamental factor in all existence. The most vital word in any or all languages is "life." Without life there could be no existence. In man's estimation life is so great a thing that he often uses the word "living" as representing all existence. But life is not all of existence. Love, substance, power, intelligence, these all play their part; and above all is man, spiritual man.

When man riots in the realm of ideas ("birds of

the heavens") and loses sight of God in the pursuit of his art, he becomes unbalanced. This applies to all who are so enamored of the outer that they lose dominion over the inner.

When man fails to master his sensations and gives himself up to the uncontrolled enjoyment of life, he is losing his dominion and must suffer the consequences of transgressing the law. Listen to the voice of wisdom and keep a steady rein on "every beast of the field": the life forces in the natural world.

Man should therefore be ever on the alert to maintain his dominion and mastery over all the ideas of the mind and sensations of the body. The wise man never gives himself up to pleasure seeking in the world or in his body. Everything has its use in the divine economy, and man as the master builder should ever be seeking to carry out the divine plan. .

In considering a practical application of this allegory, let every man ask himself, Am I entangled in the coils of the serpent of sense? The Scripture says that the serpent was the most subtle of all the beasts of the field that the Lord God created. That subtle sensuous feeling that thrills you is the beast of the field. The elemental life forces of your body are minute serpents. The reproductive elements in your body are in the form of minute serpents. These serpents are very obedient to your thought. By thinking about some sense pleasure you can concentrate them in the function of life giving, and they will blend all their energies to give you pleasure. But remember that in so doing you may be robbing some other function of its life, and it will deteriorate in consequence.

The person who gives up to the pleasures of sex

eats from the tree of life until the body is depleted
in every function; even sex itself dies of its own ignorance.

What is the remedy? Conservation, mastery, control.
Man must control every one of the elemental forces of
his being. In other words, instead of being tempted by
the devil of sensation, instead of yielding completely
to the pleasure of living, he must study the object of
life as a whole.

There are two ways of living open to man. One is
Satan's way: through experience of evil man gains by
contrast a concept of good. The other is God's way:
through consciousness of good, man sees that evil is
unreal and unnecessary. Every man and woman in the
world is following one or the other of these two courses
in the development of his individuality. Good and evil
seem to be pitted against each other in the world, but
it is not necessary for man to eat of the tree of good
and evil; he need not have a knowledge of evil in order
to realize the allness of good. If he follows God's way,
which is to know the good first, last, and always, his
mind will become so charged with good that evil will
be to him totally unreal.

You will find men on every side meeting temptation
in God's way, by knowing the good, affirming the good,
and living it according to their faith in God. I know
men who have never taken a drink of whiskey. They
have not found it necessary to become intoxicated in
order to experience the feeling of sobriety. They have
better dominion over their appetites than those who
have given up to Satan's way of experience. There are
men in the world who are living a pure life. They
know the joy of purity in the sex dominion. They have

proved that dominion over sex, under the guidance of Spirit, is a necessary part of the regeneration taught by Jesus. "For there are eunuchs, that were so born from their mother's womb: and there are eunuchs, that were made eunuchs by men: and there are eunuchs, that made themselves eunuchs for the kingdom of heaven's sake."

> *Gen. 3:1-5.* Now the serpent was more subtle than any beast of the field which Jehovah God had made. And he said unto the woman, Yea, hath God said, Ye shall not eat of any tree of the garden? And the woman said unto the serpent, Of the fruit of the trees of the garden we may eat: but of the fruit of the tree which is in the midst of the garden, God hath said, Ye shall not eat of it, neither shall ye touch it, lest ye die. And the serpent said unto the woman, Ye shall not surely die: for God doth know that in the day ye eat thereof, then your eyes shall be opened, and ye shall be as God, knowing good and evil.

The serpent is sense consciousness. It may also be called desire, sensation, or the activity of life in external manifestation apart from the divine source of life. "Woman" represents love or feeling in the individual consciousness and symbolizes the soul. Desire for sensation or activity in the external first tempts the soul, the center of feeling and emotion. The temptation of sense is at first very subtle, entering the consciousness to stir up doubt and slyly asking the question "Why not?"

From the center of one's being the life-giving, ever-bearing tree of the Spirit of God spreads its branches into every department of mind and body. Its fruits are intelligence to the mind, substance to the body, and life to the entire being. The warning given by Jehovah

God was that man should not eat of (appropriate) the fruit of this tree. In spiritual revelation we discern that man's cardinal mistake is to appropriate the pure essence of God in order to experience selfish sensuous pleasure.

The serpent is slyly suggesting to the soul that it indulge in the pleasures of sense and that the experience will result in a deeper understanding of God and His laws. The individual can always find arguments that to his own mind justify indulgence. This tendency may be described as sensation beguiling man from his Garden of Eden consciousness.

> *Gen. 3:6-7.* And when the woman saw that the tree was good for food, and that it was a delight to the eyes, and that the tree was to be desired to make one wise, she took of the fruit thereof, and did eat; and she gave also unto her husband with her, and he did eat. And the eyes of both were opened, and they knew that they were naked; and they sewed fig-leaves together, and made themselves aprons.

Woman, the intuitive or feeling side of man's nature, discerns that activity in ideas begets knowledge, but the knowledge gained is not necessarily of a divine nature. Love or feeling (woman) acting independently of wisdom (man) is not reliable.

The "eyes" are the perceptive faculty of mind, and unless the perception is established in Truth one sees or perceives duality. When one delights in knowledge that is less than Truth, one's capacity to receive inspiration direct from Divine Mind is lessened or lost. Both love (woman) and wisdom (man) become involved in a counterfeit knowledge through "eating" ideas inappropriate to the divine nature.

In the Scriptures figs are representative of the "seed" of man. This seed is in its original essence mind energy, and when ideas are kept in contact with Divine Mind, the seed of man is the life stream in its original purity. Man's sin is the misappropriation of ideas, which leads to sensation. When man and woman are joined—that is, one in sin—they are unclothed of the garment of Truth or "naked."

When wisdom and love, man and woman, are joined in the consciousness that God inspires all their thoughts and acts, the gross sensations of the flesh will be "lifted up," that is, glorified. "I, if I be lifted up from the earth, will draw all men unto myself." This is the "holy marriage."

> *Gen. 3:8-12.* And they heard the voice of Jehovah God walking in the garden in the cool of the day; and the man and his wife hid themselves from the presence of Jehovah God amongst the trees of the garden. And Jehovah God called unto the man, and said unto him, Where art thou? And he said, I heard thy voice in the garden, and I was afraid, because I was naked; and I hid myself. And he said, Who told thee that thou wast naked? Hast thou eaten of the tree, whereof I commanded thee that thou shouldest not eat? And the man said, The woman whom thou gavest to be with me, she gave me of the tree, and I did eat.

The "cool of the day" represents the relaxation or emptiness that follows sense expression. After the high tide of sensation has subsided, the voice of Jehovah God, commonly called conscience, is heard. Man is convinced that he has acted out of harmony with divine law. After experiencing sensation the picture visualized by the conscious mind is impressed on the life stream and sets up a subconscious tendency. Consciousness would hide from facing this situation, taking refuge amongst the "trees of the garden" (other sensations), but this is not the way to redemption. Every idea is to be dealt with. All error is forgiven when Truth is brought to bear on it, and if this method is pursued, only constructive thought habits will be put into activity in the subconscious realm of mind.

Jehovah God walks continually in the garden (the body) calling unto Adam (life), and when man raises his thoughts and feelings Godward, he contacts the inspiration of Being and builds again the immortal consciousness.

The soul or "woman" is the feminine aspect of man. It is through the affections (love) that man becomes involved in sensation. When a desire of the soul (woman) presses for attention, man often gives way to his feelings instead of raising them, through wisdom, to conform to higher principles.

In Truth feeling must be disciplined and refined and desire for sense pleasure eliminated. When consciousness is purified through the knowledge of Truth and thought force is established in harmonious relation to divine ideas, the woman (feeling) will be joined with man (wisdom) and the holy marriage (generation of divine ideas) will again be consummated. "Therefore shall a man leave his father and mother, and shall cleave unto his wife: and they shall be one flesh," writes the author of Genesis, and Jesus verifies it in Matthew 19:5: "For this cause shall a man leave his father and mother, and shall cleave to his wife;

and the two shall become one flesh." Indescribable joy is the heritage of those who submit their sex relations to God in prayer.

> *Gen. 3:13-14.* And Jehovah God said unto the woman, What is this thou hast done? And the woman said, The serpent beguiled me, and I did eat. And Jehovah God said unto the serpent, Because thou hast done this, cursed art thou above all cattle, and above every beast of the field; upon thy belly shalt thou go, and dust shalt thou eat all the days of thy life.

Man, ever seeking an excuse for sin, puts the blame on God for endowing him with sensation. Sensation is itself a divine creation, and all God's creation was pronounced "good." This brings us to the root cause of the appetite that craves stimulants and goes to excess in seeking satisfaction. Through listening to the serpent of sense, man goes beyond the limit set by natural or divine law and becomes a glutton and drunkard of sensation. The remedy is for him to take up the problem from a spiritual standpoint in the knowledge that sensation is a mental quality that can be satisfied only by his cultivating the spiritual side of his nature.

When the desire for sensation leads man to dissipate the precious fruit of the tree of life in his earthly garden, the whole nervous system is depleted and loses its capacity to contact the higher life current and supermind wisdom. Then man feels a lack of something; he is "naked." Sensation is no longer a heavenly ecstasy but a fleshly vibration, and crawls on its "belly," eating "dust" all the days of its life.

We often wonder why God cursed the serpent since He created him for the very purpose of enabling man

to have sensation. The author of Genesis discerned that
certain principles were in operation; that when the
creative life which Jehovah God breathed into man's
nostrils was taken away, there would be a fall from
divine union and man would have to suffer certain
conditions that would follow. So the curse was not
imposed directly by Jehovah but as a result of man's
breaking certain laws.

> *Gen. 3:15-19.* And I will put enmity between
> thee and the woman, and between thy seed and her
> seed: he shall bruise thy head, and thou shalt bruise
> his heel. Unto the woman he said, I will greatly
> multiply thy pain and thy conception; in pain
> thou shalt bring forth children; and thy desire shall
> be to thy husband, and he shall rule over thee. And
> unto Adam he said, Because thou hast hearkened
> unto the voice of thy wife, and hast eaten of the
> tree, of which I commanded thee, saying, Thou shalt
> not eat of it: cursed is the ground for thy sake;
> in toil shalt thou eat of it all the days of thy life;
> thorns also and thistles shall it bring forth to thee;
> and thou shalt eat the herb of the field; in the sweat
> of thy face shalt thou eat bread, till thou return
> unto the ground; for out of it wast thou taken: for
> dust thou art, and unto dust shalt thou return.

The seed of the woman is from God; it is the
spiritual life that comes from the fountainhead. The
seed of the serpent is fallen sense consciousness, and
there is enmity between the two. The effect, as set forth
in the text describing the suffering common to most
women, needs no metaphysical interpretation. The interpretation usually given is that the "seed" that bruised
the head of the serpent was Jesus. But these verses
were written long before the time of Jesus, so they must
refer to certain principles. The heel represents the ac-

tivity of the will in the body. When one is willful the tendency is to force the heel into the ground. When you do that you are determined.

When you make up your mind that you are not going to be governed by your sensations, you plunge the whole man into spiritual consciousness, through which you are protected from sense. All through the account of the fall of man are found these promises of redemption, implications that man has within him a saving consciousness.

The story of Eve symbolizes the truth that instead of bringing forth ideas in the realm of supersubstance, the feminine is compelled to clothe its ideas with flesh and bring them forth in the earthly consciousness.

Having lost consciousness of God as its guiding light, the soul turns to its highest concept of wisdom, the intellect (husband).

The intellect, having lost contact with its inner light, is no longer possessed of the ability to ideate direct from God, and man is forced to cultivate the ground and toil physically. Jesus demonstrated man's spiritual ability when, direct from the ether as a substance base, He produced the fishes and loaves to feed more than five thousand persons.

Gen. 3:20. And the man called his wife's name Eve; because she was the mother of all living.

The name *Eve* means "elemental life," "life," "living." Eve represents the soul region of man and is the mother principle of God in expression through which life is evolved. The I AM (wisdom) puts feeling into what it thinks, and so Eve (feeling) becomes the "mother of all living." Back of feeling is the pure life essence of God. Adam and Eve symbolize the I AM individualized in life and substance. They are the primal elemental forces of Being itself.

The Hebrew verb *hoh*, "to be being" luminous, absolute life, which forms the basis of the name *Ihoh* (Jehovah) is the basis also of the word Eve; however, due to a slight change in characters and a hardening of the vowels, it no longer represents absolute life, but the struggle of elementary existence. This indicates the struggle of the soul to regain its perfect state of existence in the Absolute, God.

Gen. 3:21. And Jehovah God made for Adam and for his wife coats of skins, and clothed them.

Man originally was connected with the warm currents of spiritual life, but when these currents were broken by thoughts of separation, he required protection from external invading thoughts, hence the "coats of skins." This need is evidenced by the outer skin covering the sensitive nerves of our body and the danger of infection when this covering is broken. When spiritual thought becomes supreme in consciousness the "coat of skins" gives way to the manifestation of the spiritual body spoken of by Paul. Corruptible flesh is the manifestation of corrupt ideas in mind. "Be ye transformed [changed in form] by the renewing of your mind."

Gen. 3:22-24. And Jehovah God said, Behold, the man is become as one of us, to know good and evil; and now, lest he put forth his hand, and take also of the tree of life, and eat, and live for ever— therefore Jehovah God sent him forth from the garden of Eden, to till the ground from whence he was taken. So he drove out the man; and he placed

at the east of the garden of Eden the Cherubim,
and the flame of a sword which turned every way,
to keep the way of the tree of life.

"Jehovah God" is Divine Mind identified as the
Christ Mind or I AM man. "Good and evil," primarily
representing the two poles of Being, are opposite but
not adverse to each other. Man developed divine consciousness—came into an understanding of ideas in
their relation to Being itself—and when he became
involved so intensely in the feeling or negative side of
his nature, he lost consciousness of the equilibrium of
the Christ Mind. Will became independent of wisdom,
and an unbalanced condition in both mind and body
was set up. And "lest he put forth his hand [appro-
priating power of mind], and take also of the tree of
life, and eat, and live for ever," using the forces of
Being toward the expression of a consciousness adverse
to the Christ Mind, omnipresent wisdom closed the
door to the within until man should again enter into
the "garden" by establishing the divine consciousness,
Christ, the Way.

The "garden" symbolizes the spiritual body in which
man dwells when he brings forth thoughts after the
pattern of the original divine ideas. This "garden" is
the substance of God. "Eden" is a state of perfect relations among the ideas of Being. The "garden of Eden"
is the divine consciousness. Having developed a consciousness apart from his divine nature, man must "till
the ground from whence he was taken"—that is, come
into the realization of God as the substance of his
being—and express ideas in harmony with Divine
Mind. Wisdom and love are joined in God, and a perfect balance is struck in consciousness between know-

ing and feeling when man spiritualizes his thoughts.

The "east" is the within. "Cherubim" refers to protection of the sacred life. The inner spiritual life is protected from the outer, coaser consciousness. The "flame of a sword" is the divine idea or Word of God. Man unites with the inner Word or sacred life through the Christ Mind.

> *Gen. 4:1-2.* And the man knew Eve his wife; and she conceived, and bare Cain, and said, I have gotten a man with *the help of* Jehovah. And again she bare his brother Abel, and Abel was a keeper of sheep, but Cain was a tiller of the ground.

The story of Cain and Abel is an allegory of the movement of certain departments of the soul or consciousness. The name *Cain* means "possession." This refers directly to that part of human consciousness which strives to acquire and possess selfishly. Cain was a tiller of the soil, which shows that he is of the earthly domain. The name *Abel* means "breath," which places Abel in the air or spiritual realm. The two are brothers, that is, are closely related in the consciousness. Abel does not represent the high spiritual consciousness but the life energy that controls the animal functions: he was a sheep raiser. The Hindu metaphysics would call Abel the animal soul and Cain the physical body. Paul would call Abel the "creature" and Cain "the flesh."

> *Gen. 4:3-4a.* And in process of time it came to pass, that Cain brought of the fruit of the ground an offering unto Jehovah. And Abel, he also brought of the firstlings of his flock and of the fat thereof.

Making sacrifices unto Jehovah is symbolic of a refining process that is constantly going on in consciousness. Jehovah is the one universal Mind, which is the receptacle of all ideas and receives all. When you have a thought of love and good will, you set free invisible emanations that are impregnated with these ideas. These ascend to a higher realm and form a part of your spiritual soul, at the same time relating you to Jehovah, who is the presiding oversoul of the race. This is the inner meaning of the offering of sacrifices to Jehovah.

Everything in nature is going through this refining process, and there is a constant ascension of substance to mind and of mind to Spirit. We are taught that a time will finally come when the whole universe will be resolved back into its original essence in God.

> *Gen. 4:4b-15.* And Jehovah had respect unto Abel and to his offering: but unto Cain and to his offering he had not respect. And Cain was very wroth, and his countenance fell. And Jehovah said unto Cain, Why art thou wroth? and why is thy countenance fallen? If thou doest well, shall it not be lifted up? and if thou doest not well, sin coucheth at the door; and unto thee shall be its desire; but do thou rule over it. And Cain told Abel his brother. And it came to pass, when they were in the field, that Cain rose up against Abel his brother, and slew him. And Jehovah said unto Cain, Where is Abel thy brother? And he said, I know not: Am I my brother's keeper? And he said, What hast thou done? the voice of thy brother's blood crieth unto me from the ground. And now cursed art thou from the ground, which hath opened its mouth to receive thy brother's blood from thy hand; when thou tillest the ground, it shall not henceforth yield unto thee its strength; a fugitive and a wanderer shalt thou be in the earth. And Cain said unto Jehovah, My

punishment is greater than I can bear. Behold, thou
hast driven me out this day from the face of the
ground; and from thy face shall I be hid; and I shall
be a fugitive and a wanderer in the earth; and it will
come to pass, that whosoever findeth me will slay
me. And Jehovah said unto him, Therefore whosoever slayeth Cain, vengeance shall be taken on
him sevenfold. And Jehovah appointed a sign for
Cain, lest any finding him should smite him.

The thoughts of the mind are nearer to the Spirit
than are the emanations of the body. Hence the offering of Abel (mind) was more acceptable to Jehovah
than was that of Cain (body). The killing out of all
human sympathy and love by the body selfishness is
the slaying of Abel by Cain. When the body demands
possession of all the resources of mind, it reduces
existence to mere material living; it has slain Abel,
whose blood of life then cries from the earthly consciousness (ground) to Jehovah for expression.

When the selfishness of the body has killed out
the finer impulses of the mind and reduced all the
higher aspirations to a material level of existence, there
is no longer any pleasure in living. Without the mind
the body is a mere machine with little sensation and
makes no progress. Cain thus tills the ground, but it
yields him no strength.

The body feels its degradation, and those who get
into this degraded condition are usually miserable. Thus
Cain's punishment is great. He fears the vengeance of
the other faculties; fears that they may condemn the
body (Cain) for its impotency. But Jehovah, divine
law, has fixed a limit to this condemnation, and we are
warned that we must not destroy the body, however
great its sins. This mark set upon Cain to prevent his

being slain is man's consciousness of his divine origin. No matter how deep the body ego may be in transgressions, it still bears the stamp of God and can never be killed out entirely. We cannot kill life, for it is eternal; but we can allow the body ego (Cain) to kill the consciousness of life within the individual organism.

Every man, by his example and word, is his brother's keeper. Jesus said, "Even so let your light shine before men; that they may see your good works, and glorify your Father who is in heaven." This does not nullify the innate freedom of your brother, but rather strengthens your ability to co-operate with the good and make it manifest in your life.

> *Gen. 4:16-24.* And Cain went out from the presence of Jehovah, and dwelt in the land of Nod, on the east of Eden. And Cain knew his wife; and she conceived, and bare Enoch: and he builded a city, and called the name of the city, after the name of his son, Enoch. And unto Enoch was born Irad; and Irad begat Mehujael; and Mehujael begat Methushael; and Methushael begat Lamech. And Lamech took unto him two wives: the name of the one was Adah, and the name of the other Zillah. And Adah bare Jabal: he was the father of such as dwell in tents and *have* cattle. And his brother's name was Jubal: he was the father of all such as handle the harp and pipe. And Zillah, she also bare Tubal-cain, the forger of every cutting instrument of brass and iron: and the sister of Tubal-cain, was Naamah. And Lamech said unto his wives:
> Adah and Zillah, hear my voice;
> Ye wives of Lamech, hearken unto my speech:
> For I have slain a man for wounding me,
> And a young man for bruising me:
> If Cain shall be avenged sevenfold,
> Truly Lamech seventy and sevenfold.

After he had killed Abel, Cain went out from the presence of Jehovah (the body consciousness lost its contact with its spiritual source) and dwelt in the land of Nod, on the east of Eden. After any positive action of the mind there is always an apparent negative reaction. Nod, a name meaning "wandering with uncertainty," suggests the seemingly unguided activity of man's subconsciousness during periods of sleep. The fundamental idea in the word *Nod* is that of uncertainty of mind, bewilderment.

The name *Enoch* means "founder," "centralizer." Metaphysically it denotes entrance into and instruction in a new state of thought or understanding.

The name *Irad* means "self-leading passion," "blind whirling." Irad represents a state in the physical or body consciousness and organism of man, the embodiment of the stubborn, foolish, destructive, devouring—yet transitory and fleeting—emotions and desires that are the result of the sense man's ignorant, confused thoughts and beliefs.

The name *Mehujael* means "manifestation of strength," "physical demonstration of power." Metaphysically Mehujael represents the belief of the outer man that strength and power are purely physical. This belief leads to error manifestations and demonstrations of power and strength that always lead to trouble of some kind; and the outer, personal man usually attributes to God the afflictions and griefs that are the result of his own error activities.

The name *Methushael* means "man of God." Metaphysically Methushael denotes the idea that man is a spiritual and perfect being, which is inherent even in the body consciousness of man (Cain and his descendants represent the body or physical consciousness). Methushael also denotes the error thought of death, of the disintegration of the outer organism that unenlightened man thinks is desirable, inevitable, of God.

The name *Lamech* means "strength," "health," "power." Metaphysically Lamech represents the thought of strength and youth that is carnal and physical.

The name *Adah* means "beauty or comeliness," "adornment," "pleasure." Metaphysically Adah symbolizes a phase of the human soul, the love nature. Love even in limited personal consciousness and expression has its pleasing aspect ("pleasure"). The expression of it adorns one with a certain beauty of character and a grace and comeliness that are lacking in persons who are wanting in love.

The name *Zillah* means "deep," "darkness, gloom, or shadow," "screened," "veiled," "protected." Zillah represents the very great or dense obscurity of thought regarding his true spiritual nature and capabilities that exists in the soul of the individual who is still living wholly in the outer or sense consciousness. Lack of true and clear understanding at this phase of unfoldment is a protection to the individual in that it shields or screens him from experiences that he is not yet able to meet yet would have to face if it were possible for the full light of Truth to enter his consciousness at this time.

The name *Jabal* means "a stream," "a welling up," "abundance." Jabal represents the transitoriness of the outer, physical character of the man who dwells in the animal-strength consciousness. The negative aspects of the name—"wanderer," "passing away," "going out"—

all imply lack of permanence. The word *cattle* refers to animal strength. *Stream* means the "life flow."

The name *Jubal* means "principle of sound," "harmony," "melody." Jubal "was the father of all such as handle the harp and pipe"; in other words, metaphysically he represents a principle of harmony, which might find expression in musical instruments. Thus Jubal symbolizes the natural rhythm, harmony, and joy of life that are experienced when the soul radiates grace, beauty of thought and character, and comeliness (Adah, mother of Jubal), and the body is healthy and strong.

The name *Tubal-cain* means "diffusion of Cain," "diffusion of worldly possessions," "flowing of centralized might." Cain represents the sense selfishness centered by an individual in his own physical being. Tubal-cain denotes a broadening out of the selfishness represented by Cain, or the same selfishness operating on a broader, more universal base. Tubal-cain is sometimes said to have been the inventor of the art of forging metals into cutting instruments.

The name *Naamah* means "amity," "social unity," "grace," "sweet or pleasant." Metaphysically Naamah represents the animal soul in pleasing, harmonious combination with youth even though the consciousness here is of the strength and youth of the outer man.

> *Gen. 4:25-26.* And Adam knew his wife again; and she bare a son, and called his name Seth: For, *said she,* God hath appointed me another seed instead of Abel; for Cain slew him. And to Seth, to him also there was born a son; and he called his name Enosh. Then began men to call upon the name of Jehovah.

The third son of Adam and Eve, Seth, was born after the death of Abel. The name *Seth* means "compensation," "substituted"; but more particularly it carries the idea of settled, placed, set. The root idea is that of surrounding sympathetic forces which envelop a thing and define its limits. Some mystics have seen in the meaning of the name a reference to the law of destiny: that which predetermines a thing and settles the order of its occurrence.

While man is in a sense a creature of free will, yet in a larger sense he is a son of God, made in His image and likeness and destined to express and demonstrate spiritual perfection. There is in all the universe, including man, a balancing power of good, of protection, that causes readjustment and healing to supervene after every transgression of law or wandering away from that which is wholesome and true. This is set forth very clearly in Bible symbology and history. Every time man has wandered away, gone to some extreme, he has experienced a reaction and been led back to a saner standpoint. It is thus that he evolves and grows into a full consciousness of his perfect good. His growth in Christlikeness is greatly accelerated however when he comes into a knowledge of the Truth that makes him free, and begins to think and act consciously and voluntarily in harmony with it.

The spiritual idea killed out by the carnality of Cain (represented by his slaying of Abel) was reincarnated or reborn in another spiritual idea (identified with the personality of Seth), as compensation for the loss of the original concept.

"And to Seth, to him also there was born a son; and he called his name Enosh. Then began men to call upon the name of Jehovah." The name *Enosh* means "a miserable man," "mortal man." When man comes to the end of his personal resources and sees the nothingness of all his efforts in the outer, apart from Spirit, he begins to look for a higher ideal to express in his life. He calls on the name of Jehovah. It is the activity of the awakening spiritual ideas within him (Seth) that causes him first to realize the futility of his human efforts to better himself, and then to recognize the one Source of all true uplift and good.

Gen. 5. This is the book of the generations of Adam. In the day that God created man, in the likeness of God made he him; male and female created he them, and blessed them, and called their name Adam, in the day when they were created. And Adam lived a hundred and thirty years, and begat a son in his own likeness, after his image; and called his name Seth: and the days of Adam after he begat Seth were eight hundred years: and he begat sons and daughters. And all the days that Adam lived were nine hundred and thirty years: and he died.

And Seth lived a hundred and five years, and begat Enosh: and Seth lived after he begat Enosh eight hundred and seven years, and begat sons and daughters: and all the days of Seth were nine hundred and twelve years: and he died.

And Enosh lived ninety years, and begat Kenan: and Enosh lived after he begat Kenan eight hundred and fifteen years, and begat sons and daughters: and all the days of Enosh were nine hundred and five years: and he died.

And Kenen lived seventy years, and begat Mahalalel: and Kenan lived after he begat Mahalalel eight hundred and forty years, and begat sons and daughters: and all the days of Kenan were nine hundred and ten years: and he died.

And Mahalalel lived sixty and five years, and begat Jared: and Mahalalel lived after he begat Jared eight hundred and thirty years, and begat sons and daughters: and all the days of Mahalalel were eight hundred and ninety and five years: and he died.

And Jared lived a hundred sixty and two years, and begat Enoch: and Jared lived after he begat Enoch eight hundred years, and begat sons and daughters: and all the days of Jared were nine hundred sixty and two years: and he died.

And Enoch lived sixty and five years, and begat Methuselah: and Enoch walked with God after he begat Methuselah three hundred years, and begat sons and daughters: and all the days of Enoch were three hundred and sixty and five years: and Enoch walked with God: and he was not; for God took him.

And Methuselah lived a hundred eighty and seven years, and begat Lamech: and Methuselah lived after he begat Lamech seven hundred eighty and two years, and begat sons and daughters: and all the days of Methuselah were nine hundred sixty and nine years: and he died.

And Lamech lived a hundred eighty and two years, and begat a son: and he called his name Noah, saying, This same shall comfort us in our work and in the toil of our hands, *which cometh* because of the ground which Jehovah hath cursed. And Lamech lived after he begat Noah five hundred ninety and five years, and begat sons and daughters: And all the days of Lamech were seven hundred seventy and seven years: and he died.

And Noah was five hundred years old: and Noah begat Shem, Ham, and Japheth.

The name *Adam* means "red," "ruddy," "firm." Adam is the first man of the human race according to the Bible. Metaphysically Adam represents the first movement in the evolution of the man idea in its contact with life and substance. Adam also represents generic man; that is, the whole human race epitomized in the typical individual-man idea.

Adam in his original state was a spiritually illumined creation. Spirit breathed into him continually the necessary inspiration and knowledge to give him superior understanding. But he began "eating" or appropriating thoughts of two powers: God and not-God, good and evil. The result, so the allegory runs, was that he fell away from spiritual life and all that it involves.

Man is Spirit, absolute and unconditioned; but man forms an Adamic consciousness into which he breathes the breath of life; this, in its perfect expression, is the Son of man, the expression of the divine idea. This Adam is all of what we term soul, intellect, and body. We are continually at work with this Adam; we can breathe into his nostrils the breath of life, insiring him with the idea of life in all its unlimited fullness. We can lift up this Adam by infusing into him this sublime idea, and in no other way.

The name *Seth* means "substituted," "settled," "compensated." Seth represents the root idea of surrounding sympathetic forces.

The name *Enosh* means "transient man," "mortal man." Enosh represents the outer or body consciousness in its limited, material, corruptible concept of the organism.

The name *Kenan* means "self-centered one," "possession invading space." Kenan denotes the seemingly established materiality of consciousness and organism. But the higher, more spiritual thought represented by Seth is at work, and the man, though seemingly established in materiality, is reaching out of the lesser self ("possession invading space") and upward toward something that has more power to uplift, enlighten, heal, renew, and restore than anything to be found in the material. Thus Kenan brings forth Mahalalel.

The name *Mahalalel* means "mighty rising," "glory of brightness," "praise of God." Metaphysically Mahalalel denotes that in man which praises and blesses and glorifies God, the good.

The name *Jared* means "descending," "low country." Metaphysically Jared denotes the descent of Spirit through praise and acknowledgment of God (Mahalalel, father of Jared), into the seemingly earthly or physical in man ("low ground") in order to lift man wholly into spiritual consciousness (Enoch, son of Jared).

The name *Enoch* means "founder," "instructor," "repentance." Enoch walked with God and did not die.. He was translated into the spiritual consciousness. Enoch represents entrance into and instruction in the new life in Christ.

The name *Methuselah* means "man of the sword," "sting of death." Methuselah has the record of having lived in the earthly body longer than any other man. Metaphysically Methuselah denotes a quick, piercing thought or word ("sword," "dart") of life, power, and oneness with God, which while it causes a renewal of youth to a degree and serves to lengthen one's life in the body, does not become abiding enough in the consciousness at the Methuselah stage of man's unfoldment to put away the appearance of death entirely.

The name *Lamech* means "strong young man," "health," "power." Metaphysically Lamech represents the strength of youth, the vital something in us that

overcomes thoughts and tendencies leading to dissolution. The vital life principle constantly inspires us
from within to keep on living. This thought of youth
was in Lamech, the father of Noah, and it found expression in Noah. The strength and youth symbolized
by the Lamech descended from Adam through Cain is
carnal and physical. The Lamech descended from
Adam through Seth, which God sent to replace Abel,
represents a higher, a more spiritual understanding.

Lamech signifies the principle of life, which not
only tends to keep one alive in the body but also
brings about the building of a new body and re-entrance
into manifest existence for each one who lets go of
his consciousness of life in the body for a time.

The name *Noah* means "rest," "calm," "peace."
Noah was the son of Lamech, the "strong young man."
It is in the strength of our youth that we idealize
the material and attach our spiritual enthusiasm to
the things of sense. But the law of reaction sets in:
Noah (rest) finds "favor in the eyes of Jehovah." If
in the strength of your youth you have indulged in the
things of sense, the law of spiritual equilibrium (the
Lord, Jehovah) is now working itself out in a "rest"
and you may have bodily ills. Thus your race of wicked
thoughts is drowned and your earth cleansed. Noah
can also denote the obedience through which seed for a
new state of consciousness is saved. Again Noah represents the consciousness at rest in God (Gen. 6:9). In
Genesis 6:10 the sons of Noah represent typical states
of mind. Shem ("renowned") represents the spiritual;
Ham ("warm") represents the physical mind, and
Japheth ("extended") represents the intellect or reason.

Chapter IV

The Reaction to Sense Living

GENESIS 6, 7, 8, 9, 10, and 11

THE RESULT of sense living is the resistance that is a part of man's consciousness. The mind of man is constantly at work, and this work results in the production of thought forms. These thought forms assume individual definiteness; they take on personality. They are aggregated into a composite mind, which works out into the body. Whenever a new idea is introduced into the mind, the personality is disturbed. It resists; but the spiritual idea is always more powerful than the personal, and with this resistance comes more or less commotion in the consciousness.

Those who have entered into this process of spiritual evolution, or what Jesus called the regeneration, are prepared for the reception of these divine new ideas, and instead of resisting they say with Jesus, "Not my will, but thine, be done." This attitude opens the way for the easy advent into their consciousness of God ideas and leads to an inspiration or steady flow of ideas into it. In this way the sense consciousness is being transformed or lifted up, and the new man appears while the old man is sloughed off. This is crucifixion. The assimilation of the new ideas leads to resurrection and finally to ascension.

There have been many floods upon the earth, and nearly every people has traditions of a time when to them "the whole earth" was engulfed in a great deluge. Geologists are agreed that there have been many deluges in the history of the earth. But these do not necessarily refer to the Flood of Genesis, nor do they corroborate it as history.

As history the story of the great rain in Genesis is very uncertain, and from a historical standpoint we should gain but little of value from its study. But as a symbolic description of certain habits of thought both in the individual and in the race and of the result of those habits of thought in consciousness, we can profit much from the story's study.

When we observe cloud formations over the earth we can be sure that rain is indicated. The wind may blow the clouds away from the immediate vicinity, but some other part of the earth will get the rain. "Clouds" formed by ignorant or erroneous thinking also indicate a coming storm. The effect of untrue thoughts may become manifest in any part of the body.

The trials and reverses in the life of an individual can be traced to a definite cause in his thinking. In it there has been some error of belief or some confusion of thought, which in its natural course under the law has worked itself into outer expression as in apparent loss, an accident, a disappointment, or a disease. We deplore the condition, yet see in it two possibilities of good. First the manifestation has fulfilled the law and provided an avenue of escape for the pent-up error within, and secondly, it has taught a valuable lesson. There is small comfort in the thought that an earthquake has relieved a strained and abnormal condition in the earth's crust. Yet when we look a little deeper we see that a strained and abnormal condition in the race thought that had to become manifest has been relieved and the race consciousness is the better for it.

> *Gen. 6:1-7.* And it came to pass, when men began to multiply on the face of the ground, and daughters were born unto them, that the sons of God saw the daughters of men that they were fair; and they took them wives of all that they chose. And Jehovah said, My Spirit shall not strive with man for ever, for that he also is flesh: yet shall his days be a hundred and twenty years. The Nephilim were in the earth in those days, and also after that, when the sons of God came in unto the daughters of men, and they bare children to them: the same were the mighty men that were of old, the men of renown.
>
> And Jehovah saw that the wickedness of man was great in the earth, and that every imagination of the thoughts of his heart was only evil continually. And it repented Jehovah that he had made man on the earth, and it grieved him at his heart. And Jehovah said, I will destroy man whom I have created from the face of the ground; both man, and beast, and creeping things, and birds of the heavens; for it repenteth me that I have made them.

When we lower our ideals to a material basis, "the sons of God" are taking unto themselves wives of "the daughters of men:" "Jehovah saw that the wickedness of man was great in the earth, and that every imagination of the thoughts of his heart was only evil continually." When we join spiritual faculties like faith, will, and imagination to material surroundings and personalities and sensual desires, we are falling short of the law of Being, which is that these higher faculties shall draw from the formless and be joined to that realm. The Nephilim represent spiritual ideas (sons of God) uniting with psychical forces to bring forth unregenerated physical forces. To unite spiritual ideas with sensual images is in direct opposition to divine law and in the Scripture is termed "wickedness."

When the wrong use of the spiritual faculties reaches a certain limit, the law (Lord) of our being begins to regulate the consciousness. Outraged nature reacts; a destruction of the false, man-made condition sets in. This it is which is symbolized in the Book of Genesis by the "flood" of Noah.

> *Gen. 6:8-17.* But Noah found favor in the eyes of Jehovah. These are the generations of Noah. Noah was a righteous man, *and* perfect in his generations: Noah walked with God. And Noah begat three sons, Shem, Ham, and Japheth. And the earth was corrupt before God, and the earth was filled with violence. And God saw the earth, and, behold, it was corrupt; for all flesh had corrupted their way upon the earth.
>
> And God said unto Noah, The end of all flesh is come before me; for the earth is filled with violence through them; and, behold, I will destroy them with the earth. Make thee an ark of gopher wood; rooms shalt thou make in the ark, and shalt pitch it within and without with pitch. And this is how thou shalt make it: the length of the ark three hundred cubits, the breadth of it fifty cubits, and the height of it thirty cubits. A light shalt thou make to the ark, and to a cubit shalt thou finish it upward; and the door of the ark shall thou set in the side thereof; with lower, second, and third stories shalt thou make it. And I, behold, I do bring the flood of waters upon the earth, to destroy all flesh, wherein is the breath of life, from under heaven; everything that is in the earth shall die.

Lamech, the name of Noah's father, is a name

signifying "a strong young man," and the name *Noah* means "rest." In the days of our youth we idealize the material world and devote our spiritual faculties to the things of sense. This devotion becomes so complete that we no longer use our spiritual faculties for their proper functions on the spiritual plane. This results in abnormal conditions, and the balance must be restored. A reaction sets in and there is a flood of seemingly adverse experiences. But Noah (rest) finds "favor in the eyes of Jehovah."

One who has indulged the strength of youth (Lamech) in pursuing the things of sense until under the law of spiritual equilibrium he begins to require rest (Noah) may have bodily ills. The cross-currents of thought have brought about a precipitation of negation in the body consciousness, caused by wicked or error thoughts clashing with the spiritually positive ideas. This is followed by the "flood," which drowns out the material thoughts and cleanses the "earth."

Science teaches that man's body contains all the elements that are found in the earth. This gives rise to the thought of "ashes to ashes, dust to dust." Religion however goes a step farther and says that man is the epitome of Being, that he is like his Maker in spirit, soul, and body, the image and likeness of God. If man's body is of the same character as the earth, it is in some of its aspects like its prototype. The earth's surface is three fourths water and the body is about eighty per cent water. This is a major negative condition that needs but little augmenting to cause an overflow or a "flood." Only our positive spiritual thoughts hold back a deluge, and once there is an overbalance the negative is let loose and there is great destruction. There is no stopping this flood by any material means, and one who is spiritually wise will not fear it but rather rejoice in the body cleansing it brings about.

Just as the earth's waters evaporate and surround it with clouds of mist, so the mists and clouds of life surround man's body. As the physical forces move on these mists and clouds of earth, so do the mental forces move on and cause the invisible ethers to condense and flood the body with its own negative thoughts. The poetic words "A flood of thoughts came o'er me" is no metaphor but a physiological fact. When mind and body reach a certain tenseness or strained condition, the law forces a conjunction, and a flood is certain to follow. This is exemplified by what is called a "nervous breakdown." Someone has said that America is fast becoming a nation of neurotics. We certainly need this lesson of Noah (rest) to learn to let go of physical tenseness and material things. This rest can be attained only when we realize that our faculties are spiritual and must seek spiritual expression.

Man is an epitome of all that exists in Being, even as regards the Spirit of God, which is inspired in him. But man is a free agent. He can open his mind to the divine intelligence and know the creative law or he can work out his unfoldment through blind experimentation. Our race is in the experimental stage. In our ignorance we transgress the law to the very limit, and then, a great reaction sets in; a general condition that is negative to the point of dissolution. Then that in us which always looks obediently to God in an extremity is awakened and we seek the divine law. This obedient disposition is represented by Noah, through whom the seed of a new state of consciousness is saved.

> *Gen. 6:18-22.* But I will establish my covenant with thee; and thou shalt come into the ark, thou, and thy sons, and thy wife, and thy sons' wives with thee. And of every living thing of all flesh, two of every sort shalt thou bring into the ark, to keep them alive with thee; they shall be male and female. Of the birds after their kind, and of the cattle after their kind, of every creeping thing of the ground after its kind, two of every sort shall come unto thee, to keep them alive. And take thou unto thee of all food that is eaten, and gather it to thee; and it shall be food for thee, and for them. Thus did Noah; according to all that God commanded him, so did he.

The only refuge from this "flood" is the ark of Jehovah. The ark represents a positive, saving state of consciousness, which agrees with or forms a covenant with the principle of Being, with subconscious inspiration, with Christ. This ark is the product of "rest," "abiding" (Noah), in the spiritual part of us, right in the midst of the flood of error. Noah heeded not the jeers of the people about him but rested on the promise of God.

Your ark must be built on a scientific understanding of the truth as regards the presence, power, and wisdom of God. This is suggested by the mathematical dimensions prescribed for the ark. Your ark is built on affirmations of what you are in Spirit. You take with you into the ark your wife, your sons and their wives (spiritual principles inhering in the soul), and "of every living thing of all flesh, two of every sort" (male and female or positive and negative activities of life in the organism).

The idea of divine Truth must be fed with true affirmations as you are being lifted up and above the flood of error thoughts that surge about you. In due time the waters of negation will subside and enable you to walk forth and to people the "earth" of your body with new and better ideas.

In case the error thoughts destroy the body of flesh, the ark represents the new body that the mind spiritually projects and that forms the basis of the organism in the new incarnation.

The story of Noah and the Flood portrays in wonderful symbolism the manner in which one of the faculties of being operates in unfolding the perfect man. The faculty of renunciation is twofold in action: it eliminates the error, and it expands the good. The name *Noah* connotes the sweet rest and quiet comfort that come after the soul has worked out some of its problems in consciousness and has perceived that there is an original spark of divinity in man that is most sacred and holy and that man's spiritual development consists in the expansion of this original divine spark. Jehovah, the image-and-likeness man created by Elohim God, recognizes only the good and instructs His Adam man to open his consciousness to good thoughts and to cleanse his consciousness from all evil by the flood waters of denial.

Man is making his body temple an eternal dwelling place for the soul. His goal is to bring into expression the kingdom of the heavens and to establish it within himself. To do this he needs to realize that the old is constantly passing away and the new constantly coming in according to the outworking of the law. He should not resist this change but rather assist in bringing it about. We are born daily and we die daily in some phase of consciousness. Some errors may stick in our mind for a while, but when new light is born in consciousness, old thoughts are carried away by Noah's Flood.

Gen. 7:1-24. And Jehovah said unto Noah, Come thou and all thy house into the ark; for thee have I seen righteous before me in this generation. Of every clean beast thou shalt take to thee seven and seven, the male and his female; and of the beasts that are not clean two, the male and his female; of the birds also of the heavens, seven and seven, male and female, to keep seed alive upon the face of all the earth. For yet seven days, and I will cause it to rain upon the earth forty days and forty nights; and every living thing that I have made will I destroy them off the face of the ground. And Noah did according unto all that Jehovah commanded him.

And Noah was six hundred years old when the flood of waters was upon the earth. And Noah went in, and his sons, and his wife, and his sons' wives with him, into the ark, because of the waters of the flood. Of clean beasts, and of beasts that are not clean, and of birds, and of everything that creepeth upon the ground, there went in two and two unto Noah into the ark, male and female, as God commanded Noah. And it came to pass after the seven days, that the waters of the flood were upon the earth. In the six hundredth year of Noah's life, in the second month, on the seventeenth day of the month, on the same day were all the fountains of the great deep broken up, and the windows of heaven were opened. And the rain was upon the earth forty days and forty nights.

In the selfsame day entered Noah, and Shem, and Ham, and Japheth, the sons of Noah, and Noah's wife, and the three wives of his sons with them, into the ark; they, and every beast after its kind, and all the cattle after their kind, and every creeping thing that creepeth upon the earth after its kind, and every bird after its kind, every bird of every sort. And they went in unto Noah into the ark, two and two of all flesh wherein is the breath of life. And they that went in, went in male and female of all flesh, as God commanded him: and Jehovah shut him in. And the flood was forty days upon the earth; and the waters increased, and bare up the ark, and it was lifted up above the earth. And the waters prevailed, and increased greatly upon the earth; and the ark went upon the face of the waters. And the waters prevailed exceedingly upon the earth; and all the high mountains that were under the whole heaven were covered. Fifteen cubits upward did the waters prevail; and the mountains were covered. And all flesh died that moved upon the earth, both birds, and cattle, and beasts, and every creeping thing that creepeth upon the earth, and every man: all in whose nostrils was the breath of the spirit of life, of all that was on dry land, died. And every living thing was destroyed that was upon the face of the ground, both man, and cattle, and creeping things, and birds of the heavens; and they were destroyed from the earth: and Noah only was left, and they that were with him in the ark. And the waters prevailed upon the earth a hundred and fifty days.

"The rain was upon the earth forty days and forty nights." The number 40 is made up of the number 4, representing unlimited freedom of action, and the cipher, 0, representing unlimited capacity of action. This number is used where a definite time cannot be

given. "Day" and "night" represent periods of understanding and lack of understanding, succeeding
each other during the "forty" period. The number of
Noah's age, 600, represents an established degree of
spiritual unfoldment. The number 7 represents the
evolution and fulfillment of the spiritual law of man
on the natural plane.

(For further interpretation of this material see
comments on Gen. 6:8-22.)

> *Gen. 8:1-3.* And God remembered Noah, and
> all the beasts, and all the cattle that were with him
> in the ark: and God made a wind to pass over the
> earth, and the waters assuaged; the fountains also
> of the deep and the windows of heaven were
> stopped, and the rain from heaven was restrained;
> and the waters returned from off the earth contin-
> ually: and after the end of a hundred and fifty days
> the waters decreased.

This Scripture describes symbolically a change in
consciousness from the negative to the positive state.
A certain set of negative thoughts run their course and
the restorative thought forces are in evidence.

> *Gen. 8:4-6.* And the ark rested in the seventh
> month, on the seventeenth day of the month, upon
> the mountain of Ararat. And the waters decreased
> continually until the tenth month: in the tenth
> month, on the first day of the month, were the tops
> of the mountains seen.
> And it came to pass at the end of forty days, that
> Noah opened the window of the ark which he had
> made:

Ararat symbolizes resting in a state of consciousness
high above the physical plane, where one gets a wide
perspective of material things. It is the place of rest

(Noah) that one arrives at through understanding and that follows turbulence, tribulation, and a flood of negative conditions.

The number 7 represents fullness in the world of phenomena. It always refers to the divine law of perfection for the divine-natural man. As man lays hold of the indwelling Christ, the Saviour, he is raised out of the Adam consciousness. He then enters the seventh stage of his unfoldment, where he finds rest and peace. It is the seventh or perfect stage of man's natural development.

The ark reaches the seventh stage of unfoldment in a high consciousness, which brings a certain measure of peace and rest.

> *Gen. 8:7-14.* And he sent forth a raven, and it went forth to and fro, until the waters were dried up from off the earth. And he sent forth a dove from him, to see if the waters were abated from off the face of the ground; but the dove found no rest for the sole of her foot, and she returned unto him to the ark; for the waters were on the face of the whole earth: and he put forth his hand, and took her, and brought her in unto him into the ark. And he stayed yet other seven days; and again he sent forth the dove out of the ark; and the dove came in to him at eventide; and, lo, in her mouth an olive-leaf plucked off: so Noah knew that the waters were abated from off the earth. And he stayed yet other seven days, and sent forth the dove; and she returned not again unto him any more.
>
> And it came to pass in the six hundred and first year, in the first month, the first day of the month, the waters were dried up from off the earth: and Noah removed the covering of the ark, and looked, and, behold, the face of the ground was dried. And in the second month, on the seven and twentieth

day of the month, was the earth dry.

When we begin to realize that we have attained a new and high state of consciousness we are more or less in doubt as to its stability. This uncertainty is symbolized by the raven. The seven days' wait means that we test the principles of the sevenfold law.

Then we send forth the dove, which represents peace of mind and confidence in the divine law. The dove is nonresistant: we rest in the Spirit. The dove brings back a green olive leaf (which represents the beginning of a new growth). We start on a new cycle of unfoldment.

Gen. 8:15-22. And God spake unto Noah, saying, Go forth from the ark, thou, and thy wife, and thy sons, and thy sons' wives with thee. Bring forth with thee every living thing that is with thee of all flesh, both birds, and cattle, and every creeping thing that creepeth upon the earth; that they may breed abundantly in the earth, and be fruitful, and multiply upon the earth. And Noah went forth, and his sons, and his wife, and his sons' wives with him: every beast, every creeping things, and every bird, whatsoever moveth upon the earth, after their families, went forth out of the ark.

And Noah builded an alter unto Jehovah, and took of every clean beast, and of every clean bird, and offered burnt-offerings on the altar. And Jehovah smelled the sweet savor; and Jehovah said in his heart, I will not again curse the ground any more for man's sake, for that the imagination of man's heart is evil from his youth; neither will I again smite any more everything living, as I have done. While the earth remaineth, seedtime and harvest, and cold and heat, and summer and winter, and day and night shall not cease.

The altar in this case represents an abiding resolution of the spiritual-minded one (Noah) who makes a covenant with the Lord to continue to "sacrifice" his sensations or transmute them on the spiritual plane. The spiritual-minded person should have his daily meditations and prayers, during which he lifts up all his states of consciousness, both masculine and feminine, seeking to know the reality back of appearances and to restore them to the Lord. This is symbolized by the daily sacrifice of the animals that came out of the ark. Thus the body is secured against the results of another universal judgment of error thoughts.

Gen. 9:1-7. And God blessed Noah and his sons, and said unto them, Be fruitful, and multiply, and replenish the earth. And the fear of you and the dread of you shall be upon every beast of the earth, and upon every bird of the heavens; with all wherewith the ground teemeth, and all the fishes of the sea, into your hand are they delivered. Every moving thing that liveth shall be food for you; as the green herb have I given you all. But flesh with the life thereof, *which is* the blood thereof, shall ye not eat. And surely your blood, *the blood* of your lives, will I require; at the hand of every beast will I require it: and at the hand of man, even at the hand of every man's brother, will I require the life of man. Whoso sheddeth man's blood, by man shall his blood be shed: for in the image of God made He man. And you, be ye fruitful, and multiply; bring forth abundantly in the earth, and multiply therein.

Noah (the consciousness), with his sons (states of mind), after the Flood (his purification) is very closely related to God.

The "flood" cleanses man of certain cloudy states of mind, and he begins to see that he lives on three planes of consciousness, represented by Noah's three sons: Ham, whose name means "hot," typifying body mind; Shem, whose name means "renowned," typifying Spirit-mind, and Japheth, whose name means "extended and wide," typifying the intellect. He also sees that his body mind organizes a fourth plane, that of the visible flesh, Canaan.

The matter of food is also to be solved. "Every moving thing that liveth shall be food for you; as the green herb have I given you all." The wording implies that green herbs are to be the food of both man and animal. But the next command is "But flesh with the life thereof, which is the blood thereof, shall ye not eat." The importance of the living element in blood is its soul (Hebrew *nephesh*), which becomes part of man's soul when he eats the blood of animals. This is forbidden, hence to this day orthodox Hebrews drain the blood from the animal flesh before it is offered for food. It is also significant that green herbs are now recommended for food for both animals and man. When we eat of the flesh of animals as popularly prepared we appropriate the soul of the animal as well as the body, and our soul is mentally impregnated with animal tendencies. As Byron said, "the eating of meat makes me savage."

God covenants or agrees to bless the purified consciousness and its realm of ideas (seed). Every idea (living creature) that is illumined of Spirit—even an idea relating to the body consciousness (earth)—is blessed when man knows the creative law and operates in accord with it.

Once the consciousness has been cleansed and man has awakened to his spiritual nature, he is saved through obedience to divine law and is no longer subject to dissolution through negative means. This "covenant," which is eternal, is with those who give up mind and body to the keeping of divine law. The "bow" signifies the orderly arrangement of ideas in Divine Mind and their perfect manifestation. One who is poised in Truth rests in the consciousness of God's presence even in the midst of error (the cloud).

Gen. 9:8-19. And God spake unto Noah, and to his sons with him, saying, And I, behold, I establish my covenant with you, and with your seed after you; and with every living creature that is with you, the birds, the cattle, and every beast of the earth with you; of all that go out of the ark, even every beast of the earth. And I will establish my covenant with you; neither shall all flesh be cut off any more by the waters of the flood; neither shall there any more be a flood to destroy the earth. And God said, This is the token of the covenant which I make between me and you and every living creature that is with you, for perpetual generations: I do set my bow in the cloud, and it shall be for a token of a covenant between me and the earth. And it shall come to pass, when I bring a cloud over the earth, that the bow shall be seen in the cloud, and I will remember my covenant, which is between me and you and every living creature of all flesh; and the waters shall no more become a flood to destroy all flesh. And the bow shall be in the cloud; and I will look upon it, that I may remember the everlasting covenant between God and every living creature of all flesh that is upon the earth. And God said unto Noah, This is the token of the covenant which I have established between me and all flesh that is upon the earth.

And the sons of Noah, that went forth from the ark, were Shem, and Ham, and Japheth: and Ham is the father of Canaan. These three were the sons of Noah: and of these was the whole earth over-spread.

God made a covenant with Noah that the earth should not again be flooded, and the rainbow was given as a sign of this covenant. The rainbow as a token of the covenant between God and the earth involves the law of obedience. It is also symbolic of the human race and of the law of unity. The rainbow is formed of many drops of water, each of which acts as a prism, receiving light from the sun and transmitting it by refraction. Each drop represents a human being and the whole race. Only as the drops refract the sun's rays do they become visible and only as man "refracts" God does he make his demonstration.

The seven colors of the solar spectrum are produced by different rates of vibration of a universal energy that in its myriad activities makes the visible universe.

When man is like Noah, obedient to the guidance of God, he is never flooded by negative conditions. When the whole race enters into this obedience, the perfect principles of unity and God refraction and reflection will be forever established. The rainbow is the sign of this state in which we shall all form with our obedient mind a circle of natural perfection. As the rainbow connects the heavens and the earth, so the state of perfect obedience and unity in Spirit brings the earth and the kingdom of the heavens together as one.

Gen. 9:20-29. And Noah began to be a husbandman, and planted a vineyard: and he drank of the wine, and was drunken; and he was uncovered within his tent. And Ham, the father of Canaan,

saw the nakedness of his father, and told his two
brethren without. And Shem and Japheth took a
garment, and laid it upon both their shoulders, and
went backward, and covered the nakedness of their
father; and their faces were backward, and they
saw not their father's nakedness. And Noah awoke
from his wine, and knew what his youngest son
had done unto him. And he said,
Cursed be Canaan;
A servant of servants shall he be unto his brethren.
And he said,
Blessed be Jehovah, the God of Shem;
And let Canaan be his servant.
God enlarge Japheth,
And let him dwell in the tents of Shem;
And let Canaan be his servant.
    And Noah lived after the flood three hundred
and fifty years. And all the days of Noah were nine
hundred and fifty years: and he died.

Noah had planted a vineyard, and he drank of the
wine: took into his physical nature the juice of the
grape. This is symbolical of the new spiritual life that
is still contaminated by the sense consciousness. Noah
had given his attention to the cultivation of the vineyard (earth consciousness) rather than the cultivation
of the spiritual consciousness. More thoroughly to
explain what the drunkenness of Noah signifies we
must resolve the allegory into its spiritual elements.

Noah became "uncovered" or naked (lost his garment of Truth) because he mixed sense (artificial)
stimulants with the new wine of life, Spirit. His cultivation of the life force in this physical manner is
like the work of some of our physical scientists. Athletes
cultivate the physical in an effort to increase the flow
of life force and imagine that the physical side is

the whole thing. Instead of illuminating Noah or giving him life the wine put him to sleep. He was intoxicated with error thought, and this opened his consciousness to negation. The higher man saw at once that he was not expressing spiritual Truth.

Although the sons of Noah were supposed to be on a higher plane than he, yet they were also in sense consciousness in a measure, and this is especially true of Ham. Now there is a higher and lower physical consciousness, and the name of Canaan, Ham's son, is introduced to symbolize the lower physical thought, the organized body. Ham saw the ignorance and the nakedness that sense thinking had produced in his father but did nothing to remedy it, nor did he try to extenuate the uncovering in any way. To Ham the thing was more or less a joke, and he told his brothers about it, evidently in a scandalous way. This reveals that man cannot get spiritual life out of material thought.

Shem, representing the Spirit in man, and Japheth, representing the intellectual nature, have pity on their father (man) because of his exposure of his nakedness and sensuality and try to cover it up without seeing it as a reality. They put a garment over their shoulders and walk backward and spread it over their father's nakedness. They do not view the occurrence as a reality.

When Noah awoke from his wine—that is, returned to his spiritual consciousness—his first words were "Cursed be Canaan." Canaan means "lowland" and represents the body consciousness. "A servant of servants shall he be unto his brethren," he said, thus placing the stamp of materiality upon the body consciousness and showing that it cannot give spiritual life.

But Noah said to the God of Shem, "Let Canaan be his servant"; that is, let the flesh come under the dominion of the spiritual man. Of Japheth Noah said, "Let him dwell in the tents of Shem"; that is, let the intellectual man dwell under the protection of the spiritual man, not as a servant but as a younger brother. Thus the physical mind (Ham) and the body (Canaan) come under the dominion of both the intellectual man and the spiritual man, the I AM itself.

The sons of Noah represent the positive, permanent thoughts that rise above the negative, wicked conditions, even the catastrophe of death (the Flood), and come down to earth again. In other words, they are carried over and reincarnated when the soul again takes on a body of flesh.

In order to get the most from physical man we must seek to develop him along spiritual lines. When the spiritual man (Noah) begins a new cycle, a new evolution in physical consciousness (after the cleansing of the "flood") he must give attention to the impact of the ideas put into the body consciousness, select carefully his food and drink, and refuse to give himself to the sense consciousness in any way.

We find the 10th chapter of Genesis to be devoted to genealogy. It gives an account of the descendents of Noah and his three sons, Shem, Ham, and Japheth.

> *Gen. 10:1-32.* Now these are the generations of the sons of Noah, *namely,* of Shem, Ham, and Japheth: and unto them were sons born after the flood. The sons of Japheth: Gomer, and Magog, and Madai, and Javan, and Tubal, and Meshech,

and Tiras. And the sons of Gomer: Ashkenaz, and Riphath, and Togarmah. And the sons of Javan: Elishah, and Tarshish, and Kittim, and Dodanim. Of these were the isles of the nations divided in their lands, every one after his tongue, after their families, in their nations.

And the sons of Ham: Cush, and Mizraim, and Put, and Canaan. And the sons of Cush: Seba, and Havilah, and Sabtah, and Raamah, Sabteca; and the sons of Raamah: Sheba, and Dedan. And Cush begat Nimrod: he began to be a mighty one in the earth. He was a mighty hunter before Jehovah: wherefore it is said, Like Nimrod a mighty hunter before Jehovah. And the beginning of his kingdom was Babel, and Erech, and Accad, and Calneh, in the land of Shinar. Out of that land he went forth into Assyria, and builded Nineveh, and Rehoboth-Ir, and Calah, and Resen, between Nineveh and Calah (the same is the great city). And Mizraim begat Ludim, and Anamim, and Lehabim, and Naphtuhim, and Pathrusim, and Casluhim (whence went forth the Philistines), and Caphtorim.

And Canaan begat Sidon his first-born, and Heth, and the Jebusite, and the Amorite, and the Girgashite, and the Hivite, and the Arkite, and the Sinite, and the Arvadite, and the Zemarite, and the Hamathite: and afterward were the families of the Canaanite spread abroad. And the border of the Canaanite was from Sidon, as thou goest toward Gerar, unto Gaza; as thou goest toward Sodom and Gomorrah and Admah and Zeboiim, unto Lasha. These are the sons of Ham, after their families, after their tongues, in their lands, in their nations.

And unto Shem, the father of all the children of Eber, the elder brother of Japheth, to him also were children born. The sons of Shem: Elam, and Asshur, and Arpachshad, and Lud, and Aram. And the sons of Aram: Uz, and Hul, and Gether, and Mash. And Arpachshad begat Shelah; and Shelah

begat Eber. And unto Eber was born two sons:
the name of the one was Peleg; for in his days was
the earth divided; and his brother's name was Joktan. And Joktan begat Almodad, and Sheleph, and
Hazarmaveth, and Jerah, and Hadoram, and Uzal,
and Diklah, and Obal, and Abimael, and Sheba, and
Ophir, and Havilah, and Jobab: all these were the
sons of Joktan. And their dwelling was from Mesha,
as thou goest toward Sephar, the mountain of the east.
These are the sons of Shem, after their families,
after their tongues, in their lands, after their nations.

These are the families of the sons of Noah,
after their generations, in their nations: and of
these were the nations divided in the earth after the
flood.

The name *Shem* means "upright," "renowned,"
"splendor," "name." Metaphysically Shem represents
the spiritual in man.

The name *Ham* means "oblique," "curved," "inferior," "hot," "blackened." Metaphysically Ham represents the physical in man, given over to sensuality.

The name *Japheth* means "extended and wide,"
"increase," "expansion," "unfoldment," "extends without limitation." Metaphysically Japheth represents the
intellect or reason, the mental realm. To "extend without limitation" this realm would have to extend into
the spiritual.

Noah's three sons, Shem, Ham, and Japheth, represent the spiritual, the physical, and the mental in
man.

The names of the "sons of Japheth" follow:

The name *Gomer* means "organic accumulation,"
"finished or perfected," "ended." Gomer represents
human reason in its greatest perfection and completion;
but by reasoning alone man cannot reach spiritual wis-

dom and Truth or come in conscious touch with God, Spirit.

The name *Magog* means "region of God," "from the upper, i. e., north," "extreme extension." Symbolically Magog represents the satanic or selfish thought force in human consciousness warring against the true thought force that springs from the ideas that Jesus taught and demonstrated.

The name *Madai* means "sufficiency," "indefinite capacity," "middle portion." Madai represents the phase of being in man that lies between the outer or conscious thinking mind and the superconscious mind or Spirit; the psychic realm.

The name *Javan* means "the East," "the dove," "warmth," "fertility," "mire," "deception." Javan symbolizes the human or personal intellect in man and one of its governing characteristics, the deceptive, error belief that understanding is gained through the impressions of the senses in contact with the outer world and through books, teachers, and experience rather than through the Spirit of God within the soul of man. In the broadest sense Javan also represents the spiritual phase of intelligence or illumined and inspired intellect, hence the idea of the East, of fertility and productiveness.

The name *Tubal* signifies "diffusive motion," "welling," "triumphal song." Tubal represents the expanding possibilities of the consciousness of man, with the joy and the good that result from increased understanding.

The name *Meshech* means "perceptibility," "drawing out," "deducing." Meshech stands for perception through the senses, judgment according to appearances, and the work of the mind in conceiving ideas and in drawing conclusions.

The name *Tiras* means "determination of forms," "thought," "imagination," "desire." Metaphysically Tiras represents the imagination or formative faculty of man made active in the mind of the individual by the inner longing of the soul (desire), whichever leads to unfoldment Godward. As the seventh son of Japheth, Tiras represents a certain fullness or completeness of that which Japheth symbolizes, the mental phase of man's being. The power to think, to image in the mind, is the formative power in man.

The names of "the sons of Gomer," with their meaning, follow:

The name *Ashkenaz* means "fire that spreads," "latent fire," "hidden fire." Ashkenaz represents the life thought formed in Spirit, the "fire that spreads" to assist in doing away with the confused state of mind represented by Babylon. When the life thought is taken up consciously by man it extends quickly to the whole consciousness, overthrowing sense confusion and its inharmonies. Fire stands for cleansing and purification and is generally used in the Bible as a symbol of the destruction of evil and error.

The name *Riphath* signifies "centrifugal force," "spoken word," "pardon," "healing." Riphath symbolizes the power actively expressing itself through the will and the word. This power, though more mental than spiritual, is refining and healing.

The name *Togarmah* means "centralizing energy," "gravitation," "hard," "strong." Togarmah represents strength and a drawing, centralizing force or energy; a force or energy of the intellect rather than of the inner spiritual understanding and therefore characterized by very great hardness and selfishness.

The names of "the sons of Javan" are given here:

The name *Elishah* means "God firmly establishes," "uprightness of God," "God saves." Even the human reason acknowledges that God is the saving power of His people. The intellectual powers of man are human and they are deceptive. Yet they are productive on their own plane; and Elishah represents the power back of the intellect that knows God to be the one true helping, sustaining, saving power in man.

The name *Tarshish* means "precipitating force," "hard," "severity." Tarshish symbolizes the hard, unyielding, argumentative tendency that is characteristic of the purely intellectual and reasoning nature in man when unmixed with divine love and the softening influence of spiritual wisdom.

The name *Kittim* signifies "the cut off," "the rejected," "outsiders." Kittim represents a phase of the outer, sense-reasoning mind in man, as opposed to the inner, true spiritual understanding. This phase of thought must be cut off, rejected, by the individual who would progress spiritually, since it is an "outsider," uncivilized and reprobate as far as Truth is concerned.

The name *Dodanim* means "confederates," "the elect," "lovable," "pleasing." Dodanim represents unifying thoughts of a very excellent character belonging to the intellect in man.

These are the names of "the sons of Ham":

The name *Cush* means "burned," "blackened," "firelike." Cush represents the darkened thought in which man has held his body and its activities, the seemingly mortal, physical part of himself. But this all changes as he perceives the Truth and holds in mind the perfect-body idea.

The name *Mizraim* means "limitation," "bondage," "tribulation." Mizraim is symbolical of the sense belief that the life as well as the organism of man is bound in materiality and that man is subject to sorrows and to all forms of error that hinder him from receiving good.

The name *Put* signifies "state of being stifled," "asphyxiation or suffocation." Put represents the darkened, sorrowful, and very material dying state of mind and body that results from a lack of spiritual inspiration, of the inbreathing and understanding of Spirit.

The name *Canaan* means "material existence," "realized nothingness," "lowland," "inferior." Canaan thus represents the body consciousness; the fleshly organism and tendencies of man; the physical rather than the spiritual. We also think of Canaan as denoting the subconsciousness.

Here are the names of "the sons of Cush," with their meaning:

The name *Seba* signifies "radical mixture," "vital fluid," "intoxicated." Seba represents intemperate desire expressing itself in the body consciousness. The Seba thought or state of thought is not poised, moderate, or well balanced as regards anything; it goes to extremes, especially in the indulgence of the appetites and desires of the flesh.

The name *Havilah* means "struggle of elementary life," "virtue born of trial." Havilah symbolizes the effort, the travail, the trials that are necessary to bring into manifestation the inner spiritual possibilities that lie back of and are wrapped up in the seemingly material organism.

The name *Sabtah* means "determining motion," "a trun," "orbit." Sabtah represents the general cyclical trend of the activity of the sensual in man. Led away by outer seeming, man has through the exercise of his personal will set up a course of action in sense consciousness that falls short of the divine ideal and is contentious and destructive.

The name *Raamah* signifies "moved with agitation," "trembling," "quaking." Raamah represents the result or fruit of the ignorant thought of the sense man regarding his body. This result takes the shape of the nameless fears, inner trembling, and un-Godlike emotions that the sense man experiences.

The significance of the name *Sabteca* is the same as that of Sabtah but greatly intensified.

The following are the names of "the sons of Raamah":

The name *Sheba* means "rest or repose," "stability," "restoration." Sheba represents a thought of wholeness or fullness on some plane of existence. Whether this thought belongs to the inner man or the outer man depends on who the person in the Bible name Sheba is and on his descent, history, or activities. If the activities are constructive or if he owns descent from Shem he represents higher and more spiritual thoughts than if the activities are not constructive and he is descended from Ham.

The name *Dedan* means "mutual attraction," "selective affinity," "physical love." Dedan refers to a phase of physical or animal attraction and affection.

The names of the children of Cush, with their meaning, are given here:

The name *Nimrod* means "self-ruling will," "rebellion." Nimrod denotes the rule of the personal will in the animal forces of the organism; also a material belief in courage and might.

The name *Babel* signifies "court of Baal," "confusion," "chaos," "vanity." When man thinks that he can comprehend and contract the divine in outer or purely mental or psychic ways the result is always confusion.

The name *Erech* means "long," "extended," "slack"; in a good sense, "prolonged," "lasting." Erech represents a state of consciousness in which, because of long and extended material thinking the natural, inherent wholeness and goodness of man is conceived by him entirely in terms of the material, bringing about the disastrous results of error in body and affairs.

The name *Accad* signifies "castle," "fortress," "highland." Accad represents a fixed state of belief that protection, great strength, exalted position, and superiority are to be attained through the intellectual and the physical alone.

The name *Calneh* signifies "complete concentration," "centralized ambition." Calneh represents selfishness, a centering in self; also confidence in material conditions rather than trust in God.

The name *Shinar* signifies "two rivers," "divided stream," "divided mind." Shinar represents a belief in two powers, an evil as well as a good one, and the error results.

Assyria represents the reasonings, philosophical as well as physical, that do not recognize a spiritual head of the universe but are based on sense observation.

The name *Nineveh* means "exterior growth," "co-

ordination," "education of youth." Nineveh represents
the seat of the natural animal forces in man's body
consciousness. The people of Nineveh were not will-
fully wicked; they were only awaiting spiritual instruction that would turn their attention away from the
outer and material to God.

Rehoboth-Ir ("broad places," "enlargements,"
"forums") symbolizes thoughts of a broadening, increasing nature, principally on the intellectual or mental plane in the individual.

The name *Calah* signifies "completed," "integrity,"
"an ancient." Calah represents a state of consciousness
built about the belief that age (in terms of years) and
experience bring balanced judgment and fullness or
perfection.

The name *Resen* means "executive power," "control from above," "restraint." Resen indicates recognition by the natural man that there is a higher guiding, ruling, judging, restraining power in his life than
that of the purely human and material.

The name *Ludim* signifies "travails," "conception,"
"nativity or physical birth." Ludim represents man's
material beliefs regarding the origin and continuation
of the race; also the expression of these beliefs.

The name *Anamim* means "statues," "rockmen,"
"fountains." Anamim represents hard, material
thoughts about life ("fountains"). Such thoughts aid
in building a corruptible body, a mere statue in so far
as its being truly alive through union with the divine
source of all life is concerned.

The name *Lehabim* means "inflamed uprisings,"
"passionate." Lehabim represents the life of the seemingly material and physical organism activated wholly

by the tendencies and desires of the outer animal
man.

Naphtuhim ("the opened," "the hollow," "the
empty ones") represent empty thoughts of lack,
thoughts that the physical man is wholly material.

The name Pathrusim signifies "region of the south,"
"broken into fragments," "dust." The Pathrusim represent thoughts belonging to a state of mind that,
though there is good in it, is still in darkness so far as
the individual is consciously or subconsciously concerned.

The name *Casluhim* signifies "tried for atonement,"
"forgiveness of sins," "hopes of life." The thought
represented by Casluhim is that man's outer consciousness evolves, unfolds, Godward by means of trials,
testings, and experience.

The name *Philistines* signifies "transitory," "migrating," "wandering." The Philistines represent forces
foreign to Spirit. The five great cities of the Philistines
ruled by "lords" denote the five senses under the dominion of thoughts foreign to Spirit (strangers, foreigners).

The name *Caphtorim* means "converts," "conver-
ters." Caphtorim represents changing, growing, unfolding thoughts that belong to the seemingly physical in
man.

The name *Sidon* signifies "catching of fish," "pro-
viding," "hunter." Sidon symbolizes a great increase of
ideas on the animal plane of thought or being in the
individual.

The name *Heth* means "sundered," "broken," "terrified." Heth represents a very active thought of fear,
the result of thinking apart from Spirit.

The name *Jebusite* signifies "trodden down," "conquered," "profaned." A Jebusite represents the spiritual or peace center in consciousness (Jerusalem) in subjection to purely sense and carnal thoughts, beliefs, and desires.

The name *Amorites* signifies "mountaineers," "highlanders." The Amorites represent the race thought of the generation of the flesh. Sex and procreation are very strongly rooted in man's consciousness and have been elevated by man in personal thought to the very heights.

The name *Girgashite* signifies "belonging to that which is dense," "marshy ground." A Girgashite represents the material state of thought that unawakened man holds concerning himself and especially concerning his material organism.

The name *Hivite* signifies "physical existence," "life born of effort," "wickedness." A Hivite represents the thoughts belonging to the carnal consciousness in man.

The name *Arkite* means "fugitive," "blind passions." An Arkite represents thoughts pertaining to the carnal consciousness in man.

The name *Sinite* means "clayey," "muddy," "hateful passions." A Sinite represents thoughts missing the mark, falling short of the divine law.

The name *Arvadite* means "avarice," "plunder," "pirate's den." An Arvadite represents a retreat or refuge or unstable, erring, destructive thoughts in a mixed, confused, ever-changing consciousness of man.

The name *Zemarite* signifies "hunger for dominion or thirst for power," "despot." A Zemarite represents rebellious, tyrannical, despotic thoughts and desires belonging to the "mind of the flesh" consciousness in unredeemed man, the outer seeking dominion.

The name Hamathite means "inclosed," "held together," "fortress." A Hamathite represents confidence in material conditions rather than trust in God.

The name. *Gerar* signifies "a sojourn," "a lodging place," "an encampment." Gerar symbolizes subjective substance and life. In the beginning of man's journey Spiritward this substance and life are in possession of the sense nature (Philistines), and the ruling ego of the sense nature lives in the region of this place.

The name *Gaza* means "strength," "power," "stronghold," Gaza represents strength on a purely physical or sense plane.

The name *Sodom* signifies "consumed with fire," "hidden wiles," "covered conspiracies." Sodom represents an obscure or concealed thought or habit in man.

The name *Gomorrah* means "overbearing," "tyranny," "oppression." Gomorrah represents a state of mind in man that is submerged in sense and is very tyrannical in its nature.

The name *Admah* means "silent," "unrelenting," "a tomb," "a fortress." Admah represents the seeming strength and merciless sureness of the death thought and condition that enters into man's experience as the result of his carnal, material, adverse thoughts and activities.

The name *Zeboiim* signifies "wars," "plunderings," "rendings with the teeth." Zeboiim refers to ravenous appetites, sensual passions, the wild-beast nature holding sway deep in the subconsciousness of many.

The name *Lasha* signifies "bursting forth," "fountains," "for looking upon." The cities that are mentioned in the text with Lasha as being on the southern border of Canaan are representative of the subconscious substance and life in man ruled over and actuated by various phases of the subjective carnal, sense mind. Lasha symbolizes the bursting forth of this inner substance and life into greater activity in consciousness. Lasha also refers to the penetration by higher ideals, truer understanding, of a seemingly mortal and material state of the subjective substance and life in unawakened man.

The names of the children of Shem, with their meaning, are listed here:

The name *Eber* signifies "passed over," "overcome," "a shoot." Eber represents the germination in man's consciousness of the spiritual phase of his being.

The name *Elam* signifies "eternal or everlasting," "fully developed." Elam symbolizes thoughts of the abidingness, resourcefulness, and creative power of Truth, of that which is of God, Spirit.

The name *Asshur* signifies "a step," "level ongoing," "observance of laws," "harmonious." Asshur typifies mental recognition that the entire man, spirit, soul, and body, is free, is of spiritual origin, and is not bound by any limitation of matter.

The name *Arpachshad* signifies "providential regeneration," "realm of astrology." Arpachshad represents the belief in man that his good depends wholly on something outside of himself—his ruling star, fate, providence—instead of depending on the power of his own thoughts to establish within himself and his world what he wills.

The name *Lud* signifies "desire to bring forth," "conception," "creation." Lud represents man's earliest conception of the truth that he is the offspring of God.

The name *Aram* means "highland," "high or ex-

alted." Aram symbolizes the intellect, which has its
foundation in Spirit; but in unawakened man it is
linked up entirely with the outer or material realm
so that it reasons from the basis of the senses instead
of acknowledging Divine Mind as the source of all intelligence.

The names of "the sons of Aram," with their meaning, follow:

The name *Uz* means "growing might," "formative power," "plan." Uz denotes the process of thought
by which man arrives at a conclusion (be it true or
erroneous) and establishes it in consciousness.

The name *Hul* means "circle," "ecstasy," "travail,"
"fear." Hul stands for that in the intellect of man
which seeks to conform to both the spiritual and outer-
sense ideas of wisdom and understanding.

The name *Gether* means "abundance," "pressed
out," "vale of trial." Gether represents man's belief
that much physical effort is needed to make a living and
to acquire abundance; thus he experiences hard labor
and many inharmonies.

The name *Mash* signifies "pressing out by contrac-
tile force," "harvest of fruits." In Mash we see the
intellect in the role of obtaining knowledge. The intellect is not naturally receptive to spiritual understanding. It is aggressive in its nature and it works very
hard in the outer seeking to obtain by force, by personal determination, and by much persistent study
and research the knowledge that it desires. The very
pressure of its outer seeking does open to it something
of the inner light and intelligence of Spirit, though in
its ignorance it usually takes to itself the honor of
having worked out the ideas that come to it from Spirit.

However fruit is realized in increased knowledge.

The name *Shelah* means "security," "peace," "demand," "prayer." Shelah represents a sense of peace, harmony, and security that has come about by prayer, affirmation, and desire centered in that which is good and true.

The names of the children of Eber, with their meaning, are given here:

The name *Peleg* means "separation through grace," "cleaving," "dividing." Peleg represents man's first realization of the difference and seeming separation between his apparently material organism and his inner spiritual ideals. Thus was the "earth divided," and the individual began to recognize his higher nature.

The name *Joktan* signifies "that which is diminished," "lessened," "of little concern." Joktan represents the lessening to the vanishing point of error in the consciousness and life of the unfolding individual.

The following are the names, with their meaning, of the children of Joktan:

The name *Almodad* signifies "measure of God," "the agitator." Almodad represents a certain discernment of the boundless possibilities that are open to man if he makes practical application of Truth. This understanding however proves to be a disturbing element ("agitator") in consciousness because it is not definite enough to bring about the real change of mind that is needed to establish peace and order and to bring forth spiritual fruit.

The name *Sheleph* means "reaction," "refraction," "drawing out." Sheleph represents a working out from within of the spiritual in man; or at least a striving of Spirit within man for greater expression in and through the individual.

The name *Hazarmaveth* means "village of death," "court of death." Hazarmaveth symbolizes a central thought or group of thoughts belonging to the sense mind of man and having as its ruling idea a strong belief in death. Its conception of justice ("court") is always active on the negative, condemnatory, and destructive side.

The name *Jerah* signifies "he will breathe," "he will become inspired," "moon." Jerah represents the light (understanding) of the inspired intellect, or to the capacity of the intellect of man for being illumined by Spirit and for radiating the light of Spirit, divine understanding.

The name *Hadoram* signifies "powerful," "pompous," "majestic." Hadoram represents the lifting up of the outer, sense mind of man, and the attributing of power and might to it as though it were man's highest source of light and good.

The name *Uzal* signifies "continual going forth," "divine spark." Uzal represents the continual unfoldment that takes place in the progressively inclined individual because of his natural tendency to conform to the divine ideal or divine spark within him, which is ever urging him on to higher light, new understanding, purer thoughts and ways.

The name *Diklah* means "palm tree," "palm grove," "ethereal lightness." Diklah denotes the inherent belief of man's inner, spiritual, or true self that complete victory over all error and complete triumph in understanding and life are his heritage.

The name *Obal* signifies "extreme attenuation of matter," "stripped," "barren." Obal denotes the barrenness, nakedness, and nothingness of all that is not founded in Truth.

The name *Abimael* means "a father from God," "father of abundance." Abimael stands for the thought of man as being descended from God; also for the thought of abundance as coming from God. At a certain stage of man's unfoldment however the thought represented by Abimael is not established in consciousness with enough positiveness to produce spiritual results.

The name *Ophir* signifies "a final state," "purity," "ashes." Ophir symbolizes that which remains after the deeper purification by fire has taken place. Through purification by the Christ Spirit, by the baptism of fire, all that is true is refined, purified, and elevated to its rightful place in the kingdom, while the dross or error of the carnal, adverse mind is reduced to dust and ashes.

The name *Jobab* signifies "fullness of joy," "trumpet call of victory," "desert," "wail of tribulation." Here Jobab represents a certain fulfillment of the seeming mortal and an entrance into that which the positive, spiritual meanings of the name denotes: a realization of dominion over error and a rejoicing in Truth.

The name *Mesha* means "harvest of spiritual fruits," "heaped-up fullness of being," "refuge," "freedom." Mesha symbolizes a place in consciousness wherein the inner life forces of the organism are freed from the dominion of carnal thought, thus raising them to higher and more spiritual expression.

The name *Sephar* means "remembering," "engraving," "book." The east always represents the within, and a mountain denotes a high plane of thought. In the consciousness of the individual, Sephar represents that high place within the spiritual realm of his being where a record is kept of all the thoughts, ideals, tendencies, desires, and activities to which he has given attention, even to those that belong to the seemingly changeable and unestablished phase of his consciousness (the Arabian tribes that were descended from Joktan).

> *Gen. 11:1-9.* And the whole earth was of one language and of one speech. And it came to pass, as they journeyed east, that they found a plain in the land of Shinar; and they dwelt there. And they said one to another, Come, let us make brick, and burn them thoroughly. And they had brick for stone, and slime had they for mortar. And they said, Come, let us build us a city, and a tower, whose top *may reach* unto heaven, and let us make us a name; lest we be scattered abroad upon the face of the whole earth. And Jehovah came down to see the city and the tower, which the children of men builded. And Jehovah said, Behold, they are one people, and they have all one language; and this is what they begin to do: and now nothing will be withholden from them, which they purpose to do. Come, let us go down, and there confound their language, that they may not understand one another's speech. So Jehovah scattered them abroad from thence upon the face of all the earth: and they left off building the city. Therefore was the name of it called Babel; because Jehovah did there confound the language of all the earth: and from thence did Jehovah scatter them abroad upon the face of all the earth.

Here is related the building by the descendents of Noah of a city and a tower that was to reach to heaven.

"And the whole earth was of one language and of one speech," which indicates that there was unity in the interchange of intelligence and purpose but that it was based on materiality: "And they had brick for stone, and slime had they for mortar." They built the city and the tower; but Jehovah confounded their language and they were scattered abroad "upon the face of all the earth."

According to Ferrar Fenton's translation of the Bible in modern English, the word *Jehovah* should be translated "chief." The chief was the priest or ruling religious power. So it was not Jehovah who confused the tongues of the people but their religious leaders. This is true today.

Interpreted in individual consciousness, it is not Spirit that leads man astray but man's interpretation of the message of Spirit as molded by man's mentality. In other words, it was the Adversary or personal ego of the people that asserted its disintegrating nature and destroyed the work of their hands.

The name *Babel* means "confusion." Babel represents the mental chaos that is the result of thinking from a wholly material standpoint.

Whether the story of the building of Babel and the scattering of its people be history or allegory matters little; it illustrates the ephemeral character of man's work exemplified times beyond number in the buried cities of the past. Not only cities but great nations have occupied large areas of this earth, only to be swept away.

This universal scattering of the nations that bravely set out to build cities and civilizations planned to reach to heaven and endure forever, should make thinking persons pause and inquire the cause of such stupendous failure. The fact is that the foundations of their cities were material instead of spiritual; there was an excess of "stone, and slime."

However every great nation has claimed God as its originator and often its temporal heads as ruling by divine right. As long as these nations had faith in this divine source they prospered, but when the personal element began to assert itself, decline set in, the nation collapsed, and its people scattered.

This is not only the history of cities and nations but also of numerous colonies of Utopian pattern for the betterment of men. Their plans are perfect and appear to be based on laws that will work toward universal happiness and prosperity. But they fail because their leader is some human being, and there is often some other human being in the colony who is ambitious to rule. Politics and party strife then enter and break down the unity that is so necessary to the success of any enterprise.

History shows that often just preceding a great national collapse dictators or "chiefs" assume the power personally to make and enforce the laws for the people. This condition repeats itself in world affairs and presages a breakdown of man-made civilization. The towers of Babel totter and philosophic onlookers foretell a lapse of the human family into primitive savagery.

That the principles on which the governments of the world are based are inadequate to meet the needs of a world nation is patent to anyone who studies the economic and moral status of various countries. God created all men of one blood, according to the Scriptures, and that universal bond of humanity is asserting

itself in the tremendous increase in facilities for inter-
course among men of every country. The struggle for
separate national existence must be broken down, and
a new and larger understanding of race solidarity
established.

We see that history is repeating itself on a larger
scale than ever before and is again ready to scatter
the inhabitants of Babel who have attempted to build
to heaven without God. After the breaking up of the
present materially founded governments, the spiritually
wise will get together and form a federation based on
the principles laid down by Jesus Christ, and we shall
then enter into that universal peace and security called
the millennium. "And this gospel of the kingdom shall
be preached in the whole world for a testimony unto
all the nations; and then shall the end come." The
prophecies of Jesus, as set forth symbolically in Matthew 24, undoubtedly point to their fulfillment at this
time, and the "tribulations" there recited are upon us.
But we need not be fearful or troubled if we are depending on God to take care of us. "The race is not
to the swift, nor the battle to the strong," "but he that
endureth to the end, the same shall be saved."

Gen. 11:10-32. These are the generations of Shem.
Shem was a hundred years old, and begat Arpachshad
two years after the flood: and Shem lived after he
begat Arpachshad five hundred years, and begat sons
and daughters.

And Arpachshad lived five and thirty years, and
begat Shelah: and Arpachshad lived after he begat
Shelah four hundred and three years, and begat sons
and daughters.

And Shelah lived thirty years, and begat Eber:
and Shelah lived after he begat Eber four hundred

and three years, and begat sons and daughters.

And Eber lived four and thirty years, and begat Peleg: and Eber lived after he begat Peleg four hundred and thirty years, and begat sons and daughters.

(For interpretation of the foregoing names see comment on Gen. 10.)

And Peleg lived thirty years, and begat Reu: and Peleg lived after he begat Reu two hundred and nine years, and begat sons and daughters.

And Reu lived two and thirty years, and begat Serug: and Reu lived after he begat Serug two hundred and seven years, and begat sons and daughters.

And Serug lived thirty years, and begat Nahor: and Serug lived after he begat Nahor two hundred years, and begat sons and daughters.

And Nahor lived nine and twenty years, and begat Terah: and Nahor lived after he begat Terah a hundred and nineteen years, and begat sons and daughters.

And Terah lived seventy years, and begat Abram, Nahor, and Haran.

Now these are the generations of Terah. Terah begat Abram, Nahor, and Haran; and Haran begat Lot. And Haran died before his father Terah in the land of his nativity, in Ur of the Chaldees. And Abram and Nahor took them wives: the name of Abram's wife was Sarai; and the name of Nahor's wife, Milcah, the daughter of Haran, the father of Milcah, and the father of Iscah. And Sarai was barren; she had no child. And Terah took Abram his son, and Lot the son of Haran, his son's son, and Sarai his daughter-in-law, his son Abram's wife; and they went forth with them from Ur of the Chaldees, to go into the land of Canaan; and they came unto Haran, and dwelt there. And the days of Terah were two hundred and five years: and Terah died in Haran.

The name *Reu* means "leading to pasture," "shepherd," "friend." Reu represents the co-operative feeling, the feeling of friendship, evolving in the individual consciousness into a sense of loving, active, responsibility for the welfare of others.

The name *Serug* means "interwoven," "tendril," "strength." Serug represents the budding, sprouting, and development of spiritual. "seed" or Truth ideas deep down in the subconsciousness by way of preparation for the saving work in the body. In the Serug phase of man's unfoldment the work is done mostly in secret, with now and then just a ray of light breaking through to consciousness.

The name *Nahor* signifies "angry," "passionate," "piercing," "slaying." Nahor denotes the piercing and breaking up of the sense consciousness hitherto unpenetrated by Truth so that the way may be opened for a new line of thought activity (Abram). This activity may be more of the subconscious than of the conscious mind. Much turmoil often accompanies this inner first breaking up of lesser ideals because of the efforts of the outer, limited, emotional self ("angry," "passionate").

The name *Haran* means "strong," "mountaineer," "exalted." Haran symbolizes an exalted state of mind, wherein Truth is lifted up in consciousness and the individual is strengthened in his determination to go on toward fuller spiritual enlightenment and upliftment.

(For Abram, Sarai, Terah, and Lot see interpretation of Gen. 12. For Canaan see the interpretation of Gen. 10.)

The name *Ur* (of the Chaldees) signifies "light."

"Orient," "brightness or brilliance," "fire or blaze."
Ur therefore symbolizes the activity of the understanding or intelligence in man; the inner spiritual part of
man's being, whence true light shines forth into the
entire consciousness.

The name *Milcah* means "queen," "rule," "coun-
sel." Milcah symbolizes the soul in the act of expressing dominion, wisdom, good judgment.

The name *Iscah* signifies "who looks upon," "scans
abroad," "discerns." Iscah represents the soul in the
act of being attentive to the things of Spirit.

Chapter V

The Initial Step Toward Redemption

GENESIS 12, 13, and 14

ACCORDING to Jesus, when a man turns toward a new country, a new state of consciousness, he must quicken his faith. Formerly he has had faith in material processes; he has attached himself to material things. Thus Abraham long lived in the sense world or consciousness, represented by Sodom and Gomorrah. His higher ideal, Jehovah, urged him to flee from that world and not to move back but to detach his mind from the things of sense and turn his face toward the light. This new land that the Lord desired him to go to represents new ideas and their manifestation, a new relationship to the substance of things. When the new ideas begin to multiply in man's mind, his environment changes; as Paul says, "if any man is in Christ, *he is* a new creature." But the beginning is to believe further than you can see or feel in terms of the senses. A man often finds it necessary to go into a "new country" that he knows nothing about; and he has to trust the Lord to carry him through. "Blessed *are* they that have not seen, and *yet* have believed." To put faith in things spiritual is the essential step.

The call of Abraham is considered the initial step in a great plan for the redemption of the Adam race from its material, sensual consciousness, called the fall of man. From any mortal viewpoint the time seems long and the way tortuous, but we may, if we will, enter into the mind of the Spirit, where one day is as a thousand years and a thousand years are as one day, and here we see the whole plan worked out in a definite, systematic, and orderly way.

Every detail in Abraham's experience has a definite counterpart in the life of each one who is bringing forth the Christ in man. A study of these things is therefore of great importance to all who seek the realization of sonship. To them it is given to understand "the mystery which hath been hid for ages and generations."

Abraham represents faith, the first great faculty developed or "called out" by man in the unfoldment of his spiritual nature or Christ Mind. Faith is that faculty by which we know God as omnipresent Spirit substance. This substance is man's supply, as discerned by the author of Hebrews when he said, "Faith is the substance of things hoped for." By faith we appropriate the spiritual substance of whatever things we desire, thus taking the first step necessary to their manifestation. Abraham, rich in faith, increased his substance until it was very great.

Volumes might be written about faith in its relation to the conscious, subconscious, and superconscious departments of mind; or about its centers of action in the body. Abraham represents faith in its early establishment in consciousness, and his life portrays the different movements of this faculty on the various planes of action in man's being. In order to understand the lessons that Abraham's life has for us, a certain familiarity with each plane of consciousness is necessary.

That in the individual which is called "I" may be

termed attention. It is in reality the spiritual man. It is the inherent capacity of the "I" to recognize ideas and through the law of Being to form ideas into states of consciousness. By forming these new states and setting up action in their various departments, the "I" (attention) can then leave them, as the millwright leaves the mill he has constructed over a waterfall. Nature carries on the work once it is established.

So we find ourselves in possession of states of consciousness that may seem to be ignorant. There are, for instance, the subconscious states that have to do with the processes of digestion, assimilation, circulation, respiration, elimination, and the like. We could not be in possession of an organism having these various powers of mind unless at some point in our experience we had established them. If we consciously assumed these powers ourselves, it is plainly possible that we could again go back of them and become familiar with their subconscious action.

Thus it is a question of attention whether or not we shall know about these various planes of mental activity. If we fix our thoughts for but ten minutes a day on the heart, we shall know in a short time what is going on at that center. So with every department of the organism. Whatever the process being carried on by an organ in the body, we may be assured that a center of intelligence is located somewhere in the vicinity of it, and by continually focusing our attention there we may become familiar with its office and work.

Abraham represents man in the first awakening of his faith, when he is dominated by it. The very name has come to be almost a synonym for faith. Abra-

ham was dwelling in a realm of limited thought, and
he was called out by Spirit into a great expansion of
all his thoughts and powers through faith. All the
people and places mentioned in connection with his
history have a symbolical meaning. They represent
other faculties and phases of mind that are called into
expression along with faith.

> *Gen. 12:1-5.* Now Jehovah said unto Abram,
> Get thee out of thy country, and from thy kindred,
> and from thy father's house, unto the land that I will
> show thee: and I will make of thee a great nation,
> and I will bless thee, and make thy name great; and
> be thou a blessing: and I will bless them that bless
> thee, and him that curseth thee will I curse: and in
> thee shall all the families of the earth be blessed. So
> Abram went, as Jehovah had spoken unto him; and
> Lot went with him: and Abram was seventy and five
> years old when he departed out of Haran. And
> Abram took Sarai his wife, and Lot his brother's son,
> and all their substance that they had gathered, and
> the souls that they had gotten in Haran; and they
> went forth to go into the land of Canaan; and into
> the land of Canaan they came.

The movement in consciousness represented in this
Scripture is that of an individual who has been spiritually inactive or laggard. The name of Abraham's
father Terah signifies "loitering." The Lord or spiritual impulse within presses forth to religious activity.
It virtually says, "Get thee out of thy country, and
from thy kindred, and from thy father's [loiterer's]
house, unto the land that I will show thee."

When this call comes, lofty ideas begin to possess
the mind. The name in its original form, Abram,
means "exalted father." Faith in the unseen God and

in divine guidance inspires lofty thoughts that become part of the consciousness without special effort when man is obedient to the call of Spirit. To those who depend on the evidence of the senses it may be blind faith, but it works out beautifully in the life of those who are true to it.

When Abraham went to seek a new country (consciousness) in response to the call of the Spirit, Lot went with him. The name *Lot* means "hidden," "concealed," "covert," and Lot represents the negative side of faith. When faith (Abraham) expands in consciousness (in a new and greater country), its old subconscious element (Lot) expands also. Lot may also be said to symbolize the part of man that is still in darkness; in other words, the natural or animal man. This part of man's nature he cannot escape, but must take with him into the new country. He can, however, by association, lift it up and increase its capacity, as Abraham "lifted up" and aided Lot, for we read that Lot prospered as well.

(For further interpretation of Abraham and Lot see commentary on Gen. 13.)

> *Gen. 12:6-9.* And Abram passed through the land unto the place of Shechem, unto the oak of Moreh. And the Canaanite was then in the land. And Jehovah appeared unto Abram, and said, Unto thy seed will I give this land: and there builded he an altar unto Jehovah, who appeared unto him. And he removed from thence unto the mountain on the east of Beth-el, and pitched his tent, having Beth-el on the west, and Ai on the east: and there he builded an altar unto Jehovah, and called upon the name of Jehovah. And Abram journeyed, going on still toward the South.

In this instance Canaan represents the pure elements of the natural body. Moreh represents the mind that is receptive to Truth; a tabernacle. In a tabernacle state of mind the constructive methods that are always characteristic of the divine are revealed, and in this state of mind protection and strength (oak tree) are realized, and victory is assured.

The "oak of Moreh" may also be said to represent a nerve center in the body, and the tabernacle an aggregation of cells.

The name *Shechem* means "inclining," "shoulder." Shechem represents man's wholly material thoughts about himself and the universe, which tend to make life a burden.

The name *Beth-el* means "house of God." Beth-el represents the understanding that all seemingly material things in reality have their origin in Spirit.

The name *Ai* means "heap of ruins." Ai refers to egotism and self-confidence without recognition of Spirit. These qualities are counterfeits of faith; they are destructive of the building of a truly spiritual character and must be put away so that the individual may come into a knowledge of his unity with God.

> *Gen. 12:10.* And there was a famine in the land: and Abram went down into Egypt to sojourn there; for the famine was sore in the land.

There was a famine in Abraham's land, and this caused him to go down into Egypt. Egypt represents the realm of substance and life in the depths of the body consciousness. In a sense this is a region of darkness and mystery, yet it is a great kingdom rich in substance and essential to the preservation of the body.

It refers to the vitality of the abdominal region. Those who have not attained an all-round understanding of the divine law do not know how to affirm the flow of a steady current of life from below to feed the flame of intelligence above, and therefore they have periods of bodily exhaustion. In this condition they seem to lose divine guidance and are plunged into apparent darkness (Egypt). This is a very necessary adjustment however.

> *Gen. 12:11-20.* And it came to pass, when he was come near to enter into Egypt, that he said unto Sarai his wife, Behold now, I know that thou art a fair woman to look upon: and it will come to pass, when the Egyptians shall see thee, that they will say, This is his wife: and they will kill me, but they will save thee alive. Say, I pray thee, thou art my sister; that it may be well with me for thy sake, and that my soul may live because of thee. And it came to pass, that, when Abram was come into Egypt, the Egyptians beheld the woman that she was very fair. And the princes of Pharaoh saw her, and praised her to Pharaoh: and the woman was taken into Pharaoh's house. And he dealt well with Abram for her sake: and he had sheep, and oxen, and he-asses, and men-servants, and maid-servants, and she-asses, and camels. And Jehovah plagued Pharaoh and his house with great plagues because of Sarai, Abram's wife. And Pharaoh called Abram, and said, What is this that thou hast done unto me? why didst thou not tell me that she was thy wife? why saidst thou, She is my sister, so that I took her to be my wife? now therefore behold thy wife, take her, and go thy way. And Pharaoh gave men charge concerning him: and they brought him on the way, and his wife, and all that he had.

Here again we see the result of a lack of spiritual

understanding. Pharaoh represents "the sun." He is the ruler of the solar plexus, the sun center in the subconscious mind. This is obscurity or "Egypt" to the conscious mind. Pharaoh's (the sun's) being in Egypt points to the truth that the light of the sun of righteousness is veiled by our life on the lower or sense plane. Pharaoh also signifies the whole house, the whole body consciousness; he is the force that rules the body under the natural regime.

Sarai represents the soul not yet regenerated and under divine law should not be allowed to unite with Pharaoh (physical sensation). Not having the divine understanding when he was drawn down into Egypt (seat of the vital processes), Abram allowed Sarai (his unregenerate love, affection, and emotion) to become united with Pharaoh (the dominating physical ego) and this brought plagues upon the land of Egypt (bodily ills).

Metaphysicians regenerating their bodies through the power of the spoken word should heed this lesson. When quickening, cleansing, and readjusting the cells at their life center, they should silently declare:

"The sensation of the flesh cannot hold my love, for my love is the daughter of God, and we are joined in purity and pure desire in my Father's house."

Thus they may escape the plagues of Egypt and the rebuke of Pharaoh: "What is this that thou hast done unto me? why didst thou not tell me that she was thy wife?"

> *Gen. 13:1.* And Abram went up out of Egypt, he, and his wife, and all that he had, and Lot with him, into the South.

Abram went up out of the land of Egypt, "and Lot

with him"; for the time had not yet come when Abram could part with Lot (the subjective) and dwell in the Promised Land (the purely spiritual consciousness).

Lot can also be said to symbolize the part of man's consciousness that is still spiritually undeveloped. In other words, Lot represents the natural or animal man. Abram still had much growth to make before he could sustain a consciousness of Spirit. He was unable as yet to cross out the material side of his nature. He still had faith in materiality and a dual vision as to the fulfillment of the Scriptures. He saw the negative as well as the positive; evil as well as good.

Until the Christ Mind is firmly established in the individual he retains a certain residue of faith in negative appearances. This divided state of mind causes confusion and discord.

> *Gen. 13:2-4.* And Abram was very rich in cattle, in silver, and in gold. And he went on his journeys from the South even to Beth-el, unto the place where his tent had been at the beginning, between Beth-el and Ai.

Abram (faith) while in Egypt accumulates rich substance ideas, which are necessary for a well-balanced mind and body. Bethel (house of God) represents the perfect body ideal. Ai (heap of rubbish) represents the physical manifestation with an increased appreciation and possession of life and substance (cattle, silver, and gold).

The return from Egypt is symbolical of man's return to his divine-natural consciousness. This was not a single event; it is something that occurs again and again in the Bible story, and is repeated in the case of every individual who comes into a realization of his spiritual oneness with God. The whole nation ot Israel was called out of Egypt to assume its destiny of bringing forth the fruit unto righteousness and life everlasting, to play a part in the restitution of the race to its Edenic state. This is the essence of the covenant. Jesus came up out of Egypt where His parents had taken Him as a child. Abram (faith) did not remain long in Egypt (sense consciousness).

> *Gen. 13:5-7.* And Lot also, who went with Abram, had flocks, and herds, and tents. And the land was not able to bear them, that they might dwell together: for their substance was great, so that they could not dwell together. And there was a strife between the herdsmen of Abram's cattle and the herdsmen of Lot's cattle: and the Canaanite and the Perizzite dwelt then in the land.

It was Abraham rather than Lot who suggested the separation. When man reaches a certain point in his spiritual development he realizes that he must let go of everything that retards his progress. Lot is typical of the natural man, always eager to take the best for himself. He chose the plain of the Jordan because it was "like the land of Egypt."

True faith in God is separated from all negative belief that the body is material, impure, or transient. The herdsmen of Abraham were separated from the herdsmen of Lot. The time comes when by reason of the increase of faith or substance these two types of mind cannot dwell together: "the land was not able to bear them." So the senses of the man who has centered his faith on the invisible are by degrees separated from the appeal of his lower nature and become true herdsmen of his enduring thoughts. As a true seer his vision is fixed on the changeless reality inhabiting all form, the substance of which all visible manifestation is but the configuration. His ear becomes attuned to the unbroken harmony of life that is permeating his mind and body and the world about him. He learns so to direct his thought of Spirit substance that if a belief in material imperfection should find lodgment in his consciousness one touch of his mind would release the hidden spring that opens the way to healing of the body.

> *Gen. 13:8-12.* And Abram said unto Lot, Let there be no strife, I pray thee, between me and thee, and between my herdsmen and thy herdsmen; for we are brethren. Is not the whole land before thee? separate thyself, I pray thee, from me: if *thou wilt take* the left hand, then I will go to the right; or if *thou take* the right hand, then I will go to the left. And Lot lifted up his eyes, and beheld all the Plain of the Jordan, that it was well watered every where, before Jehovah destroyed Sodom and Gomorrah, like the garden of Jehovah, like the land of Egypt, as thou goest unto Zoar. So Lot chose him all the Plain of the Jordan; and Lot journeyed east: and they separated themselves the one from the other. Abram dwelt in the land of Canaan, and Lot dwelt in the cities of the Plain, and moved his tent as far as Sodom.

When we put our faith wholeheartedly in spiritual reality and follow our ideal without wavering, we are willing to allow sense consciousness the choice of its own field of action. Abraham gave Lot his choice of land. When we withdraw our interest from the natural man, there is a separation. True thought and untrue thought cannot intermingle.

Canaan means "lowland," but it is here that Abraham lived after his separation from Lot. Is it not significant that this "lowland" became the Promised Land, the land "flowing with milk and honey"? True faith, which works through love, has power to refine the body and so make it the promised land of the soul. When man rediscovers this lost domain, the promises of the Scriptures will be fulfilled.

Every faculty of the mind has an active and a passive side, an objective and a subjective, a positive and a negative. Abraham represents the faculty of faith in its positive expression. To complete the symbol we find Lot ("hidden," "concealed") representing the negative or undeveloped aspect of faith. His domain is the flesh. He accompanied Abraham into Egypt and back again. When they separated, Lot chose to dwell in the "Plain of the Jordan . . . like the land of Egypt, as thou goest unto Zoar." The river Jordan here symbolizes the descending flow of thought running through the organism from head to foot. When mortal beliefs rule the individual, the life flow is muddy with sense concepts and turbulent with materiality. The Jordan is noted as a muddy stream. Zoar ("smallness," "littleness") represents that which is inferior. We should beware how we link our I AM consciousness with the faith that is established in the flesh, typified by Lot.

(For Sodom and Gomorrah see interpretation of Gen. 10).

> *Gen. 13:13-18.* Now the men of Sodom were wicked and sinners against Jehovah exceedingly. And Jehovah said unto Abram, after that Lot was separated from him, Lift up now thine eyes, and look from the place where thou art, northward and

> southward and eastward and westward: for all the
> land which thou seest, to thee will I give it, and to
> thy seed for ever. And I will make thy seed as the
> dust of the earth: so that if a man can number the
> dust of the earth, then may thy seed also be num-
> bered. Arise, walk through the land in the length of
> it and in the breadth of it; for unto thee will I give
> it. And Abram moved his tent, and came and
> dwelt by the oaks of Mamre, which are in Hebron,
> and built there an altar unto Jehovah.

Hebron ("community," "alliance," "friendship")
represents an association of ideas; in other words, concentration. Spiritual unfoldment always causes one
to direct toward God's children everywhere a kindly
feeling that is constant, deep, tender. Ability to do this
is one of the indispensable qualifications of every successful spiritual leader.

Mamre ("firmness," "vigor," "strength") refers to
the front brain, the seat of conscious thought. The lesson here is that faith in God (Abraham) brings about
the right relationship among all the associated faculties, and withal an enduring firmness, vigor, and
strength. Mamre in the sense of "fatness," "abundantly supplied," "well-fed," refers to a consciousness
of substance and riches. The qualities represented by
Mamre are not of the highest spiritual consciousness,
the Christ Mind, but they belong more to the spiritually
awakening intellect of the individual.

In Truth a person does not have to change his
residence in order to enter a new country. "The land
which thou seest" refers to a new concept of substance.
When we deny our attachment to matter and material
conditions and affirm our unity with spiritual substance,
we enter the new consciousness of real substance.

Substance is not confined to matter; it is the idea that is the firm foundation of all that we conceive to be permanent.

Abraham's moving his tent signifies that the center of consciousness changed; in this case from a lower to a higher plane.

Gen. 14:1-11. And it came to pass in the days of Amraphel king of Shinar, Arioch king of Ellasar, Chedorlaomer king of Elam, and Tidal king of Goiim, that they made war with Bera king of Sodom, and with Birsha king of Gomorrah, Shinab king of Admah, and Shemeber king of Zeboiim, and the king of Bela (the same is Zoar). All these joined together in the vale of Siddim (the same is the Salt Sea). Twelve years they served Chedorlaomer, and in the thirteenth year they rebelled. And in the fourteenth year came Chedorlaomer, and the kings that were with him, and smote the Rephaim in Ashteroth-karnaim, and the Zuzim in Ham, and the Emim in Shaveh-kiriathaim, and the Horites in their mount Seir, unto El-paran, which is by the wilderness. And they returned, and came to En-mishpat (the same is Kadesh), and smote all the country of the Amalekites, and also the Amorites, that dwelt in Hazazon-tamar. And there went out the king of Sodom, and the king of Gomorrah, and the king of Admah, and the king of Zeboiim, and the king of Bela (the same is Zoar); and they set the battle in array against them in the vale of Siddim; against Chedorlaomer king of Elam, and Tidal king of Goiim, and Amraphel king of Shinar, and Arioch king of Ellasar; four kings against the five. Now the vale of Siddim was full of slime pits; and the kings of Sodom and Gomorrah fled, and they fell there, and they that remained fled to the mountain. And they took all the goods of Sodom and Gomorrah, and all their victuals, and went their way.

Amraphel ("keeper of the treasures," "speaker of mysteries") represents the belief of unawakened man that in generation, in physical reproduction, he is fulfilling the creative law of Being.

Shinar ("two rivers," "divided stream," "divided mind") represents a belief in two powers, an evil as well as a good power, and error results.

Arioch ("lionlike," "venerable") represents the seeming power, strength, and ("lionlike") dominion that sex lust has over man; also the belief so prevalent among all peoples that the secret desires and habits pertaining to the sex life must be good and must have been ordained of God because of ages of acceptance and practice. Therefore they are regarded as sacred ("venerable").

Ellasar ("strong rebellion," "oath of Assyria," "oak of Assyria") represents a state of consciousness whose central thought and belief has to do with sex on the physical plane. It does not look to Spirit for its strength and power but trusts in the "mind of the flesh."

Chedorlaomer ("handful of sheaves," "roundness of a sheaf") represents the generative function of the body given over to the expression of sex lust.

Elam ("hidden," "concealed," "everlasting") represents thoughts of the abidingness, resourcefulness, and creative power of Truth. The natural man may not know the truth of his being; it may be hidden under the debris of sense thought and belief. It will come to light in due time however and will bring forth its fruit of perfection in the life of every individual.

Tidal ("veneration," "awe," "fear") represents the prominent place that sensuality has in the material and carnal states of consciousness that belong to the outer, animal man; also the fearfulness that results from sense expression.

Goiim ("Gentiles," "people, especially foreign") represents the carnal, material thoughts and states of consciousness that belong to the outer man (Gentile).

Bera ("spontaneous gift," "son of desire," "son of evil") represents the directing thoughts and desires of the sensual state of consciousness denoted by Sodom. (For Sodom see interpretation of Gen. 10.)

Birsha ("son of wickedness," "son of impiety," "fat with evil") was King of Gomorrah in Abraham's time. The name *Gomorrah* means "material force," "tyranny," "oppression." Gomorrah denotes a state of mind that is adverse to the law of Spirit. This state of mind has to do with the submerged or hidden subconscious phase of man's sensual life. Birsha represents the ruling thought in this state of consciousness in the individual.

Shinab ("sharpened desire," "father of mutation," "father of transgression") represents the presiding thought of the state of consciousness denoted by Admah.

Admah ("dumb," "unrelenting," "tomb") represents the seeming strength and mercilessness of the death thought and condition that enters into man's experience as the result of his carnal, material, adverse thoughts and activities.

Shemeber ("superior brilliance," "high flight," "superior name") represents the innate spiritual ideal implanted in man from the beginning that causes him to grow, unfold, and unceasingly desire and seek to attain a higher and better understanding.

Zeboiim ("wars," "rending with the teeth") represents ravenous appetites, sensual passions, the wild-beast nature holding sway in the subconsciousness. The fact that Shemeber was King of Zeboiim shows that the perfect-man idea of God is implanted in the physical being of man as well as in his more inner spiritual consciousness.

Zoar ("reduced," "lessened") denotes inferiority. It was one of the wicked cities of the plain belonging to Moab (carnal mind).

Bela ("swallow up," "utterly consume or destroy") represents the destructive tendencies in consciousness. The city of Bela symbolizes a group of destroying, consuming thoughts. It suggests the destroying of letting go of error by denial, an absorption or "swallowing up" of error by Truth or of darkness by light, thus doing away with the error.

Siddim ("extensions," "stony land") represents the very lowest material idea and manifestation of substance in the sense consciousness and the body consciousness of the individual.

Rephaim ("bonds," "terrors," "giants") was the name of a people of great stature, and Rephaim represents the seeming strength of binding, fear-producing, opposing thoughts in consciousness at a certain stage of man's unfoldment into Truth.

Ashteroth-karnaim ("horned Ashteroth," "Ashteroth of two peaks") represents the state of consciousness in man that attributes double honor, authority, and power to purely intellectual understanding and capacity. In this state of consciousness man does not recognize that God instead of intellect is the source of intelligence. The intellect borrows its real light from Spirit, just as the moon, which has no light of its own, reflects light from the sun. Ashteroth refers to the moon or intellect, while Karnaim (two horns or peaks) suggests exultation and power.

Zuzim ("glittering," "flowing out like rays," "sprouting," "restless") was the name of a people "in Ham." Zuzim represents the confusion, fears, unrestrained emotions, and general terrors of the physical consciousness of "mind of the flesh," seemingly very prominent and flourishing at a certain stage in the evolution or unfoldment of the individual.

Ham ("inferior," "hot") represents the material consciousness in man.

Emim ("the terrible," "formidable people," "objects of terror," that is, "idols") was the name of a race of giants in Shaveh-kiriathaim. Metaphysically Emim represents giant terrors and fears in human consciousness that are a result of man's believing in the outer, formed world and the conditions that man has built up as being real and true.

Shaveh-kiriathaim ("plain of the twin cities," "plain of the double meetings") is the name of a place. The name *Shaveh* means "a plain," and Shaveh represents an equalized, poised state of mind and body. The name *Kiriathaim* means "double city," and Kiriathaim denotes double strength or supply. Shaveh-kiriathaim thus denotes poise and equilibrium in the consciousness and the organism, doubly established and sure.

The Horites ("cave dwellers," "dwellers in black holes"), inhabitants of Edom, represent forces in action in man's physical organism, more especially the deep-seated, subconscious, fleshly forces and tendencies.

Seir ("bristling," "hairy," "rough," "horror") represents the physical or sense consciousness in man.

El-paran ("strength of Paran," "oak of the region

of the caves") denotes the seeming strength of the multitude of confused and undisciplined thoughts and energies in man's subconscious mind that are given over to the furtherance of sense expression.

En-mishpat ("fountain of judgment," "fountain of right") symbolizes the truth that under the law of adjustment, when it reaches a certain point in expression, sense indulgence destroys the very error desires that keep it active in consciousness. Then these desires die for lack of fuel to keep them alive.

The name Kadesh means "holy," "consecrated," "a sanctuary." Kadesh represents the divine presence within the individual consciousness.

The Amalekites ("warlike," "valley dweller," "that licks up") represent the base desires of the individual; the animal forces, appetites, and passions of the subconscious mind.

(For Amorites see interpretation of Gen. 10.)

Hazazon-tamar ("a division of palms," "felling of palms," "victory divided") represents a divided mind. This mind must be conquered before one can become fearless and so gain a real victory over error. When the thoughts are divided the results are divided.

This whole Scripture reveals the working out of sense on the lowest plane of consciousness. The kings in this chapter who served Chedorlaomer for twelve years and then rebelled represent ruling thoughts in the hidden sense consciousness of man. Error fights error, destroying much of it, and the remainder is lifted up (flees to the mountain) and eventually is absorbed by Truth. We often refer to this movement of mind as a transmuting process. A close study of these verses tells us that even in battling with sex

the Spirit of the Lord is constantly working, through
the law of sowing and reaping, to unveil to man's consciousness a higher way of life.

> *Gen. 14:12.* And they took Lot, Abram's broth-
> er's son, who dwelt in Sodom, and his goods, and
> departed.

Lot and all his possessions were carried away by
Chedorlaomer and the kings with him, who symbolize
the rule of sensuality in man. These sense beliefs and
desires have seemingly overpowered the negative side of
faith that Lot symbolizes. The power of this side of
faith has been taken over to build up and sustain
flesh that is ruled over by carnal thought. But when
knowledge of this occurrence comes to the positive
side of the faith faculty in the individual (Abraham)
who has come up out of material thought (Egypt) and
passed to a higher concept of God (Hebrew), let us
see what happens. Positive faith (Abraham) gets into
action with a thought power that destroys sense rule
(Chedorlaomer and his allies) and restores negative
faith (Lot) to its rightful place in consciousness.

> *Gen. 14:13-20.* And there came one that had
> escaped, and told Abram the Hebrew: now he dwelt
> by the oaks of Mamre, the Amorite, brother of Esh-
> col, and brother of Aner; and these were confederate
> with Abram. And when Abram heard that his
> brother was taken captive, he led forth his trained
> men, born in his house, three hundred and eighteen,
> and pursued as far as Dan. And he divided himself
> against them by night, he and his servants, and
> smote them, and pursued them unto Hobah, which
> is on the left hand of Damascus. And he brought
> back all the goods, and also brought back his brother
> Lot, and his goods, and the women also, and the

> people. And the king of Sodom went out to meet him, after his return from the slaughter of Chedorlaomer and the kings that were with him, at the vale of Shaveh (the same is the King's Vale). And Melchizedek king of Salem brought forth bread and wine: and he was priest of God Most High. And he blessed him, and said, Blessed be Abram of God Most High, possessor of heaven and earth: and blessed be God Most High, who hath delivered thine enemies into thine hand. And he gave him a tenth of all.

Mamre ("strength"), Aner ("adolescent youth"), and Eshcol ("fruitfulness"), the Amorites who "were confederate with Abram," suggest thoughts of vigor and abundant substance inspired by faith. These thoughts are apparently material in expression (Amorites), yet they are friendly toward the individual's higher concepts or faith in God (Abraham), because in reality their true origin is Spirit. They lend their conception of strength and power to the aid of faith while it is gaining its victory over error.

Faith brings into action all its accumulated wisdom and understanding ("he led forth his trained men") and makes a union with the judgment faculty (Dan). Then faith strikes at the very root of sensuality, the mortal man's belief that life is material. This belief is the hiding or lurking place (Hobah) for the error thoughts symbolized by the kings who took Lot captive.

We can never fully overcome sensuality until we put away belief in materiality. We must know that our whole being, including the body, is not material but spiritual. By sowing according to belief in the flesh we reap the corruption of the flesh, but by sowing according to Spirit we reap eternal life. (Damascus also, like Hobah, signifies a state of consciousness founded on a material conception of life in the body.)

We find a rich symbology in the story of Abraham's victorious return from the battle. He was met at the "vale of Shaveh" (which means "plain," a level place, a place of equality) by Melchizedek (whose name means "king of righteousness"), priest of God, who here symbolizes the Christ consciousness in the individual. The King of Sodom also met and greeted Abraham on the "plain" of equality (Shaveh). He here represents the ruling power in the physical.

When the Christ consciousness rules in both the mind and the body, the individual is established in right thinking and right doing (righteousness). Then he has come to the place of peace, poise, equilibrium, and wholeness signified by Shaveh. When this place is reached in both the inner and the outer consciousness (Salem and Sodom) there is a great increase of substance and of life in one's realization. This increase comes from the higher spiritual mind within, the Christ, and is symbolized by the bread and the wine that Melchizedek gave to Abraham. Melchizedek blessed Abraham and blessed God, and Abraham gave him "a tenth of all." When a person realizes that his victories are gained by the power of God alone, he should willingly use a tenth of his increase of power, understanding, and substance for the furtherance of the Christ Truth.

Gen. 14:21-24. And the king of Sodom said unto Abram, Give me the persons, and take the goods to thyself. And Abram said to the king of Sodom,

> I have lifted up my hand unto Jehovah, God Most
> High, possessor of heaven and earth, that I will not
> take a thread nor a shoe-latchet nor aught that is
> thine, lest thou shouldest say, I have made Abram
> rich: save only that which the young men have eaten,
> and the portion of the men that went with me, Aner,
> Eshcol, and Mamre; let them take their portion.

Abraham refused the proffered gifts of the King of
Sodom (sense man), which teaches us that there must
be a lifting up and transmuting of the seeming material
life and substance in the body before it can be utilized
by the higher faculties of the mind. None of the credit
for the multiplication of substance and strength should
be given to the mortal in man's nature. Spirit gives all
the increase of good.

Abram represents the spiritual ego, and the King
of Sodom represents the personal, the physical ego.
The spiritual ego or spiritual man has its first development on the physical plane. The two egos, the spiritual
and the physical, are united there in appropriating
physical things, personal things, that they consider
valuable, such as appetites, passions, and other things
on the sense plane. The spiritual man advances or develops beyond that. He does not want these things, so
he gives them all to the personality, the physical ego.
Then the physical man is willing to give up anything
to the spiritual man, and he will claim that he supplied
the spiritual man. That is the glorification of the personality. The personal man claims that he is the whole
thing, that everything belongs to him. It is personal
selfishness, and the spiritual man does not want to be
told that he got anything from the physical. He gets his
things from the realm of ideas, the spiritual realm.

Man is prone to feel that the outer or sense world is the source of his good, at least a measure of it. But in order fully to realize our sonship and our divine heritage, we must hold fast to Spirit. We must see Spirit as our only cause and sustenance. We have a tendency to plead the cause of the good in our sense nature. This is characteristic of all of us. We try hard to save some of our sense thoughts and secret habits. We have indulged in them so long (and our ancestors before us did likewise, beyond the memory of man) that we cannot help thinking there is some good in them. However we, like Abraham, must keep our vision high. We must hold steadfastly to the realization that God is the one source of all, that in spirit and in truth all is good.

The young ("immature") men who went with Abram had partaken ("eaten") of the pleasures of sense. They represent the primitive understanding, and as such they are excused from the operation of the spiritual law. The plane of activity for life and strength at a certain stage of man's development is the physical, material plane. During this stage God in His grace grants to man, when his motive is pure, a degree of immunity from the effects of his ignorant transgression of the divine law.

Chapter VI

The Promise of Salvation

GENESIS 15, 16, 17, and 18

THE PROMISE of salvation is for everyone. But man must attain it. Man must be like a child at school. He must study the lessons and pay attention. Those who are following Jesus find that they have lessons every day, in mind must listen to inspiration, and like Jesus, must pray all night when the big problem comes up. If they are faithful to the Spirit they always gain the victory. The teacher is the Holy Spirit, and all get their lessons in their own way, some through inspiration, some through dreams, some through visions, some through flashes of understanding. Spirit uses the avenue most accessible and open to the student.

This avenue may change. In fact it often does as man unfolds. The majority of students get understanding through the quickening of their own spiritual mind, but as a rule they do not have faith enough to make it powerful. Here the Spirit comes to the rescue and confirms the new understanding in dreams, sometimes in visions. As one cultivates a knowledge of the symbols and a regular word is established the leading becomes definite. All doubts are erased from consciousness. Thousands of persons in this age and day have attained a state of mind in which they commune regularly with Christ.

To be saved according to the standard set up by

Jesus we must sit with Him upon His throne in the
kingdom of heavens. This kingdom is to be attained,
not after we are dead but while we are still in the
body.

Faith in things spiritual is not born full-orbed and
perfect. It has its stages of growth in man. The parable
of the mustard seed is applicable in this as in many
other instances. Up to the time of Abraham man had
a primitive consciousness of Spirit. The story of Abraham shows us how the consciousness of soul and of
the soul's relation to God dawns in the race mind, beginning a long period of growth that reaches perfection
in the Christ demonstration on the part of Jesus. Therefore Abraham's history and his varied experiences are
to be read as having to do with the evolution of the
soul. The early stages of this soul growth are symbolized in the experiences of Abraham, the typical
man of faith.

The earliest growths of faith are not deeply rooted.
We find Abraham at first living in a tent, which indicates that faith had not yet become an abiding quality
in the consciousness of man. Through certain activities
of the mind faith takes a firmer hold and finally establishes the "firmament" mentioned in the 1st chapter of
Genesis.

Abram and Sarai, as they were called before their
names were changed to Abraham and Sarah, were both
old and had no children. Symbolizing faith and soul,
respectively, they were as yet without visible fruit
(manifestation). Deep within his heart Abraham cher-
ished an intense desire for a son as heir to his own
growing faith and the perpetuation of his own spiritual
vision. This desire was later to lead to a test of his

faith in the reality of the unseen and in the power of Spirit to bring the unseen into visible manifestation.

Not only was Abraham to be himself blessed and given a great name, but he was to be a blessing to the race in turn. This required something positive of him; namely the establishment of a faith in the invisible good as being present and active to the exclusion of a negative faith in or acceptance of appearances. Thus the promise of God to Abraham was not alone the promise of a son to gratify his personal desires; it was a promise that, with a spiritual background to his life, the impossibilities confronting the natural man would no longer exist and were to be put out of mind. Abraham was the founder of the faith that "with God all things are possible."

Abraham's son and the great nation that he was to father were thus first formed in Abraham's mind by faith in the all-potency of Spirit. The formation of the Christ, the Son, in the individual follows the same law and involves the whole man, spirit, soul, and body. The changes that take place in the mind and in the body of one who begins to exercise the faculty of faith should occasion no surprise. Sense states of mind have formed groups of cells and fixed them in consciousness in certain relations that are not in accord with spiritual law. The activity of faith in mind and body breaks up these crystallized cells, builds up new combinations and establishes them in the body in divine order and harmony. Thus the soul (Sarah) that seems barren of fruit is by faith in Spirit made to bring forth joyously (Isaac).

> *Gen. 15:1-11.* After these things the word of Jehovah came unto Abram in a vision, saying, Fear

not, Abram: I am thy shield, *and* thy exceeding great reward. And Abram said, O Lord Jehovah, what wilt thou give me, seeing I go childless, and he that shall be possessor of my house is Eliezer of Damascus? And Abram said, Behold, to me thou hast given no seed: and, lo, one born in my house is mine heir. And, behold, the word of Jehovah came unto him saying, This man shall not be thine heir; but he that shall come forth out of thine own bowels shall be thine heir. And he brought him forth abroad, and said, Look now toward heaven, and number the stars, if thou be able to number them: and he said unto him, So shall thy seed be. And he believed in Jehovah; and he reckoned it to him for righteousness. And he said unto him, I am Jehovah that brought thee out of Ur of the Chaldees, to give thee this land to inherit it. And he said, O Lord Jehovah, whereby shall I know that I shall inherit it? And he said unto him, Take me a heifer three years old, and a she-goat three years old, and a ram three years old, and a turtle-dove, and a young pigeon. And he took him all these, and divided them in the midst, and laid each half over against the other: but the birds divided he not. And the birds of prey came down upon the carcasses, and Abram drove them away.

This is a lesson of encouragement to those who are faithful yet see no visible fruits of their faith. Jehovah said, "Fear not, Abram: I am thy shield, *and* thy exceeding great reward." Whoever works under the divine law is protected, and the result is sure to come. Active faith in the spiritual powers of Being is productive of tremendous results: "I will multiply your seed as the stars of heaven." The outward evidence of the inward reality may be delayed because we are holding in mind some idea that prevents the manifestation. It is estimated that the best telescopes reveal as many as two billion stars. This illustrates the generative power of faith working in the formless substance of spiritual being. Things of form are limited and can bring but limited reward. Working in the formless, one is working in the free range of the whole expanse of the heavens, and the results are like the innumerable stars, beyond all computation.

The fulfillment of this faith in God may not come at once. A way may be opened in the consciousness for its descent into externality. But keep on believing. "He believed in Jehovah; and he reckoned it to him for righteousness." Then find out why you do not have the visible evidence. Abram asked for specific evidence. He said, "O Lord Jehovah, whereby shall I know that I shall inherit it?" Then follow instructions for a sacrifice. Some ideas on the sense plane must be sacrificed, especially those that have been holding back the demonstration. A heifer, a she-goat, a ram, a turtledove, and a young pigeon are mentioned. These represent ideas of physical strength, human will, and subconscious resistance. The idea of physical strength should be given up for the realization that its source is spiritual. Sacrifice your human will, and the divine will will work its perfect way in you. Deny away all subconscious resistance to the workings of divine law. Let peace and patience pervade your mind, while ever knowing that swiftness is characteristic of all spiritual action. Look for a swift fulfillment of all that you are holding in faith, and if it be delayed, know that some sacrifices are necessary. In all this process continue to drive away, by denial, all the "birds of prey," as Abraham did. Faith is quickened and increased by a denial of all inability, which seems real to the mind of sense. Affirm that the boundless, limitless power that creates the stars, can accomplish in your world all that it has promised or that you have desired.

Abraham's greatest desire was to bring forth a son. Our greatest desire is like unto it, for it is to bring forth the Son, the Christ, in our consciousness and in our life. God's promise applies in both cases, and the method is the same: the limited ideas of sense must be sacrificed for the limitless power of Spirit.

In a dream God revealed to Abraham that his descendants should be sojourners in a strange land (Egypt) for four hundred years, and should then come into Canaan with great substance and power to claim it as their own country.

God's promises are not vague nor veiled in mystery. If they seem so or if anything about our religion seems hazy or indefinite to us, it is because our understanding has not been developed sufficiently to comprehend the fullness of it. Through his repeated contacts with God Abraham grew in understanding; in like manner we also grow by continually "practicing the presence."

Eliezer, steward of the house of Abraham, represents the highest intellectual concept of the Deity. The name *Eliezer* means "God is my help," "God is my success." Eliezer of Damascus points to the will, which directs the temporal affairs of the illumined ego (Abraham). The power of the will in the management of one's house or body is so important that egotism results, and the spiritual man sees that this must not be perpetuated, so he asks for a "son," a projection of his exalted ideals; which was fulfilled in Isaac.

> *Gen. 15:12-21.* And when the sun was going
> down, a deep sleep fell upon Abram; and, lo, a hor-
> ror of great darkness fell upon him. And he said
> unto Abram, Know of a surety that thy seed shall
> be sojourners in a land that is not theirs, and
> shall serve them; and they shall afflict them four
> hundred years; and also that nation, whom they
> shall serve, will I judge: and afterward shall they
> come out with great substance. But thou shalt go to
> thy fathers in peace; thou shalt be buried in a good
> old age. And in the fourth generation they shall
> come hither again: for the iniquity of the Amorite
> is not yet full. And it came to pass, that, when the
> sun went down, and it was dark, behold, a smoking
> furnace, and a flaming torch that passed between
> these pieces. In that day Jehovah made a covenant
> with Abram, saying, Unto thy seed have I given this
> land, from the river of Egypt unto the great river, the
> river Euphrates: the Kenite, and the Kenizzite, and
> the Kadmonite, and the Hittite, and the Perizzite, and
> the Rephaim, and the Amorite, and the Canaanite,
> and the Girgashite, and the Jebusite.

Abraham's vision is fulfilled in the enslavement of
the Children of Israel for four hundred years in Egypt
and their final deliverance.

The sun represents the light of Spirit, but we sometimes have periods when this illumination is obscured
("the sun was going down") and we become negative
in consciousness (Abraham fell into a "deep sleep" or
stupor). Thus we make contact with the subconscious
(land of Egypt), in which region abides substance.
The realm of the subconscious needs the enlightenment of Israel; Israel also needs substance to complete
its manifestation.

The name *Kenite* means "of or belonging to
Kain," "possessions," "welding." The Kenites are

thought to have been a tribe of the Midianites; therefore like the latter, they represent the carnal consciousness of man. However they possess an element not possessed by the Canaanite nations that were to be utterly destroyed. The thoughts represented by the Kenites of our text, though seemingly of the carnal or sense man, contain a measure of judgment, discrimination, and impulse toward good that brings about their final, upliftment into salvation. (One of the meanings of Midian is "judgment.")

The name *Kenizzite* means "centralized strength," "possessor," "hunter." The Kenizzites represent the thoughts of man having to do with the animal phase of his nature, with animal strength and activity.

The name *Kadmonite* means "primeval," "prototype," "eternal." The Kadmonites represent error, carnal thoughts about life.

The name *Hittite* means "broken in pieces," "sundered," "terror." The Hittites represent thoughts of opposition, resistance, and fear.

The name *Perizzite* means "rustic," "dweller in the country." The Perizzites lived in the hill country of Canaan, like the Canaanites. These tribes represent thoughts in the subconscious mind that seem to be at enmity with Spirit, but they are fundamentally part of the principle and when so recognized can be redeemed and become part of the perfect man. This is exemplified by the Israelites making friends with the Kenites.

(For Rephaim see interpretation of Gen. 14. For Amorite, Canaanite, Girgashite, and Jebusite see interpretation of Gen. 10.)

Euphrates means "fruitfulness." These tribes and nations represent the fruits of sense consciousness.

Gen. 16:1-15. Now Sarai, Abram's wife, bare him no children: and she had a handmaid, an Egyptian, whose name was Hagar. And Sarai said unto Abram, Behold now, Jehovah hath restrained me from bearing; go in, I pray thee, unto my handmaid; it may be that I shall obtain children by her. And Abram hearkened to the voice of Sarai. And Sarai, Abram's wife, took Hagar the Egyptian, her handmaid, after Abram had dwelt ten years in the land of Canaan, and gave her to Abram her husband to be his wife. And he went in unto Hagar, and she conceived: and when she saw that she had conceived, her mistress was despised in her eyes. And Sarai said unto Abram, My wrong be upon thee: I gave my handmaid into thy bosom; and when she saw that she had conceived, I was despised in her eyes: Jehovah judge between me and thee. But Abram said unto Sarai, Behold, thy maid is in thy hand; do to her that which is good in thine eyes. And Sarai dealt hardly with her, and she fled from her face.

And the angel of Jehovah found her by a fountain of water in the wilderness, by the fountain in the way to Shur. And he said, Hagar, Sarai's handmaid, whence camest thou? and whither goest thou? And she said, I am fleeing from the face of my mistress Sarai. And the angel of Jehovah said unto her, Return to thy mistress, and submit thyself under her hands. And the angel of Jehovah said unto her, I will greatly multiply thy seed, that it shall not be numbered for multitude. And the angel of Jehovah said unto her, Behold, thou art with child, and shalt bear a son; and thou shalt call his name Ishmael, because Jehovah hath heard thy affliction. And he shall be *as* a wild ass among men; his hand *shall be* against every man, and every man's hand against him; and he shall dwell over against all his brethren. And she called the name of Jehovah that spake unto her, Thou art a God that seeth: for she said, Have I even here looked after him that seeth me? Where-

fore the well was called Beer-lahai-roi; behold, it is
between Kadesh and Bered. And Hagar bare Abram
a son: and Abram called the name of his son, whom
Hagar bare, Ishmael. And Abram was fourscore
and six years old, when Hagar bare Ishmael to
Abram.

Abraham and Sarah did not doubt God's promise
of a son, but as yet their faith in the all-creativeness
and all-power of God was weak. The spiritual child
(Isaac) is brought forth only through faith.

Abraham took Sarah's maid Hagar and had a
son by her. The name *Hagar* means "wanderer," "fugitive," "to flee one's country." Metaphysically Hagar
represents the natural or animal soul in man, which is
a servant to the higher, more spiritual soul represented
by Sarah. The thoughts of the animal soul are not
lifted up to a very high plane and are therefore likely
to be sensual, selfish, or unholy, which reacts to produce a state of fear or uncertainty (wanderer). This
sensual must give way to the spiritual. It cannot stand
in the presence of the Christ Truth but flees before it.
In development from the lower to the higher there is
often a seeming contention between the spiritual and
physical. (Sarah cast out Hagar.)

Hagar's son, being the fruit of the union of faith
with natural will and affection on a lower plane of
expression, was not recognized by Jehovah as an heir
of the promise.

There is an important lesson in this for everyone
who is growing in faith and seeking to bring forth the
fruits of Spirit according to the promise. No true
spiritual demonstration is made unless the divine law
is recognized and obeyed. When we try to demonstrate

through our own personal will and effort, we find that we fall short.

Paul gives us an interpretation of this allegory in Galatians 4:21-31. He calls Sarah the freewoman and Hagar the bondmaid. We who are born of Spirit in the Christ consciousness are sons of the freewoman and the "children of promise." Those born of the bondmaid (the outer or material) are of the flesh and are cast out from the inheritance of Spirit.

Beer-lahai-roi ("the well of the living one who seeth me," "the well of the vision of life") was the name of "a fountain of water in the wilderness, by the fountain in the way to Shur," where the angel met Hagar when she fled from Sarah. Beer-lahai-roi represents the recognition by the individual that his life is divine, is spiritual ("the well of the living one that seeth me"), and is for the whole man. Even the outer or physical man and the human side of the soul are sustained by the life of God, "the living one." It was beside this well that the Lord met Hagar and instructed her to return to Sarah, and also blessed her son Ishmael, who was yet to be born. Ishmael refers to the outer or flesh consciousness. Isaac (who later lived by this well) symbolizes divine sonship. When it is understood that there is but one life and that it is everywhere present in its fullness, the entire man will be lifted up into eternal life.

Beer-lahai-roi also symbolizes God as the guiding light of both the inner and the outer man (the well of the vision of life).

The name *Bered* means "strew," "scatter," "seeding." Bered represents the sowing of ideas (seed thoughts) in the mind that the individual may begin

to act on them consciously and make them fruitful.
(For Shur and Kadesh see interpretation of Gen.
20:1.)

> *Gen. 17:1-8.* And when Abram was ninety
> years old and nine, Jehovah appeared to Abram, and
> said unto him, I am God Almighty; walk before me,
> and be thou perfect. And I will make my covenant
> between me and thee, and will multiply thee ex-
> ceedingly. And Abram fell on his face: and God
> talked with him, saying, As for me, behold, my
> covenant is with thee, and thou shalt be the father
> of a multitude of nations. Neither shall thy name
> any more be called Abram, but thy name shall be
> Abraham; for the father of a multitude of nations
> have I made thee. And I will make thee exceeding
> fruitful, and I will make nations of thee, and kings
> shall come out of thee. And I will establish my
> covenant between me and thee and thy seed after
> thee throughout their generations for an everlasting
> covenant, to be a God unto thee and to thy seed
> after thee. And I will give unto thee, and to thy seed
> after thee, the land of thy sojournings, all the land
> of Canaan, for an everlasting possession; and I will
> be their God.

"I am God Almighty; walk before me, and be
thou perfect."

According to the Scofield Bible, the word *Almighty*
is a translation of the Hebrew *El Shaddai,* one of the
names applied to God in the Old Testament. *El* means
the "Strong One," and *shad* means "the breast, invariably used in Scripture for a woman's breast. *Shaddai*
therefore means primarily 'the breasted.' God is *'Shaddai'* because He is the nourisher, the strength-giver,
and so, in a secondary sense, the satisfier, who pours
Himself into believing lives."

It was revealed to Abram that he should henceforth be called Abraham, which means "father of a multitude." The change in name always denotes a change in character so pronounced that the old name will no longer apply to the new person. We read that Jacob's name was changed to Israel, Simon's to Peter, and Saul's name was changed to Paul. The change of name applies to everyone who changes from sense to Spirit, as is indicated in Revelation 2:17: "I will give him [that overcometh sense] a white stone, and upon the stone a new name written, which no one knoweth but he that receiveth it." The new name, Abraham, "father of a multitude," when we apply it individually means that our faith is to be expressed by bringing the multitude of our thoughts into the realm of Spirit and under the guidance of the Christ.

Through Abraham God called His "chosen people." Some have thought that God's choice of a particular nation or race is out of harmony with the idea of fatherly love and impartiality toward all His children, and so have rejected part of God's purpose before they understood it in its wholeness. Justice to all is seen when the "elect" (select) are considered in their rightful place in the divine plan of redemption. The Jews are the seed of Abraham, and through them is the whole human race blessed by the coming of Jesus.

When Abraham (faith) first catches this large vision of his good, multiplied "as the stars of the heavens," he is not concerned with details, which will work themselves out later. The particular channel through which this great expression would come was not revealed to Abraham in the first promise. The specific thing, the birth of a son to Sarah to be called

Isaac, was a much later revelation. All the facts in connection with the call of Abraham, his experiences, and the several promises made to him by Jehovah God are very important to us, for the great plan of redemption cannot be understood without them. All these promises have not been fulfilled even yet, but the word of God stands sure, and there can be no failure in their fulfillment.

Jehovah on His first contact with Abraham made him a certain promise, namely that his descendants should become a great nation in which all the people of the earth would be blessed. This was rather abstract and indefinite: Abraham was to leave his old life and environment, give up his home, and go into a new and unknown land (state of consciousness).

Jehovah made His second appearance to Abraham when he was camped under the oak of Moreh, in the land of Shechem. At that time he was on his way down to Egypt, keeping the commandment "Get thee out of thy country . . . unto the land that I will show thee." Here he received Jehovah's promise "Unto thy seed will I give this land." This shows us that Abraham is progressing in understanding, that God is becoming more definite to him, and the promise more specific.

Jehovah next appeared to Abraham after he had separated himself from Lot and returned to the land of Canaan. This time the promise was still more definite, namely that Jehovah would give him and his seed forever this very land that he saw and walked upon, to the eastward, westward, northward, and southward. Nothing indefinite or theoretical about that! Yet the promise was still indefinite as regards the descendants, who were to be as numerous as the dust of the earth.

The indefinite nature of this part of the promise was due to Abraham's lack of understanding and complete faith, for somewhere in his mind was a doubting thought caused by the fact that his wife Sarah was barren. When we doubt God's promises by speculating how He can keep them, or when we set up limitations on His power, we of course fail to comprehend, and the promises seem vague and indefinite.

Canaan means "lowland"; it symbolizes the body. The redeemed body is the Promised Land, and when man rediscovers this lost domain all the promises of the Scriptures will be fulfilled.

> *Gen. 17:9-14.* And God said unto Abraham, And as for thee, thou shalt keep my covenant, thou, and thy seed after thee throughout their generations. This is my covenant, which ye shall keep, between me and you and thy seed after thee: every male among you shall be circumcised. And ye shall be circumcised in the flesh of your foreskin; and it shall·be a token of a covenant betwixt me and you. And he that is eight days old shall be circumcised among you, every male throughout your generations, he that is born in the house, or bought with money of any foreigner that is not of thy seed. He that is born in thy house, and he that is bought with thy money, must needs be circumcised: and my covenant shall be in your flesh for an everlasting covenant. And the uncircumcised male who is not circumcised in the flesh of his foreskin, that soul shall be cut off from his people; he hath broken my covenant.

Circumcision is symbolical of the cutting off of mortal tendencies, and is indicative of purification and cleanliness. One is circumcised in the true inner significance of the word only by being thoroughly purified in soul. Then, the glory of the inner soul's cleansing and purifying action works out into the outer consciousness and the body and sets one free from all sensual, corruptible thoughts and activities. "Circumcision is that of the heart, in the spirit not in the letter." Thus man becomes a new creature in Christ Jesus.

Circumcision is the first step toward the eventual elimination of generation. This was fulfilled in the life of Jesus who taught and demonstrated regeneration. He spiritualized both soul and body, and thus made the great demonstration over death. "Verily I say unto you, that ye who have followed me, in the regeneration when the Son of man shall sit on the throne of his glory, ye also shall sit upon twelve thrones, judging the twelve tribes of Israel."

> *Gen. 17:15-21.* And God said unto Abraham, As for Sarai thy wife, thou shalt not call her name Sarai, but Sarah shall her name be. And I will bless her, and moreover I will give thee a son of her: yea, I will bless her, and she shall be *a mother of* nations; kings of peoples shall be of her. Then Abraham fell upon his face, and laughed, and said in his heart, Shall a child be born unto him that is a hundred years old? and shall Sarah, that is ninety years old, bear? And Abraham said unto God, Oh that Ishmael might live before thee! And God said, Nay, but Sarah thy wife shall bear thee a son; and thou shalt call his name Isaac: and I will establish my covenant with him for an everlasting covenant for his seed after him. And as for Ishmael, I have heard thee: behold, I have blessed him, and will make him fruitful, and will multiply him exceedingly; twelve princes shall he beget, and I will make him a great nation. But my covenant will I establish with Isaac, whom Sarah shall bear unto thee at this set time in the next year.

The name *Sarai* means "bitter," "contentious," "dominative." The name *Sarah* means "princess," "noble woman," "noble lady." Sarai's name was changed to Sarah. In spiritual symbology woman represents the soul or intuitive part of man. Sarah is the higher phase of the soul. In Sarai the soul in contending for its rightful place in consciousness; the individual is just recognizing the fact that his affection and emotions are in essence divine and must not be united with material conditions but with Spirit. In Sarah this is more fully realized and expressed.

The name *Ishmael* means "whom God hears," "whom God understands." Metaphysically Ishmael represents the fruit of the thoughts of the natural man at work in the flesh. However, God hears and understands the outer man of flesh as well as the inner man of Spirit, for he too must be redeemed from error and corruption. The name *Ishmael* can also be said to denote that state of consciousness which recognizes God but which, because of the seeming opposition of the outer world, does not express itself according to the highest standards. In other words, Ishmael represents personality, which has its real source in the I AM but which goes wrong in its activity.

In its struggle to attain light, understanding, in contacting the outer or manifest world, it becomes involved in error.

The Lord Jehovah established His everlasting covenant with the promised heir of Abraham and Sarah, whose name was to be called Isaac.

> *Gen. 17:22-27.* And he left off talking with him, and God went up from Abraham. And Abraham took Ishmael his son, and all that were born

in his house, and all that were bought with his
money, every male among the men of Abraham's
house, and circumcised the flesh of their foreskins in
the selfsame day, as God had said unto him. And
Abraham was ninety years old and nine, when he
was circumcised in the flesh of his foreskin. And
Ishmael his son was thirteen years old, when he was
circumcised in the flesh of his foreskin. In the
selfsame day was Abraham circumcised, and Ishmael his son. And all the men of his house, those
born in the house, and those bought with money of
a foreigner, were circumcised with him.

When Abraham received the light in regard to
circumcision he not only conformed to the law himself
but he ordered all the male members of his family to
follow his example. Metaphysically interpreted, this
means that the central ego (Abraham) catches the light
or lays hold of the dominant idea and transmits it to
all states of consciousness in its domain.

Critics have accused religion of being too general,
abstract, and idealistic. Some have said that the teachings of Jesus are not "practical" in this age. These
critics are invariably looking at religion from a general and abstract point of view. They consider such
promises as the one made to Abraham that he should
be the father of a great nation, with descendants as
many as the stars of heaven, allegorically rather than
the terse and very definite promise "Sarah thy wife
shall bear thee a son."

From a careful study of Genesis, especially the
story of Abraham, we should be able to see that our
religion is either a purely speculative philosophy or a
practical principle applicable to daily living, depending on our point of view and our understanding of it.

Gen. 18:1-5. And Jehovah appeared unto him by the oaks of Mamre, as he sat in the tent door in the heat of the day; and he lifted up his eyes and looked, and, lo, three men stood over against him: and when he saw them, he ran to meet them from the tent door, and bowed himself to the earth, and said, My lord, if now I have found favor in thy sight, pass not way, I pray thee, from thy servant: let now a little water be fetched, and wash your feet, and rest yourselves under the tree: and I will fetch a morsel of bread, and strengthen ye your heart; after that ye shall pass on: forasmuch as ye are come to your servant. And they said, So do, as thou hast said.

Here we have a most interesting account of another of Jehovah's appearances to Abraham. This time Abraham was sitting "in the tent door," inactive because of "the heat of the day." The tent was pitched under the oaks of Mamre, and Jehovah's appearance here was the most definite of all. The oak tree denotes something strong and protective. In many places in the Bible God's protection is compared to an oak tree. We are told that God is our strength, our deliverance, our refuge from the storm. The name *Mamre* means "fatness," "firmness," "vigor," "strength," and Mamre symbolizes endurance, renewed life, and abundant substance. Thus we see that faith (Abraham) has in and around itself everything needful for growth and for its firm establishment in consciousness.

"He lifted up his eyes and looked, and, lo, three men stood over against him." Faith must "lift up" its eyes above all material things and look to the spiritual as the source of all. Having done that, it will perceive the truth in its triune aspect. Abraham saw Jehovah as "three men." Jehovah is always the central figure, but we must not lose sight of the fact that, although the one Mind is the omnipresent source of all, it manifests itself as a trinity of spirit, soul, and body, or spirit, consciousness, and substance. When faith lifts up its eyes and catches this vision, then indeed hath Jehovah appeared unto it, and His promises are sure and clear.

Abraham's bringing water to wash the feet of his guest or guests symbolizes the necessity of purifying the consciousness by the use of denials. The "morsel of bread" for the strengthening of the heart represents substance in its relation to the renewing of one's inner strength and courage; also the necessity of using affirmation (eating bread) for the growth of the soul. Abraham recognized the triune aspect of Jehovah in manifestation, for he talked to the three men as though they were one man, whom he addresses as "my lord." This "my lord" is the I AM.

If by faith in Spirit we receive the higher ideas and entertain them as though they were realities instead of "figments of the imagination," as the faithless term them, we thereby open the way for a new state of consciousness. Many Truth seekers try to visualize God by thinking of the divine master Jesus and surround themselves with pictures of Him to aid the eye of faith.

Jehovah goes into the details of His former promise to Abraham (faith) at greater length because through his faith he has now comprehended God in a more particular and practical way. At the time of the former promise Jehovah was understood in an abstract and transcendent way, and His promise was abstract and vast in scope: that Abraham should be the father of multitudes. Now Abraham (faith) sees God in His triune manifestation as spirit, soul, and body, like unto "three men," which is a definite and practical conception. The promise is renewed and made specific in its terms. Abraham is to be the father of a nation, because his wife Sarah is to give birth to a son. This is a definite promise that cannot be misunderstood by Abraham or long postponed by Jehovah.

Since the human race is made up of individuals all patterned after the one divine-idea man, we can see in the history of these Bible characters the story of their own spiritual development both as individuals and as a race. Our understanding of the life of Abraham will not be complete unless we consider it in both these relations to us.

> *Gen. 18:6-15.* And Abraham hastened into the tent unto Sarah, and said, Make ready quickly three measures of fine meal, knead it, and make cakes. And Abraham ran unto the herd, and fetched a calf tender and good, and gave it unto the servant; and he hasted to dress it. And he took butter, and milk, and the calf which he had dressed, and set it before them; and he stood by them under the tree, and they did eat. And they said unto him, Where is Sarah thy wife? And he said, Behold, in the tent. And he said, I will certainly return unto thee when the season cometh round; and, lo, Sarah thy wife shall have a son. And Sarah heard in the tent door, which was behind him. Now Abraham and Sarah were old, *and* well stricken in age; it had ceased to be with Sarah after the manner of women. And Sarah laughed within herself, saying, After I am waxed old shall I have pleasure, my lord being old also? And Jehovah said unto Abraham, Wherefore did Sarah laugh, saying, Shall I of a surety bear a child, who am old? Is anything too hard for Jehovah? At the set time I will return unto thee,

when the season cometh round, and Sarah shall have
a son. Then Sarah denied, saying, I laughed not;
for she was afraid. And he said, Nay; but thou
didst laugh.

The feast that Abraham set before Jehovah symbolizes the new vital forces in the bodily organism
(tent)—which shares in the spiritual unfoldment—
producing a new state of consciousness (Isaac) in
spite of what seems advanced age or deterioration of
bodily vigor. Isaac represents the pleasure and joy-
ousness of life. The incredulity of Abraham and
Sarah symbolizes the doubts of the natural man.

Gen. 18:16-33. And the men rose up from
thence, and looked toward Sodom: and Abraham
went with them to bring them on the way. And Jehovah said, Shall I hide from Abraham that which
I do; seeing that Abraham shall surely become a
great and mighty nation, and all the nations of the
earth shall be blessed in him? For I have known
him, to the end that he may command his children
and his household after him, that they may keep
the way of Jehovah, to do righteousness and justice;
to the end that Jehovah may bring upon Abraham
that which he hath spoken of him. And Jehovah
said, Because the cry of Sodom and Gomorrah is
great, and because their sin is very grievous; I will
go down now, and see whether they have done altogether according to the cry of it, which is come
unto me; and if not, I will know.

And the men turned from thence, and went toward Sodom: but Abraham stood yet before Jehovah.
And Abraham drew near, and said, Wilt thou consume the righteous with the wicked? Peradventure
there are fifty righteous within the city: wilt thou
consume and not spare the place for the fifty righteous that are therein? That be far from thee to do
after this manner, to slay the righteous with the

wicked, that so the righteous should be as the wicked;
that be far from thee: shall not the Judge of all
the earth do right? And Jehovah said, If I find in
Sodom fifty righteous within the city, then I will
spare all the place for their sake. And Abraham answered and said, Behold now, I have taken upon me
to speak unto the Lord, who am but dust and ashes:
peradventure there shall lack five of the fifty righteous: wilt thou destroy all the city for lack of five?
And he said, I will not destroy it, if I find there
forty and five. And he spake unto him yet again,
and said, Peradventure there shall be forty found
there. And he said, I will not do it for the forty's
sake. And he said, Oh let not the Lord be angry, and
I will speak: peradventure there shall thirty be
found there. And he said, I will not do it, if I find
thirty there. And he said, Behold now, I have taken
upon me to speak unto the Lord: peradventure there
shall be twenty found there. And he said, I will not
destroy it for the twenty's sake. And he said, Oh
let not the Lord be angry, and I will speak yet but
this once: peradventure ten shall be found there.
And he said, I will not destroy it for the ten's
sake. And Jehovah went his way, as soon as he had
left off communing with Abraham: and Abraham
returned unto his place.

The time has now arrived in the development of
spiritual consciousness when faith (Abraham) must be
fully awakened to the truth that all belief in the expression of sensuality must be entirely put away. Sodom
is to be destroyed. But the man of faith is not yet
entirely out of his sense consciousness. Sodom ("hidden
wiles") represents an obscure or concealed thought
habit. Gomorrah ("material force") represents a state
of mind adverse to the law of Spirit. These wicked
cities of the plain are located within man, and before
he can come into a realization of the promised "son"

that he desires so much he must consent to a thorough purification from the sins that go on in them. The purification is by fire and must be absolutely complete.

The remainder of the chapter concerns Jehovah's revelation to Abraham of His intention utterly to destroy Sodom and Gomorrah because of their great wickedness; also Jehovah's agreement to save Sodom if only ten righteous men could be found in it. The tendency to plead to be allowed to keep old habits of thought on the ground that there is some good in them is a characteristic of man's early stages of development. We try very hard to save some of our secret habits and sense thoughts. At first we reason that there must be quite a few good things in the old thoughts, ideas, and ways. Then we are a little less sure about there being "fifty" and we come down to "ten." But there are not even ten righteous, and the old consciousness must be destroyed. Error must be wholly wiped out of the consciousness, and the sooner we consent to accept the fullness of the regenerative law the sooner we shall enter the kingdom.

Sodom represents the very lowest form of sense desire in the procreative center. Today we derive from the word *Sodom* the name of an unmentionable vice. Yet the spiritual-minded Abraham persisted in the belief that there must be some good in Sodom. Jehovah showed him otherwise. The tendency to plead that there must be good in sense habits persists very strongly. We cannot conceive why these functions, which seem so necessary to the reproduction of the race, should not be under the divine law. We have not yet awakened to the fact that they are but an external and counterfeit expression, a degenerate imitation, of divine reproduction.

Do not hold the thought that your so-called natural functions are divine. They are great mysteries to the human consciousness, to be understood when we have acquired spiritual wisdom. The race has gone through some strange experiences, and wonderful revelations come to those who get beneath the surface of things. There are those walking the earth today who could startle the world with revelations of Truth about the things right under our eyes that we do not see. Resolutely turn your back on all the forms of sense thought and seek no excuse for them. Then you will gradually begin to see the light within the light.

All these incidents, men, and places represent states of consciousness in the individual. The men represent the human desires that are still attached to the senses (Sodom and Gomorrah); the incidents denote their method of operation, and the places indicate their sphere of activity.

Chapter VII

The Fruits of Faith

GENESIS 19, 20, 21, and 22

IN THE PRECEDING chapter we read that when Jehovah appeared to Abraham the patriarch was sitting in the door of his tent. There is a remarkable parallel here, for Jehovah appeared to Lot as he sat in the gate of Sodom.

> *Gen. 19:1-11.* And the two angels came to Sodom at even; and Lot sat in the gate of Sodom: and Lot saw them, and rose up to meet them; and he bowed himself with his face to the earth; and he said, Behold now, my lords, turn aside, I pray you, into your servant's house, and tarry all night, and wash your feet, and ye shall rise up early, and go on your way. And they said, Nay; but we will abide in the street all night. And he urged them greatly; and they turned in unto him, and entered into his house; and he made them a feast, and did bake unleavened bread, and they did eat. But before they lay down, the men of the city, *even* the men of Sodom, compassed the house round, both young and old, all the people from every quarter; and they called unto Lot, and said unto him, Where are the men that came in to thee this night? bring them out unto us, that we may know them. And Lot went out unto them to the door, and shut the door after him. And he said, I pray you, my brethren, do not so wickedly. Behold now, I have two daughters that have not known man; let me, I pray you, bring them out unto you, and do ye to them as is good in your eyes: only unto these men do nothing, forasmuch as

they are come under the shadow of my roof. And
they said, Stand back. And they said, This one fellow came in to sojourn, and he will needs be a
judge: now will we deal worse with thee, than with
them. And they pressed sore upon the man, even
Lot, and drew near to break the door. But the men
put forth their hand, and brought Lot into the house
to them, and shut to the door. And they smote the
men that were at the door of the house with blindness, both small and great, so that they wearied themselves to find the door.

As Abraham represents the positive side of faith
and Lot the negative side, it can also be said that
Abraham represents the spiritual consciousness and
that Lot is the natural consciousness, which however
is turned toward the light. Jehovah appeared to Abraham as three. Spiritual consciousness understands the
trinity of being that is spirit, soul, and body. Lot
saw Jehovah as two angels, which shows that the natural mind leaves Spirit out of consideration.

When Abraham invited the three into his tent they
accepted his hospitality without comment. But when
Lot asked the two to spend the night under his roof,
wash their feet, and partake of his food, they refused.
It took persistent urging on the part of Lot to persuade
them to abide with him.

When the unfolding nature (Lot) begins to entertain higher spiritual thoughts (angels), all the evil
and degenerate thoughts (men of Sodom) come at
once and "compass the house." They demand that
the higher thoughts be put out, or that they be admitted (into mind) to throw them out. When the
demand is refused they become violent. Man's way
is to compromise with evil thoughts by giving to them

his love and emotion, even if he does not allow them free expression in his mind. Lot offered his daughters to the men of Sodom. When carnal thoughts become strong and numerous enough (compass the house) they assert complete mastery over the individual and tell him: "Stand back . . . This one fellow came in to sojourn, and he will needs be a judge."

The angels (high spiritual thoughts) whom Lot induced to enter his house, came to his rescue. They struck the men of Sodom (carnal thoughts) with blindness so that they were thrown into confusion and their destructive efforts rendered futile, at least for the time being: blind passions that stop at nothing to gain their ends must be annihilated.

> *Gen. 19:12-23.* And the men said unto Lot, Hast thou here any besides? son-in-law, and thy sons, and thy daughters, and whomsoever thou hast in the city, bring them out of the place: for we will destroy this place, because the cry of them is waxed great before Jehovah; and Jehovah hath sent us to destroy it. And Lot went out, and spake unto his sons-in-law, who married his daughters, and said, Up, get you out of this place; for Jehovah will destroy the city. But he seemed unto his sons-in-law as one that mocked. And when the morning arose, then the angels hastened Lot, saying, Arise, take thy wife, and thy two daughters that are here, lest thou be consumed in the iniquity of the city. But he lingered; and the men laid hold upon his hand, and upon the hand of his wife, and upon the hand of his two daughters, Jehovah being merciful unto him: and they brought him forth, and set him without the city. And it came to pass, when they had brought them forth abroad, that he said, Escape for thy life; look not behind thee, neither stay thou in all the Plain; escape to the mountain, lest thou be consumed.

And Lot said unto them, Oh, not so, my lord: behold now, thy servant hath found favor in thy sight, and thou hast magnified thy lovingkindness, which thou hast showed unto me in saving my life; and I cannot escape to the mountain, lest evil overtake me, and I die: behold now, this city is near to flee unto, and it is a little one. Oh let me escape thither (is it not a little one?), and my soul shall live. And he said unto him, See, I have accepted thee concerning this thing also, that I will not overthrow the city of which thou hast spoken. Haste thee, escape thither; for I cannot do anything till thou be come thither. Therefore the name of the city was called Zoar. The sun was risen upon the earth when Lot came unto Zoar.

Jehovah's promise to Abraham was that He would save the righteous. Here Jehovah's angels invited Lot to take with him those of his household (thought people) who were ready to advance spiritually. Only Lot, his wife, and his two virgin daughters were prepared to take the step. However after the Lord had delivered them outside the walls of the city Lot (negative faith) was afraid to attempt flight to the mountain (high state of consciousness). He knew he was not fully prepared for such a step. The angels consented to let him escape to the little city of Zoar, the name of which means "reduced," "made small," "lessened." Thus Lot was given opportunity to open his mind to the light to such a degree that seeming negation was minimized in consciousness, and he was blessed with a new understanding of Truth. ("The sun was risen upon the earth when Lot came unto Zoar.")

Gen. 19:24-26. Then Jehovah rained upon Sodom and upon Gomorrah brimstone and fire from Jehovah out of heaven; and he overthrew those

cities, and all the Plain, and all the inhabitants
of the cities, and that which grew upon the ground.
But his wife looked back from behind him, and
she became a pillar of salt.

Eventually all error must be wiped out of consciousness. In our efforts to overcome the sins of the flesh
we pass through strange experiences, and wonderful
revelations come to those of us who conform to divine
law. The destruction of Sodom and Gomorrah by fire
represents a mighty purifying process that makes man
ready for a great realization of divine life.

Lot's wife was turned into a pillar of salt. Salt
is a preservative, corresponding to memory. When we
remember the pleasures of the senses and long for their
return, we preserve the sense desire. This desire will
manifest itself sometime, somewhere, unless the memory is dissolved through renunciation.

> *Gen. 19:27-29.* And Abraham got up early in
> the morning to the place where he had stood before
> Jehovah: and he looked toward Sodom and Gomor-
> rah, and toward all the land of the Plain, and be-
> held, and, lo, the smoke of the land went up as the
> smoke of a furnace.
>
> And it came to pass, when God destroyed the
> cities of the Plain, that God remembered Abraham,
> and sent Lot out of the midst of the overthrow, when
> he overthrew the cities in which Lot dwelt.

The above Scripture means that after a degree of
cleansing or destruction of sense we mentally review
our experiences and recognize that nothing is really
destroyed but rather transmuted (Abraham beheld
the result). Through faith we take stock of the progress
we have made and find that we are getting a consciousness of radiant substance (smoke) and of a

higher life (heat). Nothing is lost. When sense consciousness is raised to a higher plane all that belongs to it is saved with it. This is represented by Jehovah's saving Lot's life.

> *Gen. 19:30-38.* And Lot went up out of Zoar, and dwelt in the mountain, and his two daughters with him; for he feared to dwell in Zoar: and he dwelt in a cave, he and his two daughters. And the first-born said unto the younger, Our father is old, and there is not a man in the earth to come in unto us after the manner of all the earth: come, let us make our father drink wine, and we will lie with him, that we may preserve seed of our father. And they made their father drink wine that night: and the first-born went in, and lay with her father; and he knew not when she lay down, nor when she arose. And it came to pass on the morrow, that the first-born said unto the younger, Behold, I lay yesternight with my father: let us make him drink wine this night also, and go thou in, and lie with him, that we may preserve seed of our father. And they made their father drink wine that night also: and the younger arose, and lay with him; and he knew not when she lay down, nor when she arose. Thus were both the daughters of Lot with child by their father. And the first-born bare a son and called his name Moab: the same is the father of the Moabites unto this day. And the younger, she also bare a son, and called his name Ben-ammi: the same is the father of the children of Ammon unto this day.

When the soul reaches a certain stage of unfoldment the natural progressive quality of faith shows a tendency toward spiritual growth. Lot here represents natural faith in a state of evolution, yet his living in a cave in the mountain denotes that this faith is still in the clutches of materiality. The feminine forces of faith (daughters of Lot) reflect the parent desire for continued perpetuation of their line. There was no other masculine principle on the plane of consciousness on which these feminine forces were functioning ("there is not a man in the earth to come in unto us after the manner of all the earth"). Through stimulating life (wine) the seed idea was implanted by the father principle (Lot) in receptive soil and brought forth fruit.

Moab, son of Lot's eldest daughter, represents the thought that perpetuates body consciousness. It is found in the idea of organized substance ("flowing from the father") but it is impregnated with the lusts of the flesh. Referring to the Moabites, Jeremiah says, "Cursed be he that doeth the work of Jehovah negligently." So Moab represents one phase of the lusts of carnal mind for expression through the flesh. While Moab pertains to the body and the most external conditions of life, there is something good in him, or at least a possibility of good.

Ben-ammi, the name of the son of Lot's youngest daughter and father of the Ammonites, means "son of my people," "son of my kindred," "son of my tribe," which points to segregation and personal selfishness. This thought is the source of the clan, then the nation. When this egotism is exalted the nation looks on itself as being superior to all other nations and proceeds to compel them to acknowledge this superiority by force of arms. The Ammonites waged constant war against the Israelites but were eventually defeated.

Gen. 20:1. And Abraham journeyed from thence toward the land of the South, and dwelt between Kadesh and Shur; and he sojourned in Gerar.

The name *Shur* means "going round about," "wall," "fortification," "ox." Shur represents the never-ceasing progress, unfoldment, and development of man. In his evolution man has apparently always moved in cycles; but each time he comes again to his starting place he seems to be a little in advance of his former state. When he begins to awaken spiritually his progress is more rapid. There is also a thought of strength and might ("wall," "ox").

The name *Kadesh* means "pure," "bright," "holy," "sacred." Kadesh represents the inherently pure, sinless, perfect, ideal state in the depths of the consciousness of every individual.

Abraham "dwelt between Kadesh and Shur; and he sojourned in Gerar." Gerar symbolizes subjective substance and life. Abraham had on one hand Kadesh —the inherently pure, sinless, ideal state—and on the other hand Shur (unceasing progress) while he had his existence in Gerar (substance and life). Thus does faith (typified by Abraham) develop in the spiritually awakening individual.

> *Gen. 20:2-13.* And Abraham said of Sarah his wife, She is my sister: and Abimelech king of Gerar sent, and took Sarah. But God came to Abimelech in a dream of the night, and said to him, Behold, thou art but a dead man, because of the woman whom thou hast taken; for she is a man's wife. Now Abimelech had not come near her: and he said, Lord, wilt thou slay even a righteous nation? Said he not himself unto me, She is my sister? and she, even she herself said, He is my brother: in the integrity of my heart and the innocency of my hands have I done this. And God said unto him in the dream, Yea, I know that in the integrity of thy heart thou hast

done this, and I also withheld thee from sinning against me: therefore suffered I thee not to touch her. Now therefore restore the man's wife; for he is a prophet, and he shall pray for thee, and thou shalt live: and if thou restore her not, know thou that thou shalt surely die, thou, and all that are thine.

And Abimelech rose early in the morning, and called all his servants, and told all these things in their ears: and the men were sore afraid. Then Abimelech called Abraham, and said unto him, What hast thou done unto us? and wherein have I sinned against thee, that thou hast brought on me and on my kingdom a great sin? thou hast done deeds unto me that ought not to be done. And Abimelech said unto Abraham, What sawest thou, that thou hast done this thing? And Abraham said, Because I thought, Surely the fear of God is not in this place; and they will slay me for my wife's sake. And moreover she is indeed my sister, the daughter of my father, but not the daughter of my mother; and she became my wife: and it came to pass, when God caused me to wander from my father's house, that I said unto her, This is thy kindness which thou shalt show unto me: at every place whither we shall come, say of me, He is my brother.

If spiritual faith through the affectional side of one's nature (Sarah) makes union with the controlling unregenerate will in the subconscious (Abimelech) there is a reversal of the progressive law and bodily ills (the plagues of Egypt) are brought forth, as we noted with reference to a previous experience of Abraham. (See interpretation of Gen. 12:10-20.) However in an instance like this, when faith, lacking understanding, would have repeated the error, the soul has progressed until the subconsciousness has come under the guidance of Spirit, and the plagues that came as a result of a former mistake are not repeated on this occasion.

Abimelech (unregenerate will) was quickened to the point where he could receive instruction through dreams. Spirit revealed to Abimelech the true relationship between Abraham and Sarah, and thus he was saved from making an unlawful union.

When Abimelech (will) faced Abraham (pioneering faith) with the fact, Abraham admitted that he had lost sight of the possibilities of the divine omnipresence and was not aware that the all-knowing Spirit could penetrate into every consciousness. "Because I thought, Surely the fear of God is not in this place." Abraham and Sarah were of the same blood and therefore he said truly, "She is my sister."

> *Gen. 20:14-18.* And Abimelech took sheep and oxen, and men-servants and women-servants, and gave them unto Abraham, and restored him Sarah his wife. And Abimelech said, Behold, my land is before thee: dwell where it pleaseth thee. And unto Sarah he said, Behold, I have given thy brother a thousand pieces of silver: behold, it is for thee a covering of the eyes to all that are with thee; and in respect of all thou art righted. And Abraham prayed unto God: and God healed Abimelech, and his wife, and his maid-servants; and they bare children. For Jehovah had fast closed up all the wombs of the house of Abimelech, because of Sarah, Abraham's wife.

This is a situation where there is apt to be contention between the soul and the body consciousness unless adjustment is made. Pioneering faith (Abraham) in union with the spiritual soul (Sarah) issues in a high realization of both soul and body. It is only the highest emanation of body consciousness that is ready for transmutation, consequently there needs to be an equalizing and adjusting power to establish peace and safety in the body consciousness in order to avoid some form of plague. To teach this truth Abimelech (the ruling power that controls the substance side of man's being), his wife, and maidservants are represented as being unproductive for a season, but as being healed through faith (Abraham interceded with God).

> *Gen. 21:1-7.* And Jehovah visited Sarah as he had said, and Jehovah did unto Sarah as he had spoken. And Sarah conceived, and bare Abraham a son in his old age, at the set time of which God had spoken to him. And Abraham called the name of his son that was born unto him, whom Sarah bare to him, Isaac. And Abraham circumcised his son Isaac when he was eight days old, as God had commanded him. And Abraham was a hundred years old, when his son Isaac was born unto him. And Sarah said, God hath made me to laugh; every one that heareth will laugh with me. And she said, Who would have said unto Abraham, that Sarah should give children suck? for I have borne him a son in his old age.

Isaac was born after Abraham and Sarah were both past the age of bringing forth. So we when born of the Spirit through faith are born not "of the will of the flesh, nor of the will of man, but of God." The natural man has no power to bring forth the "new man" in Christ Jesus. The natural man brings forth Hagar's son, who is not the chosen heir. The new man is a "new creature," begotten not of the flesh but of the divine word. This begetting represents the forming of a new state of consciousness, the consciousness referred to by

Paul when he expressed the hope to the Galatians that "Christ be formed" in them.

As one gains a certain inner satisfaction from doing a good deed, so in repeatedly following the promptings of Spirit one accumulates a fund of satisfaction that finally breaks forth in laughter. Isaac was not born until Abraham and Sarah had reached old age—had accumulated a "faith consciousness." Note the different kinds of laughter in this allegory. Abraham laughed questioningly, hopefully, when it was announced that Sarah would bear a son. Sarah laughed incredulously when the promise was announced to her. Both Abraham and Sarah, with their friends, laughed joyfully and thankfully when Isaac was born.

Religion is not the dolorous thing that many have pictured it, much to its loss and to ours as well. On the contrary religion should make man joyful. God is not to be served in the spirit of bondage to a taskmaster but in the spirit of happiness. In Deuteronomy we read: "Because thou servedst not Jehovah thy God with joyfulness, and with gladness of heart, by reason of the abundance of all things; therefore shalt thou serve thine enemies . . . in hunger, and in thirst, and in nakedness, and in want of all things." If one's prayers are not answered or one fails to demonstrate the reason may perhaps be found here.

Those who persistently exercise faith in God find there is generated in their mind a condition that gradually grows into a conviction of the permanent presence of divine substance within, and this gives rise to the most exquisite joy. Inward ecstasy is what gives the countenance of peace to the saint and of illumination and purity to the sister of mercy. It is experienced by all who pass into the second degree of faith (Isaac, son of Abraham).

Gen. 21:8-21. And the child grew, and was weaned: and Abraham made a great feast on the day that Isaac was weaned. And Sarah saw the son of Hagar the Egyptian, whom she had borne unto Abraham, mocking. Wherefore she said unto Abraham, Cast out this handmaid and her son: for the son of this handmaid shall not be heir with my son, even with Isaac. And the thing was very grievous in Abraham's sight on account of his son. And God said unto Abraham, Let it not be grievous in thy sight because of the lad, and because of thy handmaid; in all that Sarah saith unto thee, hearken unto her voice; for in Isaac shall thy seed be called. And also of the son of the handmaid will I make a nation, because he is thy seed. And Abraham rose up early in the morning, and took bread and a bottle of water, and gave it unto Hagar, putting it on her shoulder, and *gave her* the child, and sent her away: and she departed, and wandered in the wilderness of Beer-sheba. And the water in the bottle was spent, and she cast the child under one of the shrubs. And she went, and sat her down over against him a good way off, as it were a bowshot: for she said, Let me not look upon the death of the child. And she sat over against him, and lifted up her voice, and wept. And God heard the voice of the lad; and the angel of God called to Hagar out of heaven, and said unto her, What aileth thee, Hagar? fear not; for God hath heard the voice of the lad where he is. Arise, lift up the lad, and hold him in thy hand; for I will make him a great nation. And God opened her eyes, and she saw a well of water; and she went, and filled the bottle with water, and gave the lad drink. And God was with the lad, and he grew; and he dwelt in the wilderness, and became, as he grew up, an archer. And he dwelt in the wilderness

of Paran: and his mother took him a wife out of
the land of Egypt.

When Isaac was weaned (symbolizing his readiness
to take a forward step in soul responsibility) Ishmael,
Hagar's son, mocked him. Such mockery is the experience of everyone in the new birth. The thoughts
that are the fruit of the mind of flesh rise up within
him and mock the new man. Here the overcomer has
a definite work to do. The animal soul (Hagar, the
bondmaid) and the natural desires (her son) must be
cast out. As Abraham grieved when Hagar was ban-
ished, so we sometimes grieve at giving up the fruits
of material thinking brought forth by the natural man.

In the development of spiritual faculties, of which
faith (Abraham) is one, there is an ascending movement of the consciousness that is felt and understood by
the individual having the experience but that is difficult
to explain to one who has not yet entered upon that
plane of development. The faculty of faith grows
stronger with each trial, and when it is obedient to the
Lord as its divine guide, it finds an added pleasure in the
exercise of both mind and body at every upward step.
Each function of man's organism is spiritual at its
foundation, and when he exercises it as intended by
Divine Mind his every breath and every heartbeat is a
song of joy. Even the most earthly functions may be
spiritualized and become sources of unending pleasure,
while when they are under the control of the animal
mind of man they become demoralizers of the body.
Under divine guidance the retrogression produced
by mere animalism may be harmonized and purified
through the descent of the fires of Spirit. This is what
happened to Sodom and Gomorrah, which represent

the desires and activities pertaining to generation.

When we have faith in God and the ways of Spirit, we are willing to give up all our material pleasures if such be the instruction of the inner guide. This giving up is symbolized by the sacrifices so often referred to in the history of the Children of Israel. The body and its vital forces are in perpetual action, which is progressive under the divine law. When the law is disregarded there is a waning of the higher forces that brings a sense of discomfort. It is frequently through pain that we are brought to see the error of our ways. Then we should hasten to find the law of being that will give real satisfaction without inharmony.

The action of Abraham is an example of this practice. After giving up animal gratification and purifying the mind of sense thoughts (banishing Hagar and Ishmael), he experienced a greater pleasure from a more interior or spiritual action of the same function. Isaac was the fulfillment of Abraham's greatest desire. But the use of the natural functions must also be raised to a higher plane. On each of the ascending stages in bodily transmutation there is a residuum of the last preceding stage remaining in consciousness. This too must be purified so that the whole man may be a fit temple for the Holy Spirit.

The seemingly inhuman treatment of Hagar and Ishmael by Abraham and Sarah is symbolical of the activity of forces at work in the soul of man. The natural soul (Hagar), lacking real understanding of the newly awakened spiritual soul (Sarah), looks on it with a jealous and antagonistic eye. The product of the thoughts of the natural man at work in the flesh (Ishmael) reflects the natural soul's attitude and scoffs at the possibility of joy brought about through mere pleasure in spiritual life. Such an attitude brings about a separation between the spiritual state of consciousness and the natural state that depletes the supply on the natural plane.

The wilderness of Beer-sheba represents in individual consciousness the multitude of undisciplined and uncultivated thoughts. Even in this state of mind a person can hear the voice of God. God spoke to Hagar, which opened her eyes to the truth that the well of living water was close by and that she and her son would be amply sustained and prospered.

This tells us that even the outermost part of man (the body) is to be saved and to be given the chance to unfold and become efficient in all its activities.

Ishmael became an archer, which indicates that he was an expert at hitting the mark. Later he left Beer-sheba and "dwelt in the wilderness of Paran." The name *Paran* means "region of caverns," "region of searching," "place of much digging." Paran represents the multitude of seemingly confused and undisciplined thoughts of the subconscious mind; also a place or period of much earnest searching after Truth. That "his mother took him a wife out of the land of Egypt" means that Ishmael (fruits of the flesh) through Hagar (the natural soul) unites with the feminine force of materiality.

> *Gen. 21:22-34.* And it came to pass at that time, that Abimelech and Phicol the captain of his host spake unto Abraham, saying, God is with thee in all that thou doest: now therefore swear unto me here by God that thou wilt not deal falsely with me, nor with my son, nor with my son's son: but according

to the kindness that I have done unto thee, thou shalt do unto me, and to the land wherein thou hast sojourned. And Abraham said, I will swear. And Abraham reproved Abimelech because of the well of water, which Abimelech's servants had violently taken away. And Abimelech said, I know not who hath done this thing: neither didst thou tell me, neither yet heard I of it, but today. And Abraham took sheep and oxen, and gave them unto Abimelech; and they two made a covenant. And Abraham set seven ewe lambs of the flock by themselves. And Abimelech said unto Abraham, What mean these seven ewe lambs which thou hast set by themselves? And he said, These seven ewe lambs shalt thou take of my hand, that it may be a witness unto me, that I have digged this well. Wherefore he called that place Beer-sheba; because there they sware both of them. So they made a covenant at Beer-sheba: and Abimelech rose up, and Phicol the captain of his host, and they returned into the land of the Philistines. And *Abraham* planted a tamarisk tree in Beer-sheba, and called there on the name of Jehovah, the Everlasting God. And Abraham sojourned in the land of the Philistines many days.

The name *Phicol* means "spokesman for all," "all-commanding," "every tongue." Phicol was the captain of the host of Abimelech and represents the seeming all-sufficiency of sense consciousness in man at a certain stage of his evolution. He was a Philistine, a Philistine denoting sense consciousness.

The name *Beer-sheba* means "well of the oath," "well of fulfillment," "well of the seven." Abraham represents the first activity of the faith faculty in man's consciousness. Abimelech represents the will, which though unregenerate at this stage of man's unfoldment, recognizes faith and its attainments (Abraham and his possessions). Abimelech fears that he and his kingdom will be overrun by Abraham and his ever-increasing family and household. On the other hand, Abimelech's servants take by force the well that Abraham had dug. This latter means that the life forces, which have been discovered and laid hold of by faith's activity, have been utilized and corrupted by the fleshly man instead of being retained for the use of the mental and spiritual. The covenant between Abraham and Abimelech denotes the establishing of a right relation in consciousness between the spiritual and so-called material. Beer-sheba represents the establishing of this agreement ("well of the oath") between the inner and the outer, wherein faith and its adherents (higher thoughts) are given ample room in the organism and are allowed to retain possession of the well (reservoir of life) that they have been instrumental in bringing to light. On the other hand, the higher thoughts of faith realize that they must not harm or destroy the outer man (Abimelech and his kingdom).

To swear by the seven is to covenant that the thing promised will be fulfilled, the number seven representing fulfillment of the natural law.

> *Gen. 22:1-18.* And it came to pass after these things, that God did prove Abraham, and said unto him, Abraham; and he said, Here am I. And he said, Take now thy son, thine only son, whom thou lovest, even Isaac, and get thee into the land of Moriah; and offer him there for a burnt-offering upon one of the mountains which I will tell thee of. And Abraham rose early in the morning, and saddled his ass, and took two of his young men with him, and Isaac his son; and he clave the wood for the burnt-offering, and rose up, and went unto the

place of which God had told him. On the third
day Abraham lifted up his eyes, and saw the place
afar off. And Abraham said unto his young men,
Abide ye here with the ass, and I and the lad will
go yonder; and we will worship, and come again
to you. And Abraham took the wood of the burnt-
offering, and laid it upon Isaac his son; and he took
in his hand the fire and the knife; and they went
both of them together. And Isaac spake unto Abraham his father, and said, My father: and he said,
Here am I, my son. And he said, Behold, the fire
and the wood: but where is the lamb for a burnt-
offering? And Abraham said, God will provide himself the lamb for a burnt-offering, my son: so they
went both of them together.

And they came to the place which God had
told them of; and Abraham built the altar there,
and laid the wood in order, and bound Isaac his son,
and laid him on the altar, upon the wood. And
Abraham stretched forth his hand, and took the
knife to slay his son. And the angel of Jehovah
called unto him out of heaven, and said, Abraham,
Abraham: and he said, Here am I. And he said, Lay
not thy hand upon the lad, neither do thou anything unto him; for now I know that thou fearest
God, seeing thou hast not withheld thy son, thine
only son, from me. And Abraham lifted up his
eyes, and looked, and, behold, behind *him* a ram
caught in the thicket by his horns: and Abraham
went and took the ram, and offered him up for a
burnt-offering in the stead of his son. And Abraham called the name of that place Jehovah-jireh:
as it is said to this day, In the mount of Jehovah
it shall be provided. And the angel of Jehovah
called unto Abraham a second time out of heaven,
and said, By myself have I sworn, saith Jehovah,
because thou hast done this thing, and hast not
withheld thy son, thine only son, that in blessing I
will bless thee, and in multiplying I will multiply

> thy seed as the stars of the heavens, and as the
> sand which is upon the sea-shore; and thy seed
> shall possess the gate of his enemies; and in thy
> seed shall all the nations of the earth be blessed;
> because thou hast obeyed my voice.

The story of the near sacrifice of Isaac illustrates
the truth that we must be willing to give up the
pleasures of sense without question if we are to have
the consciousness of the greater satisfactions of Spirit.
Being willing and obedient in submitting our sensations
to the law of Spirit, we then find that we do not at all
sacrifice the real inner joy but only its coarser expression in physical generation (which is represented by
the ram).

It seemed to Abraham that the law of Spiritual
growth demanded the slaying of Isaac, the whole
consciousness of joy. At various stages of unfoldment
there are trials as well as triumphs, and those who have
but a transient faith in the wisdom and power of
Spirit are apt to give up and turn back before the
process is complete. (Abraham did not turn back.)
Moriah, the name of the land where Abraham was sent
to make his sacrifice, signifies the "bitterness of
Jehovah." So we find that the changes that take place
in consciousness sometimes are bitter experiences, and
it takes a strong faith to believe that good will come
out of them. Yet it always does come when there is
steadfast obedience to God and faith in His goodness.
The successful meeting of such trials gives great power
to the body and brings a sure reward. Abraham became the father of a multitude as numerous "as the
stars of the heavens, and as the sand which is upon
the sea-shore."

The child was not sacrificed although Abraham took every step in preparation. After he had successfully passed this test, the angel of the Lord repeated the promise of the covenant: "By myself have I sworn, saith Jehovah . . . and in thy seed shall all the nations of the earth be blessed; because thou hast obeyed my voice."

In the regeneration man must be willing to sacrifice his greatest pleasure in life (Isaac). But when he has given up willingly, made the spiritual surrender, he finds that it is not the joy of life that he sacrifices but only the sensuous aspect of joy.

Faith in God (Abraham) and obedience to the divine law brings forth a serene peace and joy. Christians well know that the development of faith and obedience does cause one to become inwardly happy and outwardly serene. Jesus had this inward happiness, and He tried to pass it on to His disciples: "These things have I spoken unto you, that my joy may be in you, and *that* your joy may be made full."

The name *Jehovah-jireh* means "Jehovah will see," "Jehovah will behold," "Jehovah will provide." It signifies "I am the provider." If we expect to demonstrate prosperity from without, we find it a slow process; but if we know that the I AM is the provider, we have the key to the inexhaustible resource.

Gen. 22:19. So Abraham returned unto his young men, and they rose up and went together to Beer-sheba; and Abraham dwelt at Beer-sheba.

The two young men represent masculine forces that have been trained for service under the supervision of pioneering faith.

Beer-sheba represents the establishing of a right relationship in consciousness between the spiritual and the seemingly material. Faith (Abraham) and the young masculine thoughts dwell in the state of consciousness represented by Beer-sheba, and it is in the light of this fact that the following incidents are to be understood.

> *Gen. 22:20-24.* And it came to pass after these things, that it was told Abraham, saying, Behold, Milcah, she also hath borne children unto thy brother Nahor: Uz his first-born, and Buz his brother, and Kemuel the father of Aram, and Chesed, and Hazo, and Pildash, and Jidlaph, and Bethuel. And Bethuel begat Rebekah: these eight did Milcah bear to Nahor, Abraham's brother. And his concubine, whose name was Reumah, she also bare Tebah, and Gaham, and Tahash, and Maacah.

Milcah represents the soul in its function of expressing dominion, wisdom, and good judgment. The soul of man on its feminine side is intuitional and often perceives or senses things that, while they are not perceived by the outer or more active and positive part of the individual consciousness, should be heeded by it.

Nahor symbolizes a piercing and breaking up of the individual sense consciousness hitherto unpenetrated by Truth so that a new line of thought may be brought forth.

Nahor and Milcah united to produce eight children (states of consciousness), whose names are interpreted here.

(For Uz see interpretation of Gen. 10.)

The name *Buz* means "despicable," "contempt," "despised." Buz represents a scornful, scoffing state of thought, which is despicable in the light of Truth.

The name *Kemuel* means "God stands," "God's righteousness." Kemuel symbolizes the righteousness and judgment of God in the process of becoming ascendant in individual consciousness, of growing and taking a firmer hold; also of bringing about a closer union of the true, higher, spiritual thoughts of the mind in order to establish the adjustment that is needed for the further progress of the individual.

The name *Chesed* means "an astrologer," "a magus," "wisdom." Chesed represents a certain type of wisdom, a wisdom that is psychical in its nature rather than spiritual.

The name *Hazo* means "vision," "revelation," "agreement." The arousing of a higher desire in man (Nahor) through the activity of faith (Abraham) causing the piercing of the darkness of material belief and opens the way for a new and clearer insight into Truth. This new insight is symbolized by Hazo.

The name *Pildash* means "flame of fire." Pildash represents zeal, ardor, the result of a quickening that has taken place in consciousness.

The name *Jidlaph* means "dropping," "distilling," "tearful." Jidlaph represents a very negative type of thought in man.

The name *Bethuel* means "dweller in God," "abode of God." Bethuel represents unity with God; a conscious abiding in Him.

Rebekah (the name of Bethuel's daughter) means "tying firmly," "snare," "beauty that ensnares." Rebekah represents the soul's natural delight in beauty.

Reumah (the name of Nahor's concubine means "lofty," "sublime," "pearl." Reumah symbolizes the soul or feminine principle in man elevated to a place of appreciation, of high esteem, in consciousness.

By Reumah, Nahor had four children, whose names are given here.

The name *Tebah* means "slaughter," "slaying," "life guard." Tebah represents an active thought of or strong belief in self-defense ("life guard") that is very destructive ("slaughter," i. e., of animals or persons).

The name *Gaham* means "flaming," "burning," "charring." Gaham symbolizes the heat of sense consciousness brought to a climax, a focus, and burning itself out. This is caused by the higher desires (Nahor and Reumah) that have been aroused by the awakening of faith (Abraham) in the individual. Thus a reaction sets in, the whole consciousness revolts against sense beliefs, and a measure of purification is accomplished.

The name *Tahash* means "burrowing," "diving," "ram." Tahash symbolizes an increase of life activity in the organism but an activity more of the animal than the spiritual kind.

The name *Maacah* means "squeezed," "compressed." Maacah represents an oppressively aggressive character. He is of the outer sense man.

(For Aram see interpretation of Gen. 10:27-32.)

Chapter VIII

The Mental Supplants the Physical

GENESIS 23, 24, 25, 26, 27, and 28

IT IS SELF-EVIDENT that both the physical and metaphysical sides of life are capable of manifold expression. Some metaphysicians contend that all is mind and matter is the negative of mind or nothingness. However, contemplation of the tremendous possibilities infolded in the earth makes us pause when we hear that assertion. Here beneath our feet is a crust of substance upon whose pages like a mighty book is written a record of the earth's evolution during the aeons and ages through which it has passed from mist to matter. In it the geologist finds the fossils that tell him of its physical history, and the trained psychic can hold in his hand a piece of inanimate rock and it will tell him its evolution from ether to matter. The souls of all forms from mollusk up to man have left a certain memory essence upon the substance they handled, and that essence is preserved ready to be redeemed and raised to higher levels by the minds that gave it form. Although the body of

"Imperious Caesar, dead and turned to clay

Might stop a hole to keep the wind away,"

its soul essence endures and will in the final judgment, or justification, of man's work be merged into the perfect body. Daniel pointed to this when he wrote, "Many of them that sleep in the dust of the earth shall awake."

The purchase by Abraham of the cave of Machpelah as a grave for Sarah involves this mystical soul essence. Machpelah means infolded, winding, spiral, symbolizing a condition in which great possibilities of expression are involved. Not only Sarah but Abraham himself, Isaac, Rebekah, Leah, and Jacob were buried there. All these were spiritually quickened and therefore impressed their soul qualities upon matter more definitely than the children of Heth; but all are to undergo judgment, through numerous incarnations, at the end of the ages, "some to everlasting life, and some to shame and everlasting contempt." "And they that are wise shall shine as the brightness of the firmament; and they that turn many to righteousness as the stars for ever and ever."

> *Gen. 23:1-2.* And the life of Sarah was a hundred and seven and twenty years: these were the years of the life of Sarah. And Sarah died in Kiriath-arba (the same is Hebron), in the land of Canaan: and Abraham came to mourn for Sarah, and to weep for her.

The name *Kiriath-arba* means "city of Arba," "city foursquare." Symbolically Kiriath-arba denotes the state of consciousness that attributes to material reason the perfection belonging to and coming from spiritual understanding only; that attributes strength, power, knowledge, and greatness to the outer formed world instead of knowing that all power and reality exists in Spirit, in the unformed ideas of the one Mind.

Sarah (symbolizing the spiritual soul in a certain degree of unfoldment) died in Kiriath-arba. In truth however the higher activities of the soul cannot die. It may seemingly become entangled in thoughts on the natural plane and disappear for a season from the conscious mind. However it is enjoying a period of rest in preparation for a new and higher expression.

Gen. 23:3-20. And Abraham rose up from before his dead, and spake unto the children of Heth, saying, I am a stranger and a sojourner with you: give me a possession of a burying-place with you, that I may bury my dead out of my sight. And the children of Heth answered Abraham, saying unto him, Hear us, my lord; thou art a prince of God among us: in the choice of our sepulchres bury thy dead; none of us shall withhold from thee his sepulchre, but that thou mayest bury thy dead. And Abraham rose up, and bowed himself to the people of the land, even to the children of Heth. And he communed with them, saying, If it be your mind that I should bury my dead out of my sight, hear me, and entreat for me to Ephron the son of Zohar, that he may give me the cave of Machpelah, which he hath, which is in the end of his field; for the full price let him give it to me in the midst of you for a possession of a burying-place. Now Ephron was sitting in the midst of the children of Heth: and Ephron the Hittite answered Abraham in the audience of the children of Heth, even of all that went in at the gate of his city, saying, Nay, my lord, hear me: the field give I thee, and the cave that is therein, I give it thee; in the presence of the children of my people give I it thee: bury thy dead. And Abraham bowed himself down before the people of the land. And he spake unto Ephron in the audience of the people of the land, saying, But if thou wilt, I pray thee, hear me: I will give the price of the field; take it of me, and I will bury my dead there. And Ephron answered Abraham, saying unto him, My lord, hearken unto me: a piece of land worth four hundred shekels of silver, what is that betwixt me and thee? bury therefore my dead. And

> Abraham hearkened unto Ephron; and Abraham weighed to Ephron the silver which he had named in the audience of the children of Heth, four hundred shekels of silver, current *money* with the merchant.
>
> So the field of Ephron, which was in Machpelah, which was before Mamre, the field, and the cave which was therein, and all the trees that were in the field, that were in all the border thereof round about, were made sure unto Abraham for a possession in the presence of the children of Heth, before all that went in at the gate of the city. And after this, Abraham buried Sarah his wife in the cave of the field of Machpelah before Mamre (the same is Hebron), in the land of Canaan. And the field, and the cave that is therein, were made sure unto Abraham for a possession of a burying-place by the children of Heth.

Abraham requested the children of Heth to "entreat for me to Ephron the son of Zohar" that he might give him the cave of Machpelah for a burying place for Sarah.

The name *Zohar* means "whiteness," "brightness," "nobility." Zohar represents thoughts of a pure, clear, lofty, discriminating character.

The name *Ephron* means "gazellelike," "quick," "volatile." Ephron represents a type of thought that is very impulsive, light, airy, and quick to change.

The name *Machpelah* means "equally divided," "twofold," "spiral form." Machpelah represents subconscious body substance (a field in which there was a cave). Sarah and the others buried in this cave symbolize the submergence of spiritual ideals in us. When these ideals have done their work in the conscious realm of our mind, for the time being they give way to other activities of the mind, while they sink back into the subconsciousness (cave). There they take deep root in substance and continue their work, which is not apparent to the outer, conscious, thinking part of the mind. They work out into the body consciousness in another incarnation, thus aiding in raising the whole organism to a higher plane of expression.

When going through the inner experience of releasing from consciousness some much-cherished soul quality or thought activity that has become useless for the time being, one may have a tendency to grieve and to hold to the good that seems to be becoming inactive in one's life. Then the thought activity represented by Ephron comes to one's rescue to aid one in making the necessary change and in letting go of the old. Sarah died in Hebron, and it was in Hebron that Abraham bargained with Ephron for the cave of Machpelah in which to bury Sarah. Hebron refers to the conscious mind; also to a certain "association" of thoughts. Faith (Abraham) suggests the awakening of man's mind to higher ideals, and hills denote their manifestation.

The word *Mamre* means "firmness," "vigor," "strength." The oak trees (which surrounded Mamre) in themselves denote strength and protection; but the Hebrew name for oak trees has a deeper significance than this; it comes from a root similar to the one from which is derived the word *Elohim*. Thus we are reminded of the truth that those who trust in God as their defense, their refuge, and their fortress, and who dwell in the secret place of the Most High, abide under the shadow of the Almighty, and not only are kept from all evil and its results but also continue to grow and unfold in understanding, in spirituality, in every good. The Hebrew words *ayil, elon,* and *allah* all refer to the oak or terebinth, and express the ideas of power, elevation, and expansion. The prefix *al* or *el* that begins the name Elohim, or better Ælohim, comes from the same root, which refers to the power of expansive movement, the power of extension, and is also the personal pronoun *el,* which stands for the strong one or the absolute.

Abraham's insistence on paying Ephron for the ground where Sarah was to be buried emphasizes the sufficiency of Spirit and the opulence of those who live under its law. Abraham was the possessor of an all-producing faith, and he was expected to use it on all occasions to supply his every need. Those who have a living faith in God's all-sufficiency do not beg or accept things without recompense but give value received for everything.

> *Gen. 24:1-9.* And Abraham was old, *and* well stricken in age: and Jehovah had blessed Abraham in all things. And Abraham said unto his servant, the elder of his house, that ruled over all that he had, Put, I pray thee, thy hand under my thigh: and I will make thee swear by Jehovah, the God of heaven and the God of the earth, that thou wilt not take a wife for my son of the daughters of the Canaanites, among whom I dwell: but thou shalt go unto my country, and to my kindred, and take a wife for my son Isaac. And the servant said unto him, Peradventure the woman will not be willing to follow me unto this land: must I needs bring thy son again unto the land from whence thou camest? And Abraham said unto him, Beware thou that thou bring not my son thither again. Jehovah, the God of heaven, who took me from my father's house, and

from the land of my nativity, and who spake unto
me, and who sware unto me, saying, Unto thy seed
will I give this land; he will send his angel before
thee, and thou shalt take a wife for my son from
thence. And if the woman be not willing to follow
thee, then thou shalt be clear from this my oath;
only thou shalt not bring my son thither again. And
the servant put his hand under the thigh of Abraham
his master, and sware to him concerning this matter.

The progenitor of the house of Abraham (primitive
faith) is Spirit. Abraham desired to perpetuate the
spiritual trend of consciousness. The "servant, the
elder of his house, that ruled over all that he had"
(representing the personal ego that rules over the
body or "house" consciousness), obeyed every injunc-
tion of his. Abraham (the progressive mind) desires
Isaac (his happy, joyous thoughts) to unite in marriage
with one of his kindred (Rebekah: high ideals) in the
land of Haran (exalted state of mind). Abraham
(progressive faith) then requires his obedient servant
(the personal ego ruling over the body consciousness)
to take an oath or affirm, with his hand (power) on
Abraham's thigh, that this shall be accomplished.

Yarek, the Hebrew word translated "thigh," comes
from a little used root and is sometimes used euphemis-
tically to designate the genitals. This oath was not
taken on the thigh but on the genital organs, a practice
not peculiar to the Hebrews but known to many other
primitive people. Such a custom hints at phallicism or
the worship of the physical source of life. As our courts
impress on the witness the sacredness of his oath
by having him place his hand on the Bible while
making it, so these people used the source of physical
life to enforce the sanctity of an oath.

Spiritual light comes through the activity of pioneering faith. Abraham realized that through his struggles for a higher state of consciousness (Haran) his soul had become rooted and grounded in the fundamental principles of Truth. Therefore he desired his happy, joyous thoughts (Isaac) to unite with a feminine soul force that had sprung from the original root of Spirit (his own kindred).

> *Gen. 24:10-62.* And the servant took ten camels, of the camels of his master, and departed, having all goodly things of his master's in his hand: and he arose, and went to Mesopotamia, unto the city of Nahor. And he made the camels to kneel down without the city by the well of water at the time of evening, the time that women go out to draw water. And he said, O Jehovah, the God of my master Abraham, send me, I pray thee, good speed this day, and show kindness unto my master Abraham. Behold, I am standing by the fountain of water; and the daughters of the men of the city are coming out to draw water: and let it come to pass, that the damsel to whom I shall say, Let down thy pitcher, I pray thee, that I may drink; and she shall say, Drink, and I will give thy camels drink also: let the same be she that thou hast appointed for thy servant Isaac; and thereby shall I know that thou hast showed kindness unto my master. And it came to pass, before he had done speaking, that, behold, Rebekah came out, who was born to Bethuel, the son of Milcah, the wife of Nahor, Abraham's brother, with her pitcher upon her shoulder. And the damsel was very fair to look upon, a virgin, neither had any man known her: and she went down to the fountain, and filled her pitcher, and came up. And the servant ran to meet her, and said, Give me to drink, I pray thee, a little water from thy pitcher. And she said, Drink, my lord: and she hasted, and let down her pitcher upon her hand,

and gave him drink. And when she had done giving
him drink, she said, I will draw for thy camels also,
until they have done drinking. And she hasted, and
emptied her pitcher into the trough, and ran again
unto the well to draw, and drew for all his camels.
And the man looked stedfastly on her, holding his
peace, to know whether Jehovah had made his journey prosperous or not. And it came to pass, as the
camels had done drinking, that the man took a
golden ring of half a shekel weight, and two bracelets for her hands of ten shekels weight of gold,
and said, Whose daughter art thou? tell me, I pray
thee. Is there room in thy father's house for us to
lodge in? And she said unto him, I am the daughter
of Bethuel the son of Milcah, whom she bare unto
Nahor. She said moreover unto him, We have both
straw and provender enough, and room to lodge in.
And the man bowed his head, and worshipped Jehovah. And he said, Blessed be Jehovah, the God of my
master Abraham, who hath not forsaken his lovingkindness and his truth toward my master: as for me,
Jehovah hath led me in the way to the house of my
master's brethren.

And the damsel ran, and told her mother's house
according to these words. And Rebekah had a brother,
and his name was Laban: and Laban ran out unto
the man, unto the fountain. And it came to pass,
when he saw the ring, and the bracelets upon his sister's hands, and when he heard the words of Rebekah his sister, saying, Thus spake the man unto
me; that he came unto the man; and, behold, he
was standing by the camels at the fountain. And
he said, Come in, thou blessed of Jehovah; wherefore standest thou without? for I have prepared
the house, and room for the camels. And the man
came into the house, and he ungirded the camels;
and he gave straw and provender for the camels, and
water to wash his feet and the feet of the men that
were with him. And there was set food before him to

eat: but he said, I will not eat, until I have told mine errand. And he said, Speak on. And he said, I am Abraham's servant. And Jehovah hath blessed my master greatly; and he is become great; and he hath given him flocks and herds, and silver and gold, and men-servants and maid-servants, and camels and asses. And Sarah my master's wife bare a son to my master when she was old: and unto him hath he given all that he hath. And my master made me swear, saying, Thou shalt not take a wife for my son of the daughters of the Canaanites, in whose land I dwell: but thou shalt go unto my father's house, and to my kindred, and take a wife for my son. And I said unto my master, Peradventure the woman will not follow me. And he said unto me, Jehovah, before whom I walk, will send his angel with thee, and prosper thy way; and thou shalt take a wife for my son of my kindred, and of my father's house: then shalt thou be clear from my oath, when thou comest to thy kindred; and if they give her not to thee, thou shalt be clear from my oath. And I came this day unto the fountain, and said, O Jehovah, the God of my master Abraham, if now thou do prosper my way which I go: behold, I am standing by the fountain of water; and let it come to pass, that the maiden that cometh forth to draw, to whom I shall say, Give me, I pray thee, a little water from thy pitcher to drink; and she shall say to me, Both drink thou, and I will also draw for thy camels: let the same be the woman whom Jehovah hath appointed for my master's son. And before I had done speaking in my heart, behold, Rebekah came forth with her pitcher on her shoulder; and she went down unto the fountain, and drew: and I said unto her, Let me drink, I pray thee. And she made haste, and let down her pitcher from her shoulder, and said, Drink, and I will give thy camels drink also: so I drank, and she made the camels drink also. And I asked her, and said, Whose daughter art thou? And she said, The daughter of Bethuel, Nahor's son, whom Milcah bare unto him: and I put the ring upon her nose, and the bracelets upon her hands. And I bowed my head, and worshipped Jehovah, and blessed Jehovah, the God of my master Abraham, who had led me in the right way to take my master's brother's daughter for his son. And now if ye will deal kindly and truly with my master, tell me: and if not, tell me; that I may turn to the right hand, or to the left.

Then Laban and Bethuel answered and said, The thing proceedeth from Jehovah: we cannot speak unto thee bad or good. Behold, Rebekah is before thee, take her, and go, and let her be thy master's son's wife, as Jehovah hath spoken. And it came to pass, that, when Abraham's servant heard their words, he bowed himself down to the earth unto Jehovah. And the servant brought forth jewels of silver, and jewels of gold, and raiment, and gave them to Rebekah: he gave also to her brother and to her mother precious things. And they did eat and drink, he and the men that were with him, and tarried all night; and they rose up in the morning, and he said, Send me away unto my master. And her brother and her mother said, Let the damsel abide with us *a few* days, at least ten; after that she shall go. And he said unto them, Hinder me not, seeing Jehovah hath prospered my way; send me away that I may go to my master. And they said, We will call the damsel, and inquire at her mouth. And they called Rebekah, and said unto her, Wilt thou go with this man? And she said, I will go. And they sent away Rebekah their sister, and her nurse, and Abraham's servant, and his men. And they blessed Rebekah, and said unto her, Our sister, be thou *the mother* of thousands of ten thousands, and let thy seed possess the gate of those that hate them.

And Rebekah arose, and her damsels, and they rode upon the camels, and followed the man: and the servant took Rebekah, and went his way. And Isaac came up from the way of Beer-lahai-roi; for he dwelt in the land of the South.

A declaration of Truth is always demonstrated in mind and body. Paul says the man is not without the woman in the Lord. In the above Scripture the law is in process of being fulfilled (the oath or affirmation made by Abraham's servant is here being demonstrated.

Abraham's servant journeyed into the land of Mesopotamia in search of a wife for Abraham's son Isaac and was led by Jehovah to the city of Nahor, where he found Rebekah.

The state of consciousness represented by Mesopotamia lies close to the spiritual, at least close enough to be open to the divine urge for light and higher attainment ("country between," "middle region," "middle land"). Otherwise it could not have been the home of Rebekah and her brother Laban, nor of Abraham at the time when he received from God the revelation directing him to come out from his people into another country (to enter into a higher and more spiritual state of mind) that he might possess his divine inheritance.

Nahor denotes the arousing of a more lofty desire in man through the activity of faith (Abraham). These greater aspirations pierce the darkness of materiality and aid in bringing about a new trend of thought ("eager," "piercing," "slaying").

Bethuel, father of Rebekah, represents conscious unity with Spirit. Milcah, mother of Rebekah, represents wisdom and good judgment through the intuitional or feminine nature.

The name *Rebekah* means "tying firmly," "noosed cord," "beauty that ensnares." Rebekah represents the soul's natural delight in beauty. This essence of the soul is continually going forth and making contact with the harmonious and the beautiful.

Abraham's servant adorned Rebekah with rings and bracelets of gold, which appealed to her love of the beautiful. This no doubt influenced her in her decision to make the journey to the house of Abraham. Metaphysically Rebekah's taking this step represents an esthetic feminine force within the soul penetrating down into the subconscious and there making union with life and substance. The servant (personal ego) guided Rebekah into Beer-lahai-roi, in the "land of the South" (the subconscious), where Isaac dwelt.

(For further interpretation of Beer-lahai-roi see comments on Gen. 16:1-15.)

Through the inherent love of the harmonious thousands are blessed and many hearts of "hate" are directed into other channels of expression ("let thy seed possess the gate of those that hate them").

Gen. 24:63-67. And Isaac went out to meditate in the field at the eventide: and he lifted up his eyes, and saw, and, behold, there were camels coming. And Rebekah lifted up her eyes, and when she saw Isaac, she alighted from the camel. And she said unto the servant, What man is this that walketh in the field to meet us? And the servant said, It is my master: and she took her veil, and covered herself. And the servant told Isaac all the things that he had done. And Isaac brought her into his mother Sarah's tent, and took Rebekah, and she became his wife; and he loved her: and Isaac was comforted after his mother's death.

The happy Isaac consciousness claimed its counterpart in Rebekah. Faith and obedience (Abraham) bring forth joy, and joy (Isaac) is linked with the beauty of nature without. The devout, joyous soul readily makes union with the natural, harmonious expression of Spirit, and in the joy of spiritual realization the thoughts are lifted up in exaltation and praise. "And Isaac went out to meditate in the field at the eventide: and he lifted up his eyes, and saw . . . And Rebekah lifted up her eyes . . . and he loved her." Thus is portrayed the union of the devout, joyous nature with the soul of love.

The joyous soul, when established in spiritual faith and poise, is screened from contact with inharmonies: "and she took her veil, and covered herself."

Isaac led Rebekah into his mother Sarah's tent. This signifies that the soul powers symbolized by Isaac and Rebekah are ever penetrating into the physical, here represented by the tent.

> *Gen. 25:1-4.* And Abraham took another wife, and her name was Keturah. And she bare him Zimran, and Jokshan, and Medan, and Midian, and Ishbak, and Shuah. And Jokshan begat Sheba, and Dedan. And the sons of Dedan were Asshurim, and Letushim, and Leummim. And the sons of Midian: Ephah, and Epher, and Hanoch, and Abida, and Eldaah. All these were the children of Keturah.

The name of Abraham's second wife, Keturah, means "incense," "perfume," "aloeswood." Keturah represents a soul consciousness that aspires to higher things even though still in sense.

To Abraham Keturah bare six sons. Zimran represents a positive expression of joy, harmony, **and** grace, the first conscious result of a union in the individual of awakening faith (Abraham) with the aspiration of the soul for higher bodily attainment (Keturah). Jokshan represents a sly, treacherous, deceitful tendency that often exists in the sense mind of man and that places the individual who gives way to it in difficult situations. Medan and Midian represent the sense of dominion that to a degree is founded on discrimination and understanding but that is still full of contention and strife. Ishbak typifies the transitoriness of human ambition and its results. Shuah denotes an exceedingly depressed, downcast state of thought.

The meaning of the names of the six sons of Abraham and Keturah point to divided thought; the thoughts are partly good thoughts and partly limited thoughts, thoughts of the sense mind. The descendants of these sons became enemies of the Israelites. While the trend of thought represented by them may to a certain extent be helpful to the natural man at a certain stage of his unfoldment, the time comes when they must be released from the mind so that the real, true thoughts and activities (Israelites) may have full sway in the consciousness.

Jokshan begat Sheba, who represents wholeness or fullness on various planes of existence ("return to an original state," "repose," "equilibrium"), and Dedan ("mutual attraction," "physical love," "low"), who represents a phase of physical or animal attraction and affection. This must give way to true love, which is spiritual in its character and is unselfish and pure.

Dedan had three sons. Asshurim represents the reasoning power of faith operating in sense consciousness. The reasoning of the intellect, guided by the senses, may seem almost invincible at times, but it does not endure. Only spiritual ideas and their manifestation are truly strong, powerful, and abiding. The second son of Dedan was Letushim, who represents the sense of being oppressed and hard driven that all persons in the lower, earthly consciousness experience much of the time. In the Letushim consciousness advancement is slow and is gained by means of hard experiences. The third son of Dedan was Leummim, who symbolizes great increase and multiplication of thoughts in consciousness but without real spiritual quickening.

Midian had five sons. Ephah represents darkened and obscured phases of thought and soul in which the Spirit of God is working—over which Spirit is brooding —that Truth may blossom forth and come to fruition in due time. Midian's second son was Epher, who represents thoughts on the animal plane of consciousness in man that are active but young and inexperienced. His third son was Hanoch, who represents entrance into a higher consciousness than has been known and experienced before. The fourth son, Abida, represents the belief that knowledge comes through the senses. The judgment of the senses, based on outer appearances, produces discordant thoughts, jealousies, and the like. Midian's fifth son Eldaah ("whom God has called"), represents a central thought that responds in a measure to the quickening presence of Spirit although it belongs to the sense phase of man consciousness. It perceives that God is the source of understanding, yet it does not bring forth definite fruit in consciousness.

> *Gen. 25:5-6.* And Abraham gave all that he had unto Isaac. But unto the sons of the concubines, that Abraham had, Abraham gave gifts; and he sent

them away from Isaac his son, while he yet lived,
eastward, unto the east country.

Isaac was the product of Abraham's spiritual consciousness, while the sons of the concubines were the
product of his personal consciousness. Hence Isaac
(meaning divine sonship) was the rightful heir to all
that Abraham had.

> *Gen. 25:7-11.* And these are the days of the
> years of Abraham's life which he lived, a hundred
> three-score and fifteen. And Abraham gave up
> the ghost, and died in a good old age, an old man,
> and full *of years,* and was gathered to his people.
> And Isaac and Ishmael his sons buried him in the
> cave of Machpelah, in the field of Ephron the son
> of Zohar the Hittite, which is before Mamre; the
> field which Abraham purchased of the children of
> Heth: there was Abraham buried, and Sarah his
> wife. And it came to pass after the death of Abra-
> ham, that God blessed Isaac his son; and Isaac dwelt
> by Beer-lahai-roi.

Machpelah was a field "before Mamre" that Abraham bought from Ephron, of the children of Heth.
Machpelah represents the subconscious body substance.
As in the case of Sarah, when the aggregation of
thoughts symbolized by Abraham has done its perfect
work in the conscious realm of mind, it gives way for
the time being to other activities of the mind and sinks
back into the subconsciousness. (See comments on Gen.
23:3-20.)

The name *Mamre* means "firmness," "vigor,"
"strength." The lesson here is that faith in God
(suggested by Abraham) brings about the right relation among all the faculties, establishing firmness,
vigor, and strength.

After Abraham's passing God blessed Isaac, and he dwelt in Beer-lahai-roi by the well of the same name. The name *Beer-lahai-roi* means "the well of the living one." Isaac symbolizes divine sonship. When the individual realizes that life is omnipresent and eternal and that Spirit is its source he has laid the foundation for its manifestation throughout his whole being.

> *Gen. 25:12-18.*   Now these are the generations of Ishmael, Abraham's son, whom Hagar the Egyptian, Sarah's handmaid, bare unto Abraham: and these are the names of the sons of Ishmael, by their names, according to their generations: the first-born of Ishmael, Nebaioth; and Kedar, and Adbeel, and Mibsam, and Mishma, and Dumah, and Massa, Hadad, and Tema, Jetur, Naphish, and Kedemah: these are the sons of Ishmael, and these are their names, by their villages, and by their encampments; twelve princes according to their nations. And these are the years of the life of Ishmael a hundred and thirty seven years: and he gave up the ghost and died, and was gathered unto his people. And they dwelt from Havilah unto Shur that is before Egypt, as thou goest toward Assyria: he abode over against all his brethren.

The first-born of Ishmael was Nebaioth. Nebaioth represents the outer, sensate, or material consciousness, reflecting the light of the inner, true ideas that are born of Spirit ("heights"), and realizing the possibility of bringing forth abundant good ("cultivation of the soil," "fruitfulness," "germinations") through the power of the word of understanding ("prophetic utterances," "inspired words").

The second son of Ishmael was Kedar. Kedar represents a confused, unsettled, disturbed, obscure thought yet one with a degree of power that belongs to the outer or sense side of consciousness.

The third son of Ishmael was Adbeel. Adbeel represents a yearning of the soul for something higher and better. This yearning will bring forth fruit in time, when it has been subjected to the necessary education and training. Though not always recognized as coming from God, this discipline is brought about by the working of the divine law.

The fourth son, Mibsam, represents a perception or sensing, to a degree, of the joys and beauties of Spirit: the power to perceive, discriminate, detect, estimate.

The fifth son, Mishma, represents a receptive, attentive, obedient attitude in the outer or sense consciousness.

The sixth son, Dumah, represents the condition that man calls death; also the state of man wherein he is dead through his trespasses and sins.

The seventh son, Massa, represents the ushering in of a new thought regarding that in man which has hitherto been deemed by him to be wholly material and so doomed to death and dissolution. This new thought is a prophecy that the seemingly physical body will ultimately be lifted up and saved alive. Massa represents a. type of thought that lays hold of, retains, and transports this truth ("divine declaration," "a lifting up,") into the outer organism, the seemingly mortal part of the individual.

Ishmael's eighth son was Hadad. Hadad symbolizes the setting up as all-powerful of the intellect in its spiritually unawakened state. Back of the intellect however, back of every expression of intelligence or understanding, there exists the hidden principle of all light, all wisdom, all knowledge: God, Spirit.

The ninth son, Tema, represents abundant substance and life, firmness, faithfulness, and Truth stored in the subconsciousness.

The tenth son, Jetur, represents an idea of order, solidity, strength, that which keeps within bounds; the idea or belief that the individual can be kept in orderly existence only when limited to certain lines of thought and action, only when his thoughts, beliefs, and acts are fenced in. The sense man's way of making the individual better is always to limit him by means of outer rules and regulations; it knows nothing of true spiritual freedom and guidance, which alone can bring about real strength, unity, and adjustment in consciousness.

The eleventh son, Naphish, symbolizes the activity of the very breath of life by which every living creature is animated and inspired, consciously or unconsciously.

The twelfth son, Kedemah, represents the inner or true being of man, divine principle; that which exists from everlasting to everlasting, man's true spiritual or Christ self.

Ishmael represents the thoughts that are the fruit of the personal or carnal in man. Kedemah, the youngest of his twelve sons, symbolizes the individual's turning within to his inner or true being, which is spiritual, eternal. This makes us think of Paul's words in I Corinthians 15:46, 47: "Howbeit that is not first which is spiritual, but that which is natural; then that which is spiritual. The first man is of the earth, earthy: the second man is of heaven." God, Spirit, and the Christ, who is man's true inner self, are first; otherwise the outer man could not be. In outer expression and manifestation however the physical man appears to come first, and he seems to run the full gamut of experience in the outer consciousness before he finally turns about and begins to seek within his own inner being to find God, Spirit, his true source and sustenance.

> *Gen. 25:19-22.* And these are the generations of Isaac, Abraham's son: Abraham begat Isaac: and Isaac was forty years old when he took Rebekah, the daughter of Bethuel the Syrian of Paddanaram, the sister of Laban the Syrian, to be his wife. And Isaac entreated Jehovah for his wife, because she was barren: and Jehovah was entreated of him, and Rebekah his wife conceived. And the children struggled together within her; and she said, If it be so, wherefore do I live? And she went to inquire of Jehovah.

When Isaac (representing serenity, peace, joy) was forty years old he took Rebekah to be his wife. Rebekah symbolizes the soul's natural delight in beauty. She was the daughter of Bethuel, who symbolizes unity with God, a conscious abiding in Him, and the sister of Laban, who symbolizes an exalted state of mind.

> *Gen. 25:23-28.* And Jehovah said unto her,
> Two nations are in thy womb,
> And two peoples shall be separated from thy bowels:
> And the one people shall be stronger than the other people;
> And the elder shall serve the younger.
> And when her days to be delivered were fulfilled, behold, there were twins in her womb. And the first came forth red, all over like a hairy garment; and she called his name Esau. And after that came forth

> his brother, and his hand had hold on Esau's heel;
> and his name was called Jacob: and Isaac was three-
> score years old when she bare them.
>   And the boys grew: and Esau was a skilful
> hunter, a man of the field; and Jacob was a quiet
> man, dwelling in tents. Now Isaac loved Esau, be-
> cause he did eat of his venison: and Rebekah loved
> Jacob.

The inner joyous life current (Isaac) gradually builds up a physical body of great vitality and at the same time develops an active mentality. These two phases of life, the mental and the physical, are represented by Isaac's twin sons Jacob and Esau. They were twins, but Esau was slightly the older, which fact under the Hebrew law gave him the rights of the eldest son and made him Isaac's heir. Metaphysically this denotes the physical vigor comes first at this stage of development but that the mind accompanies it as a close second. Jacob had hold of Esau's heel when they were born, showing that the mental is directly connected with the physical and holds it in check at all times, even from the beginning.

Isaac loved Esau better than he loved Jacob. When we remember that Isaac represents joy in the individual consciousness we can understand why the physical man seems to supply the needs of joy better than does the mental. Esau continually brought venison (substance to nourish the animal appetite) to please his father.

Rebekah loved Jacob better than she loved Esau. The exalted mother principle (Rebekah) loves its expression (Jacob) better than the physical expression (Esau) and seeks the blessing of the father principle (Isaac) upon it.

Esau's birthright is the body and the all-round

development to which it is entitled. It is an inheritance of potential mental powers, which rightly used will lift the physical man out of the fleshly consciousness to the higher consciousness of the allness of Divine Mind. Under the natural law of evolution the physical man (Esau) is brought forth first and has precedence over the intellectual man (Jacob). However in this allegory the physical man is overwhelmed by his desire for creature comforts ("pottage") and does not sufficiently value the mind power that has been given to man. The mental man, being on a higher plane, naturally draws to himself the finer forces of being. In consequence Jacob (the intellect) acquires precedence over Esau (the body consciousness).

> *Gen. 25:29-33.* And Jacob boiled pottage: and Esau came in from the field, and he was faint: and Esau said to Jacob, Feed me, I pray thee, with that same red *pottage;* for I am faint: therefore was his name called Edom. And Jacob said, Sell me first thy birthright. And Esau said, Behold, I am about to die: and what profit shall the birthright do to me? And Jacob said, Swear to me first; and he sware unto him: and he sold his birthright unto Jacob.

The ambitious ideas of the intellect forge far ahead of the growth of the body. Instead of supplying the body with its natural substance, which is spiritual, it gives the body consciousness intellectual ideas (boiled pottage). (Esau was named Edom, "red," because he sold his birthright for the red pottage. Edom pertains to the outer man, the physical phase of man's consciousness and organism.) This results in a temporary separation in consciousness between the mind and the body. Esau went his way, and Jacob became a man rich in the world's goods. Under divine law, however, they were twins and the separation was only apparent. They were to become united again and share all the blessings that Jacob (intellect) had gained.

We must remember that the "birthright" that Esau so willingly bartered away for a mess of pottage meant not only a right to the material goods of his father Isaac but to the spiritual blessings of the covenant of Abraham, which descending on him, should through him bless the world. Instead of "Abraham, Isaac, and Esau" the immortal words would be "Abraham, Isaac, and Jacob." To a "profane person" (Heb. 12:16) this would have no meaning, for spiritual blessings are visionary and unreal to him.

The name *Jacob* means "supplanter." In the development of the spiritual consciousness the supplanting quality finds its true office in replacing selfishness with unselfishness. We who seek to bring the ideal into active expression in our life know that to do this we must put into the place occupied by willful self-seeking an unwavering faith in the unseen God. The sensual must be supplanted by the spiritual, the apparent by the ideal. The fact that Jesus approvingly cited the Jewish tradition in His words "Many shall come from the east and the west, and shall sit down with Abraham, and Isaac, and Jacob, in the kingdom of heaven" proves the value of this supplanting power or power that man has to change his mind and so remake his consciousness and his life.

Jacob, representing a limited concept of the I AM, is ambitious to receive orignal inspiration and is unwilling to let appetite and passion rule. Therefore as the whole scheme of development is from lower to higher, Jacob (intellect) must supplant Esau (the immature consciousness of the natural man that is moved by desire).

It is by the work of conscious re-creation of his life after the pattern of the divine ideal that man gains self-dominion and becomes a citizen of the kingdom of the heavens, the inner kingdom of peace and power.

> *Gen. 26:1-11.* And there was a famine in the land, besides the first famine that was in the days of Abraham. And Isaac went unto Abimelech king of the Philistines, unto Gerar. And Jehovah appeared unto him, and said, Go not down into Egypt; dwell in the land which I shall tell thee of: sojourn in this land, and I will be with thee, and will bless thee; for unto thee, and unto thy seed, I will give all these lands, and I will establish the oath which I sware unto Abraham thy father; and I will multiply thy seed as the stars of heaven, and will give unto thy seed all these lands; and in thy seed shall all the nations of the earth be blessed; because that Abraham obeyed my voice, and kept my charge, my commandments, my statutes, and my laws. And Isaac dwelt in Gerar: and the men of the place asked him of his wife; and he said, She is my sister: for he feared to say, My wife; lest, *said he,* the men of the place should kill me for Rebekah; because she was fair to look upon. And it came to pass, when he had been there a long time, that Abimelech king of the Philistines looked out at a window, and saw, and, behold, Isaac was sporting with Rebekah his wife. And Abimelech called Isaac, and said, Behold, of a surety she is thy wife: and how saidst thou, She is my sister? And Isaac said unto him, Because I said, Lest I die because of her. And Abimelech said, What is this thou hast done unto us? one of the people might easily have lain with thy wife, and thou wouldest have brought guiltiness upon

us. And Abimelech charged all the people, saying,
He that toucheth this man or his wife shall surely
be put to death.

The soul established in a consciousness of serenity,
peace, laughter, joy (Isaac), accepts spiritual things
as real. God's promise is: "I will be with thee, and will
bless thee; for unto thee, and unto thy seed, I will
give all these lands, and I will establish the oath which
I sware unto Abraham thy father; and I will multiply
thy seed as the stars of heaven, and I will give unto
thy seed all these lands; and in thy seed shall all the
nations of the earth be blessed." When there is a need
of substance the serene, joyous side of the soul through
mind activity penetrates into the subconsciousness
(Gerar), where there is an abundance of all things.
But here the personal will (Abimelech) rules. When a
mind is not strong enough to work from principle or
has not faith enough to trust God, it exposes the beautiful and gracious side of its nature (Rebekah) to the
undisciplined sense consciousness, the law is broken,
and plagues result. In this case however personal will
has received enough light to preceive the truth and the
threatened harm is averted.

Gen. 26:12-22. And Isaac sowed in that land,
and found in the same year a hundredfold: and Jehovah blessed him. And the man waxed great, and
grew more and more until he became very great:
and he had possessions of flocks, and possessions of
herds, and a great household: and the Philistines
envied him. Now all the wells which his father's
servants had digged in the days of Abraham his
father, the Philistines had stopped, and filled with
earth. And Abimelech said unto Isaac, Go from
us; for thou art much mightier than we. And Isaac

departed thence, and encamped in the valley of
Gerar, and dwelt there.

And Isaac digged again the wells of water,
which they had digged in the days of Abraham
his father; for the Philistines had stopped them
after the death of Abraham: and he called their
names after the names by which his father had called
them. And Isaac's servants digged in the valley,
and found there a well of springing water. And
the herdsmen of Gerar strove with Isaac's herdsmen,
saying, The water is ours: and he called the name of
the well Esek, because they contended with him. And
they digged another well, and they strove for that
also: and he called the name of it Sitnah. And he
removed from thence, and digged another well;
and for that they strove not: and he called the name
of it Rehoboth; and he said, For now Jehovah hath
made room for us, and we shall be fruitful in the
land.

Isaac was working according to law, and he was
prospering. The Isaac faculty in man has a double
mission. Isaac was the connecting link between Abraham and Israel; that is, between faith in God and rulership or manifestation of God. His activity in "unstop-
ping" the wells dug by Abraham allegorizes the re-
opening of the hidden springs of life and the keeping
of the soul consciously connected with its inner source.
Isaac was not a well digger so much as a well "re-
opener." Abraham had dug the wells. Faith delves
into the deep things of Spirit and unearths the pure
life essence. In the beginning of spiritual unfoldment
however the outer senses (Philistines) suppress or
crowd out this fine substance and life of Spirit. The
Philistines represent evil material thoughts that "fill
with earth" the channels of spiritual expression.

Isaac's first well was named Esek, a name signifying "violence" or "contention." A warring takes place in the valley (the subconsciousness) between the Philistine herdsmen (the animal desires) and Isaac's servants (the awakening spiritual thoughts). The new energy and vigor of life that man gains by his conscious contact with Spirit is sought by the sense desires to be used at once for their gratification and pleasure. They would take this fine essence and energy to build up sense rather than to build up the spiritual nature. Thus contention and strife arise.

The second well was called Sitnah, a name that also signifies "strife" and "hatred." The material sense thoughts (Philistines) do not give up easily but follow the individual a long way on his path to development of a spiritual consciousness. However we read that Isaac's third well, called Rehoboth (a name signifying "broad places" or "enlargements"), was not taken by the Philistines. Material thoughts cannot continue to follow and annoy the man who is persistent in his determination to find the "water of life."

Gen. 26:23-33. And he went up from thence to Beer-sheba. And Jehovah appeared unto him the same night, and said, I am the God of Abraham thy father: fear not, for I am with thee, and will bless thee, and multiply thy seed for my servant Abraham's sake. And he builded an altar there, and called upon the name of Jehovah, and pitched his tent there: and there Isaac's servants digged a well.

Then Abimelech went to him from Gerar, and Ahuzzath his friend, and Phicol the captain of his host. And Isaac said unto them, Wherefore are ye come unto me, seeing ye hate me, and have sent me away from you? And they said, We saw plainly that Jehovah was with thee: and we said, Let there now be an oath betwixt us, even betwixt us and thee, and let us make a covenant with thee, that thou wilt do us no hurt, as we have not touched thee, and as we have done unto thee nothing but good, and have sent thee away in peace: thou art now the blessed of Jehovah. And he made them a feast, and they did eat and drink. And they rose up betimes in the morning, and sware one to another: and Isaac sent them away, and they departed from him in peace. And it came to pass the same day, that Isaac's servants came, and told him concerning the well which they had digged, and said unto him, We have found water. And he called it Shibah: therefore the name of the city is Beer-sheba unto this day.

This Scripture interprets itself very definitely within the soul of man. Isaac (spiritual peace, joy) under the guidance of Jehovah is conscious of the I AM pioneering faith (symbolized by Abraham). In this "place" in mind a new order is established, which denotes the willingness to give up the lower for the higher, the personal for the impersonal, the animal for the divine.

At this stage of the allegory appears Abimelech, King of the Philistines (representing metaphysically the unregenerate will of the sense man). With him he brings Ahuzzath (selfishness) and Phicol ("speech") and tries to make an agreement with Isaac. The will (Abimelech) believes that it is the rightful ruler of man and that all the rich substance that comes to man from Spirit is for the gratification of sense desires. Having witnessed the ever-increasing power and possessions of Isaac, who represents divine sonship, Abimelech (the will) fears the loss of his own rule and possessions.

The divine Son, the Christ, does not destroy but fulfills and saves. Error eventually brings on its own destruction, but the error seems to flourish along with the good during a certain period of development; the wheat and tares are allowed to grow together until the harvest. The harvesttime came when the Israelites under Joshua took possession of the Promised Land. Even then the Philistines made several successful comebacks and had to be defeated again and again.

There were seven wells altogether, culminating in the one named Beer-sheba, "well of the oath" or "seventh well." The opening up of these seven wells symbolizes the establishment of a right relation in consciousness between the seven creative centers in natural man and the spiritual powers of the Christ man. The whole allegory illustrates the struggle going on within man for the possession of the life generated in his body. This struggle takes place between the higher and the lower nature of the individual—the spirtual soul and the animal soul—at a certain stage of his development. Beer-sheba is the place where the altar of victory is set up and God is given the thanks.

> *Gen. 26:34-35.* And when Esau was forty years old he took to wife Judith the daughter of Beeri the Hittite, and Basemath the daughter of Elon the Hittite: and they were a grief of mind unto Isaac and to Rebekah.

When Esau (the body consciousness) reaches the age of forty years (the number forty denoting a certain degree of completeness) he takes two wives (makes union with two forces), Judith and Basemath. Judith (the feminine consciousness of prayer and praise) is the daughter of Beeri (limitation). Basemath (the

ability to receive intuitively spiritual understanding
and guidance) is the daughter of Elon (materiality and
transitoriness). Because of the limiting, unenduring,
material character of these forces, this union for a
season is bound to bring trial and grief to the higher
spiritual forces (Isaac and Rebekah) finding expression
through the body consciousness (Esau).

The Bible narrative about Jacob and Esau has always been read historically, and theologians have had
trouble trying to excuse Jacob and Rebekah for their
apparent duplicity in their dealings with Isaac and
Esau. When read in the light of spiritual understanding
or considered as part of the history of the unfoldment
of the individual soul, the incidents lose their aspect
of duplicity and we find that they are a description of
the subtle working of the soul in spiritual evolution
under the guidance of Divine Mind. The soul is progressive. It must go forward. The soul must meet and
overcome its limitations.

> *Gen. 27:1-17.* And it came to pass, that when
> Isaac was old, and his eyes were dim, so that he
> could not see, he called Esau his elder son, and
> said unto him, My son: and he said unto him, Here
> am I. And he said, Behold now, I am old, I know
> not the day of my death. Now therefore take, I pray
> thee, thy weapons, thy quiver and thy bow, and go
> out to the field, and take me venison; and make me
> savory food, such as I love, and bring it to me, that
> I may eat; that my soul may bless thee before I die.
> And Rebekah heard when Isaac spake to Esau his
> son. And Esau went to the field to hunt for venison,
> and to bring it. And Rebekah spake unto Jacob her
> son, saying, Behold, I heard thy father speak unto
> Esau thy brother, saying, Bring me venison, and
> make me savory food, that I may eat, and bless thee

before Jehovah before my death. Now therefore, my son, obey my voice according to that which I command thee. Go now to the flock, and fetch me from thence two good kids of the goats; and I will make them savory food for thy father, such as he loveth: and thou shalt bring it to thy father, that he may eat, so that he may bless thee before his death. And Jacob said to Rebekah his mother, Behold, Esau my brother is a hairy man, and I am a smooth man. My father peradventure will feel me, and I shall seem to him as a deceiver; and I shall bring a curse upon me, and not a blessing. And his mother said unto him, Upon me be thy curse, my son; only obey my voice, and go fetch me them. And he went, and fetched, and brought them to his mother: and his mother made savory food, such as his father loved. And Rebekah took the goodly garments of Esau her elder son, which were with her in the house, and put them upon Jacob her younger son; and she put the skins of the kids of goats upon his hands, and upon the smooth of his neck: and she gave the savory food and the bread, which she had prepared, into the hand of her son Jacob.

Jacob was very dear to the heart of his mother. Rebekah symbolizes the beautiful and esthetic side of man's nature, the divine-natural. In keeping with the mother principle, in which these twin states of mind gestated and grew, she desires that the mental take precedence over the animal. The seeming trickery on the part of Rebekah and Jacob is an illustration of how we are moved by emotional states of consciousness and how, in our half-blind understanding, we accept their suggestions. The fact is that the soul (woman, Rebekah) is constantly making suggestions to us in dreams, visions, and intuitive flashes. These suggestions may sometimes be for our highest good and sometimes they may not be. Spiritual understanding must determine this point and decide whether we should follow them or not. Rebekah represents the love of the ideal, and it is only through Jacob, the mental, that the ideal can be realized.

The mind feels that its claim to the control of life should come before the claims of physical sense. By its superior quickness, aided by the soul's (Rebekah's) love of mental acumen, the mental tricks the physical and secures the blessing of substance and the acknowledged authority in the organism. Then the head rules the heart in us until the touch of Spirit (Jacob's wrestling with the angel) arouses the soul to action and there is another supplanting, this time of the intellect's sterile claims, which are taken over by the soul. In reality the physical body has an equal right with the intellect to the uplifting and refining influence of Spirit. Being twins, they should be treated as equals, the law of the first-born should not be allowed to operate, but should be blessed and established in the substance of all good things.

The difference between Esau and Jacob is given to us in Jacob's own words: "Behold, Esau my brother is a hairy man, and I am a smooth man." The Semitic word for "hairy," translators tell us, has a connotation of intemperance or licentiousness. In the Epistle to the Hebrews Paul calls Esau a "fornicator, or profane person." This may be taken in a literal sense or in the sense of one who commits spiritual adultery; that is, who is unfaithful to God, divine love. The name *Esau* also signifies "one swept away" or "one who rushes forward wildly and implusively." He is the very antipode of Jacob, "the smooth," clean, reliable man. The word *smooth* is used in the story of David's victory over Goliath: David took "five smooth stones out of the brook."

Esau is unfortunately no uncommon type. As for "smooth" men, very few are smooth to start with. It is the constant rubbing, cutting, and reshaping that makes them at last "the polished corners of the temple," good and beautiful after the pattern of heaven.

The denunciations of Esau by the prophets Jeremiah, Obadiah, and Malachi were not directed against a man of that name but against the course of conduct exemplified by him. Therefore it might well appear to Malachi, interpreting the name metaphorically, that God loved Jacob and hated Esau because Jacob symbolized the mental man and Esau the physical or animal man.

> *Gen. 27:18-40.* And he came unto his father, and said, My father: and he said, Here am I; who art thou, my son? And Jacob said unto his father, I am Esau thy first-born; I have done according as thou badest me: arise, I pray thee, sit and eat of my venison, that thy soul may bless me. And Isaac said unto his son, How is it that thou hast found it so quickly, my son? And he said, Because Jehovah thy God sent me good speed. And Isaac said unto Jacob, Come near, I pray thee, that I may feel thee, my son, whether thou be my very son Esau or not. And Jacob went near unto Isaac his father; and he felt him, and said, The voice is Jacob's voice, but the hands are the hands of Esau. And he discerned him not, because his hands were hairy, as his brother Esau's hands: so he blessed him. And he said, Art thou my very son Esau? And he said, I am. And he said, Bring it near to me, and I will eat of my son's venison, that my soul may bless thee. And he

brought it near to him, and he did eat: and he
brought him wine, and he drank. And his father
Isaac said unto him, Come near now, and kiss me,
my son. And he came near, and kissed him: and
he smelled the smell of his raiment, and blessed him,
and said,
See, the smell of my son
Is as the smell of a field which Jehovah hath blessed:
And God give thee of the dew of heaven,
And of the fatness of the earth,
And plenty of grain and new wine:
Let peoples serve thee,
And nations bow down to thee:
Be lord over thy brethren,
And let thy mother's sons bow down to thee:
Cursed be every one that curseth thee,
And blessed be every one that blesseth thee.

And it came to pass, as soon as Isaac had made
an end of blessing Jacob, and Jacob was yet scarce
gone out from the presence of Isaac his father, that
Esau his brother came in from his hunting. And he
also made savory food, and brought it unto his
father; and he said unto his father, Let my father
arise, and eat of his son's venison, that thy soul
may bless me. And Isaac his father said unto him,
Who art thou? And he said, I am thy son, thy first-
born, Esau. And Isaac trembled very exceedingly,
and said, Who then is he that hath taken venison,
and brought it me, and I have eaten of all before
thou camest, and have blessed him? yea, *and* he shall
be blessed. When Esau heard the words of his father,
he cried with an exceeding great and bitter cry, and
said unto his father, Bless me, even me also, O my
father. And he said, Thy brother came with guile,
and hath taken away thy blessing. And he said, Is not
he rightly named Jacob? for he hath supplanted me
these two times: he took away my birthright; and,
behold, now he hath taken away my blessing. And
he said, Hast thou not reserved a blessing for me?

And Isaac answered and said unto Esau, Behold, I
have made him thy lord, and all his brethren have I
given to him for servants; and with grain and new
wine have I sustained him: and what then shall I do
for thee, my son? And Esau said unto his father,
Hast thou but one blessing, my father? bless me,
even me also, O my father. And Esau lifted up his
voice, and wept. And Isaac his father answered and
said unto him,
Behold, of the fatness of the earth shall be thy
    dwelling,
And of the dew of heaven from above;
And by thy sword shalt thou live, and thou shalt
    serve thy brother;
And it shall come to pass, when thou shalt break
    loose,
That thou shalt shake his yoke from off thy neck.

Jacob represents the man of spiritual insight: he is
not exactly spiritual but is beginning to see the possibilities of mind and is going forward. In Truth Jacob
represents the illumined intellect. Isaac was not a
spiritual man, but he represents one of the stages in
the evolution of spiritual man. When this evolution
comes into manifestation and pours out its essence
upon the natural man (Esau), the spiritual quality
in the natural man is stimulated. It moves forward
and outdistances the physical, but the physical is not
destroyed.

Isaac placed his blessing on Jacob. The real point
is that the blessing imparts an inward impetus or an
inspiration to the real, spiritual man. It stimulates the
intellect (Jacob) first, which then supplants or takes
precedence over the physical. This is the reason why
intellectual people apparently get ahead; but "the
last shall be first, and the first shall be last."

The body is entitled to an equal blessing, as given by Isaac to Esau.

"And it shall come to pass, when thou shalt break loose,

That thou shalt shake his yoke from off thy neck."

In other words, when the body begins to realize its innate capacity the yoke of the mind is broken. This phase of man's evolution may be said to be in evidence in the struggle between capital and labor, or mind and body. Also there is a recognition by the scientific world of a principle in the body that directs it in the matter of food, healing, and in a general instinctive knowing of all matters pertaining to its welfare.

> *Gen. 27:41-46.* And Esau hated Jacob because of the blessing wherewith his father blessed him: and Esau said in his heart, The days of mourning for my father are at hand; then will I slay my brother Jacob. And the words of Esau her elder son were told to Rebekah; and she sent and called Jacob her younger son, and said unto him, Behold, thy brother Esau as touching thee, doth comfort himself, *purposing* to kill thee. Now therefore, my son obey my voice; and arise, flee thou to Laban my brother to Haran; and tarry with him a few days, until thy brother's fury turn away; until thy brother's anger turn away from thee, and he forget that which thou hast done to him: then I will send, and fetch thee from thence: why should I be bereaved of you both in one day?
>
> And Rebekah said to Isaac, I am weary of my life because of the daughters of Heth: if Jacob take a wife of the daughters of Heth, such as these, of the daughters of the land, what good shall my life do me?

When cheated of its due the body rebels, as Esau

did, and the outraged cells react in a disorderly way on the mind. Insane asylums bear witness to the fact that a neglected body will destroy the channels through which the mind is meant to function perfectly in man. The threat of Esau against the life of Jacob represents the inward rebellion that we feel when we change our modes of thought. The physical cannot be ignored. It must have its place in the all-round, fully developed man. This truth is illustrated by Esau. He became rich. He had many possessions, and he was the head of a race.

To avoid an open conflict Rebekah (the soul) ordered Jacob to flee to her brother Laban at Haran. The name *Laban* means "white," "shining," and the name Haran "exalted," "mountaineer." This clearly indicates that the attention must be centered on exalted states of mind and united with spiritual wisdom and understanding.

> *Gen. 28:1-9.* And Isaac called Jacob, and blessed him, and charged him, and said unto him, Thou shalt not take a wife of the daughters of Canaan. Arise, go to Paddan-aram, to the house of Bethuel thy mother's father; and take thee a wife from thence of the daughters of Laban thy mother's brother. And God Almighty bless thee, and make thee fruitful, and multiply thee, that thou mayest be a company of peoples; and give thee the blessing of Abraham, to thee, and to thy seed with thee; that thou mayest inherit the land of thy sojournings, which God gave unto Abraham. And Isaac sent away Jacob: and he went to Paddam-aram unto Laban, son of Bethuel the Syrian, the brother of Rebekah, Jacob's and Esau's mother.
>
> Now Esau saw that Isaac had blessed Jacob and sent him away to Paddan-aram, to take him a wife

from thence; and that as he blessed him he gave
him a charge, saying, Thou shalt not take a wife of
the daughters of Canaan; and that Jacob obey his
father and his mother, and was gone to Paddan-
aram: and Esau saw that the daughters of Canaan
pleased not Isaac his father, and Esau went unto
Ishmael, and took, besides the wives that he had,
Mahalath the daughter of Ishmael Abraham's son,
the sister of Nebaioth, to be his wife.

A man's marrying a wife symbolizes the union of
the ego with certain ideals. If these ideals are spiritual,
then spiritual character is developed with all its qualities. If the union is with inferior ideals, like that of
Esau, the fruit may be large in quantity, but it will
be of inferior quality. Jacob was admonished to go to
Paddan-aram ("tableland"), to the house of Bethuel
("dweller in God"), and to take a wife from among
the daughters of Laban ("shining," "pure"). Paddan-
aram represents levelheadedness, poise in Spirit; and
Laban, with whom Jacob (the unfolding ego) seeks
association, represents a clear state of mind in which
higher understanding is dominant. Thus the way is
pointed to a unification with the love principle in its
higher aspects. Jacob had exalted ideals, divine aspirations, and now it was necessary that love should become one of his attributes. High ideals, spiritual aspirations, and pure motives are necessary to the union that
the I AM makes with the soul.

Esau took Mahalath, daughter of Ishmael and sister of Nebaioth, to be his wife. The Ishmaelites represent the offspring of the natural, unillumined races
(states of mind). Nebaioth denotes the outer, sensate,
or material consciousness. Mahalath symbolizes a peace-

ful, harmonious, tuneful attitude of the soul, found in expression on the carnal and also on a higher plane.

> *Gen. 28:10-17.* And Jacob went out from Beer-sheba, and went toward Haran. And he lighted upon a certain place, and tarried there all night, because the sun was set; and he took one of the stones of the place, and put it under his head, and lay down in that place to sleep. And he dreamed; and, behold, a ladder set up on the earth, and the top of it reached to heaven; and, behold, the angels of God ascending and descending on it. And, behold, Jehovah stood above it, and said, I am Jehovah, the God of Abraham thy father, and the God of Isaac: the land whereon thou liest, to thee will I give it, and to thy seed; and thy seed shall be as the dust of the earth, and thou shalt spread abroad to the west, and to the east, and to the north, and to the south: and in thee and in thy seed shall all the families of the earth be blessed. And, behold, I am with thee, and will keep thee whithersoever thou goest, and will bring thee again into this land; for I will not leave thee, until I have done that which I have spoken to thee of. And Jacob awaked out of his sleep, and he said, Surely Jehovah is in this place; and I knew it not. And he was afraid, and said, How dreadful is this place! this is none other than the house of God, and this is the gate of heaven.

On his journey to Haran—which had a double purpose: to escape the wrath of the disappointed Esau, and "to take him a wife"—Jacob came to a certain place where he tarried all night, "because the sun was set." He took one of the stones that abounded in the place for use as a pillow and lay down to sleep. This incident illustrates the fact that when we are going through an emotional experience that is leading us upward to a

higher spiritual consciousness we may not understand what is happening, may have no light on it
("the sun was set"), but if like Jacob we tarry there
in the darkness in meditation, the messengers of God—
ideas of Truth—will come to us in the subconsciousness
(dreams).

Jacob's act of placing a stone under his head symbolizes the effort of the understanding to put itself in a
position to unravel the meaning of matter and material
conditions. In the very midst of seeming materiality
and darkened understanding the visions of the night
reveal the ladder reaching from earth to heaven and
the angels of God (spiritual thoughts) ascending
it and descending it. The ladder represents the step-by-
step realization by means of which man assimilates the
divine ideas of Truth that come to him from Jehovah.
Jehovah promised the land to Jacob and his seed and
assured Jacob of His continued presence and power:
"Behold, I am with thee, and will keep thee whitherso-
ever thou goest, and will bring thee again into this
land; for I will not leave thee . . . And Jacob awaked
out of his sleep, and he said, Surely Jehovah is in this
place; and I knew it not."

God is right here in our midst. Understanding,
when turned toward the omnipresent light of Spirit,
opens its eyes to the astonishing fact that the seemingly
material bodies and temporal surroundings conceal
the immanent God. Jacob said, "How dreadful is this
place! this is none other than the house of God, and
this is the gate of heaven." When divine wisdom reveals to us that our seemingly physical body is "none
other than the house of God," we are at first afraid.
It seems "dreadful" that we have made the Father's

house a "den of robbers."

> *Gen. 28:18-22.* And Jacob rose up early in the morning, and took the stone that he had put under his head, and set it up for a pillar, and poured oil upon the top of it. And he called the name of that place Beth-el: but the name of the city was Luz at the first. And Jacob vowed a vow, saying, If God will be with me, and will keep me in this way that I go, and will give me bread to eat, and raiment to put on, so that I come again to my father's house in peace, and Jehovah will be my God, then this stone, which I have set up for a pillar, shall be God's house: and of all that thou shalt give me I will surely give the tenth unto thee.

In the morning of this new understanding even the temporal surroundings become holy in our sight. Like Jacob we set up the common things, the stones upon which we slept in ignorance, and pour the oil of joy and gladness upon them. Then we name the place (our body temple and its affairs) Bethel, the "house of God." Jacob took the stone that he had used for a pillow and made a pillar of it. Instead of whining over the hardness of his experience he blessed it and made it a sustaining point in his mind.

Jacob was awestruck by the tremendous thought of omnipresence: what seems so commonplace may be the very house of God, and thinking some true thought or doing some loving act may be the gate of heaven. Jacob's vow to be more faithful to God and to give Him one tenth of all he received is a recognition of God as the source of all that man requires and also of the need of a constant reminder of this fact; hence the agreement to give back the tithe. Those who practice tithing testify that it leads them into an understanding of the relation of God to material affairs that they can get in no other way. When a person feels that he has God for a partner in all his financial affairs, he is never afraid of failure or lack.

In his inner consciousness man can make an agreement of this kind with the Mind of Spirit and can keep it in his everyday affairs. Many metaphysicians write out such contracts and put them away in the full assurance that the terms will be carried out by both contracting parties, God and man. It is found by nearly everyone who tries this plan that the agreement is fulfilled. If you would have your material affairs prosper, agree with Jehovah to give one tenth of your income to some work dedicated to God. If you keep your part of the agreement, you may rest assured that the Lord will keep His and abundantly prosper you, that your financial affairs will be taken care of without worry or strain on your part, and that you will come into a land where peace and plenty go hand in hand.

When there is recognition in fact by the mental (Jacob) of the true nature of the body's essence and of the spiritual nature of all life, then we begin the ascent from self to selflessness. We are then willing to give of our thought substance to God, and the house of God (the body) bears witness to the sincerity of our vow.

The natural seeks to hold onto all that it can gain by fair or unfair means, but the heart self, as soon as it has had a vision of the infinite, seeks in its turn to give. In this dream Jacob heard the voice of God saying, "To thee will I give . . ." When he awoke and came to himself, his quickened heart echoed in thankful responsiveness, "I will surely give . . . unto thee."

Chapter IX

Man Develops Spiritual Faculties

GENESIS 29, 30, and 31

AN ALLEGORY is a description of one thing under the image of another. It suggests but does not specifically state a meaning. A key to its interpretation is necessary, and this is usually given in the proper names that are used. By the employment of such symbols the Bible describes man in his wholeness, spirit, soul, and body. The names of men, places, tents, temples in every case have a meaning relative to the character of man. Mental states are thus described, and it is important that the individual who seeks spiritual wisdom for his regeneration shall be able to understand the allegory by use of the key hidden in the names.

An example of this is the name *Jacob,* which means "supplanter," one who gradually supplants and takes the place of the natural man in the consciousness of the individual and of the race. To accomplish this great work it is necessary that the individualized I AM shall have certain experiences and develop certain faculties essential to the higher-type man that is to follow.

Mystics tell us that man passes through twelve stages in his spiritual development. Each of these is a particular state of consciousness developed by a presiding ego or faculty. The last and highest state of consciousness is that complete, twelve-sided spiritual character attained by Jesus. This final attainment of the twelvefold man reveals the spiritual man, the image and likeness created in the beginning. These states may all be active in the individual consciousness at the same time, but the dominant one will indicate the point the person has reached in his development.

Jacob was overdeveloped intellectually and robbed his body (Esau) of its rightful heritage of life. This wrong was atoned for when he divided his accumulated wealth with Esau. In the meantime he had developed the spiritual side of his life and had brought forth a number of faculties (sons).

> *Gen. 29:1-15.* Then Jacob went on his journey; and came to the land of the children of the east. And he looked, and, behold, a well in the field, and, lo, three flocks of sheep lying there by it; for out of that well they watered the flocks: and the stone upon the well's mouth was great. And thither were all the flocks gathered: and they rolled the stone from the well's mouth, and watered the sheep, and put the stone again upon the well's mouth in its place. And Jacob said unto them, My brethren, whence are ye? And they said, Of Haran are we. And he said unto them, Know ye Laban the son of Nahor? And they said, We know him. And he said unto them, Is it well with him? And they said, It is well: and, behold, Rachel his daughter cometh with the sheep. And he said, Lo, it is yet high day, neither is it time that the cattle should be gathered together: water ye the sheep, and go and feed them. And they said, We cannot, until all the flocks be gathered together, and they roll the stone from the well's mouth; then we water the sheep. While he was yet speaking with them, Rachel came with her father's sheep; for she kept them. And it came to pass, when Jacob saw Rachel the daughter of Laban his mother's brother, and the sheep of Laban his mother's brother, that Jacob went near, and rolled the stone from the

well's mouth, and watered the flock of Laban his mother's brother. And Jacob kissed Rachel, and lifted up his voice, and wept. And Jacob told Rachel that he was her father's brother, and that he was Rebekah's son: and she ran and told her father.

And it came to pass, when Laban heard the tidings of Jacob his sister's son, that he ran to meet him, and embraced him, and kissed him, and brought him to his house. And he told Laban all these things. And Laban said to him, Surely thou art my bone and my flesh. And he abode with him the space of a month. And Laban said unto Jacob, because thou art my brother, shouldest thou therefore serve me for nought? tell me, what shall thy wages be?

Metaphysically interpreted, Jacob's journeying toward the east is a way of saying that the illumined intellect is penetrating deeper into the inner spiritual consciousness. The well of water symbolizes an innate spiritual life capacity in the body consciousness. The three flocks of sheep represent three states of physical existence, each on its own plane expressing the innocent, obedient activity of life. The people Jacob visits are living in Haran, the name of which means "strong," "exalted," "mountaineer"; the people being not necessarily spiritual but having high ideals. Their concepts are limited in expression ("they put the stone again upon the well's mouth in its place"). Laban represents the unsophisticated natural man whose pure high ideals are expressed by Rachel and Leah (they shepherd his sheep or thoughts). Jacob (related through his mother to this divine-natural plane of consciousness) now makes a closer contact that brings about prosperity for all concerned.

Gen. 29:16-30. And Laban had two daughters: the name of the elder was Leah, and the name of the younger was Rachel. And Leah's eyes were tender; but Rachel was beautiful and well-favored. And Jacob loved Rachel; and he said, I will serve thee seven years for Rachel thy younger daughter. And Laban said, It is better that I give her to thee, than that I should give her to another man: abide with me. And Jacob served seven years for Rachel; and they seemed unto him but a few days, for the love he had to her.

And Jacob said unto Laban, Give me my wife, for my days are fulfilled, that I may go in unto her. And Laban gathered together all the men of the place, and made a feast. And it came to pass in the evening, that he took Leah his daughter, and brought her to him; and he went in unto her. And Laban gave Zilpah his handmaid unto his daughter Leah for a handmaid. And it came to pass in the morning that, behold, it was Leah: and he said to Laban, What is this thou hast done unto me? did not I serve with thee for Rachel? wherefore then hast thou beguiled me? And Laban said, It is not so done in our place, to give the younger before the first-born. Fulfil the week of this one, and we will give thee the other also for the service which thou shalt serve with me yet seven other years. And Jacob did so, and fulfilled her week: and he gave him Rachel his daughter to wife. And Laban gave to Rachel his daughter Bilhah his handmaid to be her handmaid. And he went in also unto Rachel, and he loved also Rachel more than Leah, and served with him yet seven other years.

When unselfish love touches the heart, self drops out of the mind. Love in the heart lifts us out of the time limitations of sense consciousness into the joy of the eternal present. When we forget ourselves in the service of love, the selflessness of God takes possession of our being. Yet the selfless man is ever the self-possessed man, such is the paradox of spiritual law. The higher self in man loves the pure natural soul (Rachel) and works joyously to possess it. The higher self also loves the human part of the soul (Leah) with an objective love and feeds it with the enduring substance of true thought. Jacob was true to Leah. We can sustain the whole consciousness in health and unfailing strength by recognizing it as the essence of invisible substance.

The love story of Jacob and Rachel is one of the most beautiful in all literature. Jacob served her father seven years for her hand and was then disappointed because he had to marry her elder sister Leah. He then served seven more years for Rachel, which because of his great love for her seemed but a few days.

The name *Bilhah* means "bashfulness," "timidity," "tenderness." Bilhah represents a tendency of the soul toward self-abasement.

The name *Zilpah* means "distilling," "leaking." Zilpah symbolizes the unfolding soul of man in which as yet too much of the human is in evidence.

Gen. 29:31-35. And Jehovah saw that Leah was hated, and he opened her womb: but Rachel was barren. And Leah conceived, and bare a son, and she called his name Reuben: for she said, Because Jehovah hath looked upon my affliction; for now my husband will love me. And she conceived again, and bare a son: and said, Because Jehovah hath heard that I am hated, he hath therefore given me this *son* also: and she called his name Simeon. And he conceived again, and bare a son; and said, Now this time will my husband be joined unto me, because I have borne him three sons: therefore was his name called

Levi. And she conceived again, and bare a son: and she said, This time will I praise Jehovah: therefore she called his name Judah; and she left off bearing.

The first child born to Leah was Reuben. At his birth she cried, "Jehovah hath looked upon my affliction." The emphasis is on the word *looked,* and we find that the name *Reuben* means "a son seen," "vision of the son." Thus the mother revealed the character of the faculty represented by the child, and this is likewise true in the case of each of the sons.

The first faculty brought forth in man's spiritual development is vision, the ability to discern the reality of Spirit that lies back of every form or symbol in the material world. Like Jacob all Truth seekers are anxious to develop faith (Benjamin) to remove mountains and imagination (Joseph) to mold substance to their desires, but also like Jacob they must bring forth the faculties of seeing, hearing, feeling, praise, judgment, strength, power, understanding, zeal, and order on the spiritual plane.

Simeon, the second son of Leah, represents hearing or, in a broader sense, receptivity. When man is receptive to the inflow of Spirit nothing can keep his good from him, and he is in a position to make rapid strides in his development.

When Levi, the third son, was born, Leah exclaimed, "Now this time will my husband be joined unto me." The emphasis is on the word *joined.* Levi means "uniting," which in the body is feeling, in the soul compassion, and in the spirit love. The faculty of love is the unifying principle in consciousness. It connects our forces with that on which we center our attention. When our attention is focused on Spirit, these faculties become spiritualized. When we elevate love (Levi) to the plane of Spirit (John), it draws to us all that the soul requires. When it is kept on the lower plane as feeling or emotion it often leads to selfishness, to indulgence, even to violence.

The fourth son of Jacob and Leah was Judah. In the Hebrew this name means "praise Jehovah." In Spirit this is prayer and the faculty of accumulating spiritual substance. In sense consciousness this faculty becomes acquisitiveness, the desire to accumulate material things, and if the self is dominant the faculty "hath a devil" (Judas).

> *Gen. 30:1-8.* And when Rachel saw that she bare Jacob no children, Rachel envied her sister; and she said unto Jacob, Give me children, or else I die. And Jacob's anger was kindled against Rachel: and he said, Am I in God's stead, who hath withheld from thee the fruit of the womb? And she said, Behold, my maid Bilhah, go in unto her; that she may bear upon my knees, and I also may obtain children by her. And she gave him Bilhah her handmaid to wife: and Jacob went in unto her. And Bilhah conceived, and bare Jacob a son. And Rachel said, God hath judged me, and hath also heard my voice, and hath given me a son: therefore called she his name Dan. And Bilhah Rachel's handmaid conceived again, and bare Jacob a second son. And Rachel said, With mighty wrestlings have I wrestled with my sister, and have prevailed: and she called his name Naphtali.

Rachel and Bilhah represent soul attitudes. The name *Rachel* means "journeying," "migrating," which indicates a transitory state. In this instance Rachel was finding fault with Jacob (I AM). Such an attitude thwarts the inflow of Spirit. This is why Rachel had not conceived.

Bilhah was modest and teachable, consequently receptive to Spirit. This receptivity opens the door to spiritual inspiration, whose fruit is good judgment (Dan) and strength of character (Naphtali). That there is a close relation between the physical, mental, and spiritual aspects of strength is shown by the fact that the back becomes tired when thoughts of the burdens of materiality are held. The realization that all strength is primarily spiritual relieves this condition, and strength is restored. ("Lo now, his strength is in his loins," says Job.) Man retards his spiritual growth by his material thinking and his mental clinging to the things of the world. The faculties of judgment and strength find expression in the physical or more outer consciousness of man, but their true origin is Spirit, and their spiritual nature and spiritual activity are in due time established. The higher expression of this faculty is symbolized by Jesus' apostle Andrew.

Jacob and his sons lived several hundred years before the time of Jesus, hence represent the earlier stages of man's development. They were natural men living by sense and emotion, yet possessing great spiritual possibilities. In the same way our faculties in the first stages of their unfoldment express themselves on the lower planes of sense. Like everything else with which we have to deal, they have a physical, a mental, and a spiritual side to bring into manifestation.

The faculties evolve on three planes. Jacob being a type of the illumined mental, his sons especially portray ideals. By developing our ideals we may attain to a high degree of human perfection. But before we can become anything more than human or mortal our faculties must be spiritualized and put to work on the heavenly plane. Just as the sense man has reached his present stage by the development of the senses, so the divine man must evolve by the development of his spiritual powers. The faculties involved are essentially the same, differing only as regards the plane on which they are expressed, since body, soul, and spirit are really one, and are separated only in consciousness.

> *Gen. 30:9-13.* When Leah saw that she had left off bearing, she took Zilpah her handmaid, and gave her to Jacob to wife. And Zilpah Leah's handmaid bare Jacob a son. And Leah said, Fortunate! and she called his name Gad. And Zilpah Leah's handmaid bare Jacob a second son. And Leah said, Happy am I! for the daughters will call me happy: and she called his name Asher.

Leah's maid Zilpah (whose name means "distilling," "extracting an essence") was the mother of the next two sons, Gad and Asher. Gad symbolizes power, which at this stage of development is on the personal plane. Divine Mind gives man power over his thoughts and ideas and the forces of the soul. In the higher consciousness this power is exercised over the self and inner conditions rather than over other persons and the world without. The higher expression is shown by the apostle Philip.

Asher symbolizes understanding, which corresponds to wisdom in the realm of Spirit (Thomas). Through his knowing faculty man acquires a body of knowledge by study and observation of the world without. Through the same faculty he acquires wisdom by being receptive to the Spirit within. Tennyson brings out this difference clearly when he says, "Knowledge is earthly, of the mind; but wisdom is heavenly, of the soul."

Jacob now had eight sons, four by Leah, two by Bilhah, and two by Zilpah.

> *Gen. 30:14-21.* And Reuben went in the days of wheat harvest, and found mandrakes in the field, and brought them unto his mother Leah. Then Rachel said to Leah, Give me, I pray thee, of thy son's mandrakes. And she said unto her, Is it a small matter that thou hast taken away my husband? and wouldest thou take away my son's mandrakes also? And Rachel said, Therefore he shall lie with thee to-night for thy son's mandrakes. And Jacob came from the field in the evening, and Leah went out to meet him, and said, Thou must come in unto me; for I have surely hired thee with my son's mandrakes. And he lay with her that night. And God hearkened unto Leah, and she conceived, and bare Jacob a fifth son. And Leah said, God hath given me my hire, because I gave my handmaid to my husband: and she called his name Issachar. And Leah conceived again, and bare a sixth son to Jacob. And Leah said, God hath endowed me with a good dowry; now will my husband dwell with me, because I have borne him six sons: and she called his name Zebulun. And afterwards she bare a daughter, and called her name Dinah.

There is an interesting story in connection with the birth of the next son. In the Oriental household where there were several wives there were sure to be petty jealousies and naïve intrigues. Jacob spent most of his time with Rachel since she was his favorite. To get his attention Leah bargained with Rachel to keep out of the way for a while, and as a reward gave her some mandrakes or "love apples" that her son Reuben had brought in to her. Leah had great zeal and was never discouraged by her failure of her attempts to win Jacob's favor. When the child was born she called him Issachar, a name meaning "there is reward." Metaphysically he represents the faculty of zeal, active in substance and in the body consciousness.

Zeal is a strong force, the urge behind all things and the impulse to every achievement. It sets in motion all the machinery of the universe to attain the object of its desire. It should be tempered with understanding and love, else it becomes a destructive force. Even a criminal may be zealous in his work.

The spiritual side of the zeal faculty is represented by the apostle Simon the Canaanite.

It is worthy of note that Leah—metaphysically the human soul as distinguished from the more advanced soul (Rachel)—was the mother of six or one half of Jacob's sons. The last one she brought forth was Bebulun (whose name means "habitation," "neighbor") and who symbolizes the faculty of order. Order is the first law of the universe. Indeed there could be no universe unless its various parts were kept in perfect harmony. In the sense mind there is disorder, manifest in confusion of thought and action, while in Divine Mind everything is perfect order. Therefore it is most important, if we are to survive at all, that our thoughts be put in order and kept in harmony with divine intelligence.

Even in the small details of life, such as dress, conversation, eating, sleeping, and working, system and order enables one to live a richer and fuller life. But only in divine order can be found the life abundant and eternal. This order is established in our body and affairs when we live up to the higher convictions of our being under the guidance of spiritual understanding. No man-made law can be strong, true, or exact enough to insure perfect order. Only when man becomes conscious of who and what he is can he exercise his God-given dominion and bring his life into line with the principle of divine order, which is mind, idea, and manifestation. The apostle James, son of Alphaeus, symbolizes order on the spiritual plane.

The name *Dinah,* the daughter of Leah and Jacob, means "judged," "justified," "acquitted," "avenged." Dinah represents the soul side or feminine aspect of the judgment faculty in man; it might be called intuition, the intuition of the natural man.

> *Gen. 30:22-25.* And God remembered Rachel, and God hearkened to her, and opened her womb. And she conceived, and bare a son: and said, God hath taken away my reproach: and she called his name Joseph, saying, Jehovah add to me another son.
> And it came to pass, when Rachel had borne Joseph, that Jacob said to Laban, Send me away, that I may go unto mine own place, and to my country.

During all this time Jacob had been serving his father-in-law Laban in the country of Haran. This was a high or mountainous place and metaphysically denotes the high state of consciousness in which the individual is strengthened and given the determination to go forward to spiritual enlightenment and full development. Eleven of Jacob's sons were born in Haran, the last of whom was Joseph, the child of Rachel, the beloved. In the high state of spiritual consciousness man develops the faculties from the simple one of seeing to that of imagination, the faculty represented by Joseph.

> *Gen. 30:26-43.* Give me my wives and my children for whom I have served thee, and let me go: for thou knowest my service wherewith I have served thee. And Laban said unto him, If now I have found favor in thine eyes, *tarry: for* I have divined that Jehovah hath blessed me for thy sake. And he said, Appoint me thy wages, and I will give it. And he said unto him, Thou knowest how I have served thee, and how thy cattle have fared with me. For it was little which thou hadst before I came, and it hath increased unto a multitude; and Jehovah hath blessed thee whithersoever I turned: and now when shall I provide for mine own house also? And he said, What shall I give thee? and Jacob said, Thou shalt not give me aught: if thou wilt do this thing for me, I will again feed thy flock and keep it. I will pass through all thy flock to-day, removing from thence every speckled and spotted one, and every black one among the sheep, and the spotted and speckled among the goats: and *of such* shall be my hire. So shall my righteousness answer for me hereafter, when thou shalt come concerning my hire that is before thee: every one that is not speckled and spotted among the goats, and black among the sheep, that, *if found* with me, shall be counted stolen. And Laban said, Behold, I would it might be according to thy word. And he removed that day the he-goats that were ringstreaked and spotted, and all the she-goats that were speckled and spotted, every one that had white in it, and all the black ones among the sheep, and gave them into the hand of his sons; and he set three days' journey betwixt himself and Jacob: and Jacob fed the rest of Laban's flocks.
>
> And Jacob took him rods of fresh poplar, and of the almond and of the plane-tree; and peeled white streaks in them, and made the white appear

which was in the rods. And he set the rods which he
had peeled over against the flocks in the gutters in the
watering-troughs where the flocks came to drink;
and they conceived when they came to drink. And
the flocks conceived before the rods, and the flocks
brought forth ringstreaked, speckled, and spotted.
And Jacob separated the lambs, and set the faces
of the flocks toward the ringstreaked and all the
black in the flock of Laban: and he put his own
droves apart, and put them not unto Laban's flock.
And it came to pass, whensoever the stronger of the
flock did conceive, that Jacob laid the rods before
the eyes of the flock in the gutters, that they might
conceive among the rods; but when the flock were
feeble, he put them not in: so the feebler were
Laban's, and the stronger Jacob's. And the man increased exceedingly, and had large flocks, and maid-
servants and men-servants, and camels and asses.

This Scripture is quite symbolical of conditions
within ourselves.

One of the forces operative in the illumined intellect (Jacob) is the image-making faculty of the
mind. In this Scripture the activity of this faculty is
freely exemplified. The imagination has the ability
and power to throw onto the screen of visibility in
substance and life any idea that the mind conceives.
This accounts for the rapid increase in Jacob's possessions.

Jacob served Laban seven years thinking he would
get Rachel (the spiritual soul) to wife only to find
that Leah (the human soul) had been substituted. This
would indicate that Laban in one aspect of his nature
was something of a trickster. Jacob then had to work
another seven years to pay for Rachel. However, there
is only one presence, one power, one intelligence, and

one's own must come to him. When the soul looks steadily to Omnipresence, it finds that the law of equilibrium adjusts all conditions. For his hire Jacob was to take from Laban's flock all the ring-streaked and speckled and spotted cattle, all the black sheep, and all the speckled and spotted goats; which he removed some little distance. In addition to this he was to receive from the increase of Laban's flocks, which were free from these markings, all those animals which bore the same markings as Jacob's flocks.

When the strong, healthy herds were ready to conceive, Jacob placed in the gutters around the watering troughs where they came to drink rods of fresh poplar, and of almond, and of the plane tree, in which he had peeled white streaks; the flocks conceived before these rods, and they brought forth young that were ring-streaked, speckled, and spotted. When the weak flocks were ready to conceive and came to drink, he took away the rods in which he had peeled the white streaks. In the end Jacob had large, strong, healthy herds and Laban had small and weak herds.

Taking it all in all, the illumined intellect (Jacob) receives all that it deserves.

These passages in Genesis show the urge toward higher things on the part of those who received the quickening of the Spirit. Jacob, Laban, and Laban's family were of the same stock, but Jacob was more spiritually awakened, and because of his superior understanding all those with whom he was associated enjoyed increase of understanding and substance. Laban said to Jacob, "I have divined that Jehovah hath blessed me for thy sake." Separating the animals owned jointly by Laban and Jacob implies that the vital forces have

expanded to the point where finer types are possible.
These types are represented as "ringstreaked, speckled,
and spotted," and they fell to Jacob. Jacob also discovered that he could increase his "flocks" by using his
image-making faculty, focusing the mind on a certain
image when he was in creative consciousness. The sculp-
tor makes a mental image of the thing he is carving
and it appears under the impact of his hand.

Gen. 31:1-16. And he heard the words of Laban's
sons, saying, Jacob hath taken away all that was our
father's; and of that which was our father's hath
he gotten all this glory. And Jacob beheld the countenance of Laban, and, behold, it was not toward
him as beforetime. And Jehovah said unto Jacob,
Return unto the land of thy fathers, and to thy kindred; and I will be with thee.
    And Jacob sent and called Rachel and Leah to the
field unto his flock, and said unto them, I see your
father's countenance, that it is not toward me as
beforetime; but the God of my father hath been with
me. And ye know that with all my power I have
served your father. And your father hath deceived
me, and changed my wages ten times; but God
suffered him not to hurt me. If he said thus, The
speckled shall be thy wages; then all the flock bare
speckled: and if he said thus, The ringstreaked shall
be thy wages; then bare all the flock ringstreaked.
Thus God hath taken away the cattle of your father,
and given them to me. And it came to pass at the
time that the flock conceive, that I lifted up mine eyes,
and saw in a dream, and, behold, the he-goats which
leaped upon the flock were ringstreaked, speckled,
and grizzled. And the angel of God said unto me
in the dream, Jacob: and I said, Here am I. And
he said, Lift up now thine eyes, and see: all the he-
goats which leap upon the flock are ringstreaked,
speckled, and grizzled: for I have seen all that Laban

doeth unto thee. I am the God of Beth-el, where thou anointedst a pillar, where thou vowedst a vow unto me: now arise, get thee out from this land, and return unto the land of thy nativity. And Rachel and Leah answered and said unto him, Is there yet any portion or inheritance for us in our father's house? Are we not accounted by him as foreigners? for he hath sold us, and hath also quite devoured our money. For all the riches which God hath taken away from our father, that is ours and our children's: now then, whatsoever God hath said unto thee, do.

Laban and his family represent the pure natural in man, to which Jacob (spiritual illumination) brings expansion. Laban acknowledged that Jacob had brought him prosperity. But the spiritually illumined intellect (Jacob) reaps a share of the increase, and to this the natural man objects when his sons or "afterthoughts" call his attention to it.

In his dream Jehovah showed Jacob (illumined intellect) that he had finished his work in Haran (a high exalted state of consciousness on the natural plane) and now must function in a more fertile, productive soil. He must return with his possessions to the land of his nativity.

The wives for whom Jacob had labored also had their substance share and inherited part of the increase. When the mind is spiritually quickened all the faculties respond, especially the imagination, as indicated by the "ringstreaked, speckled, and grizzled" progeny.

Gen. 31:17, 18. Then Jacob rose up, and set his sons and his wives upon the camels; and he carried away all his cattle, and all his substance which he had gathered, the cattle of his getting, which he had gathered in Paddan-aram, to go to Isaac his father unto the land of Canaan.

Jacob was moving from Haran all the possessions he had acquired in Paddan-aram (the place of substance in the organism) to Canaan (the state of consciousness that to the individual is the kingdom of heaven). He took away with him a great wealth of substance, including camels, cattle, sheep, gold, and silver, and even the teraphim (highest thoughts) of that land.

"I am the God of Bethel, where thou anointedst a pillar, where thou vowedst a vow unto me: now arise, get thee out from this land, and return unto the land of thy nativity."

We recall that Bethel, "the house of God," symbolizes the consciousness in which Jacob dwelt when he beheld the ladder reaching to heaven and exclaimed, "Surely Jehovah is in this place; and I knew it not."

> *Gen. 31:19-21.* Now Laban was gone to shear his sheep: and Rachel stole the teraphim that were her father's. And Jacob stole away unawares to Laban the Syrian, in that he told him not that he fled. So he fled with all that he had; and he rose up, and passed over the River, and set his face toward the mountain of Gilead.

Gilead represents a high state of consciousness, where Spirit reveals its discerning, judging power. In this state of consciousness man refuses to allow his high ideals to become subject to error reasonings. Thus his spiritual discernment is not clouded by mortal thinking.

> *Gen. 31:22-32.* And it was told Laban on the third day that Jacob was fled. And he took his brethren with him, and pursued after him seven days' journey; and he overtook him in the mountain of Gilead. And God came to Laban the Syrian in a

dream of the night, and said unto him, Take heed
to thyself that thou speak not to Jacob either good
or bad. And Laban came up with Jacob. Now Jacob
had pitched his tent in the mountain: and Laban
with his brethren encamped in the mountain of
Gilead. And Laban said to Jacob, What hast thou
done, that thou hast stolen away unawares to me, and
carried away my daughters as captives of the sword?
Wherefore didst thou flee secretly, and steal away
from me, and didst not tell me, that I might have
sent thee away with mirth and with songs, with
tabret and with harp; and didst not suffer me to
kiss my sons and my daughters? now hast thou done
foolishly. It is in the power of my hand to do you
hurt: but the God of your father spake unto me
yesternight, saying, Take heed to thyself that thou
speak not to Jacob either good or bad. And now,
though thou wouldest needs be gone, because thou
sore longedst after thy father's house, *yet* wherefore
hast thou stolen my gods? And Jacob answered and
said to Laban, Because I was afraid: for I said, Lest
thou shouldest take thy daughters from me by force.
With whomsoever thou findest thy gods, he shall not
live: before our brethren discern thou what is thine
with me, and take it to thee. For Jacob knew not that
Rachel had stolen them.

The teraphim were household gods of the Eastern
peoples. They were images, apparently human in form,
that were used for purposes of worship in the homes
of the people. They were supposed to bring prosperity
and health and general domestic good. Even the Israelites used these images much of the time, though the
practice was of heathen origin.

Metaphysically the teraphim represent thoughts
tending to the outer only for supply, protection, and
all good (givers of prosperity, guardians of comforts,

nourishers, domestic idols); thoughts that imply trust
in the many outer channels through which one's good
comes to one instead of faith in God as one's sustenance and power of development; also the many
thoughts and desires that man entertains and gives expression to in outer ways and that should first of all
be centered in the one Presence within him.

Gen. 31:33-53. And Laban went into Jacob's tent,
and into Leah's tent, and into the tent of the two
maid-servants; but he found them not. And he went
out of Leah's tent, and entered into Rachel's tent.
Now Rachel had taken the teraphim, and put them
in the camel's saddle, and sat upon them. And Laban
felt all about the tent, but found them not. And she
said to her father, Let not my lord be angry that I
cannot rise up before thee; for the manner of women
is upon me. And he searched, but found not the
teraphim.
   And Jacob was wroth, and chode with Laban: and
Jacob answered and said to Laban, What is my tres-
pass? what is my sin, that thou hast hotly pursued
after me? Whereas thou hast felt about all my stuff,
what hast thou found of all thy household stuff?
Set it here before my brethren and thy brethren, that
they may judge betwixt us two. These twenty years
have I been with thee; thy ewes and thy she-goats
have not cast their young, and the rams of thy flocks
have I not eaten. That which was torn of beasts I
brought not unto thee; I bare the loss of it; of my
hand didst thou require it, whether stolen by day
or stolen by night. Thus I was; in the day the drought
consumed me, and the frost by night; and my sleep
fled from mine eyes. These twenty years have I been
in thy house; I served thee fourteen years for thy two
daughters, and six years for thy flock: and thou
hast changed my wages ten times. Except the God
of my father, the God of Abraham, and the Fear

of Isaac, had been with me, surely now hadst thou sent me away empty. God hath seen mine affliction and the labor of my hands, and rebuked thee yesternight.

And Laban answered and said unto Jacob, The daughters are my daughters, and the children are my children, and the flocks are my flocks, and all that thou seest is mine: and what can I do this day unto these my daughters, or unto their children whom they have borne? And now come, let us make a covenant, I and thou; and let it be for a witness between me and thee. And Jacob took a stone, and set it up for a pillar. And Jacob said unto his brethren, Gather stones; and they took stones, and made a heap: and they did eat there by the heap. And Laban called it Jegar-saha dutha: but Jacob called it Galeed. And Laban said, This heap is witness between me and thee this day. Therefore was the name of it called Galeed: and Mispah, for he said, Jehovah watch between me and thee, when we are absent one from another. If thou shalt afflict my daughters, and if thou shalt take wives besides my daughters, no man is with us; see, God is witness betwixt me and thee. And Laban said to Jacob, Behold this heap, and behold the pillar, which I have set betwixt me and thee. This heap be witness, and the pillar be witness, that I will not pass over this heap to thee, and that thou shalt not pass over this heap and this pillar unto me, for harm. The God of Abraham, and the God of Nahor, the God of their father, judge betwixt us. And Jacob sware by the Fear of his father Isaac.

Man should remember always that he does not live by bread alone, by outer ways and means, but by every word that proceeds out of the mouth of God: by the inner creative, sustaining, energizing life, love, power, strength, and intelligence of Spirit.

Laban symbolizes that which is pure and gentle. He was told in a dream what had happened, but God also revealed to him that he was not to speak good or bad to Jacob. However, he searched the tents for the teraphim without discovering them, as Rachel had placed them on the camel's back under the saddle on which she was riding. A covenant was made between Jacob and Laban. They gathered stones in a heap and they ate there. Laban called the heap Jegar-sahadutha, the Aramaic name for Galeed. *Galeed* means "massive witness," "heap of witnesses," "rock of time," "great endurance." It was the heap of stones that Jacob and Laban gathered for a witness between them when Jacob with his wives, children, and possessions left Laban to return to Esau and to Jacob's own country. It was also called Mizpah, "watchtower," and thus signifies the watchtower of prayer, while Galeed signifies the witness that Spirit with man bears to Truth. By following the true Jehovah Spirit in ourselves we shall always deal justly with every phase of our consciousness and of our entire organism, as well as with persons. "This heap be witness, and the pillar be witness, that I will not pass over this heap to thee, and that thou shalt not pass over this heap and this pillar unto me, for harm."

> *Gen. 31:54, 55.* And Jacob offered a sacrifice in the mountain, and called his brethren to eat bread: and they did eat bread, and tarried all night in the mountain. And early in the morning Laban rose up, and kissed his sons and his daughters, and blessed them: and Laban departed, and returned unto his place.

Jacob offered a sacrifice, and he and his brethren ate bread together. The sacrifice consisted of an animal slaughtered as an offering to the deity in man, symbolizing the surrender to Spirit of the animal forces that they may be transmuted into higher states of consciousness. Eating bread means joining in communion, partaking of spiritual substance. Early in the morning Laban arose and kissed his sons and his daughters in token of affection. Then he invoked divine favor upon them and returned to his place.

Chapter X

The Spiritual Gains Precedence of the Mental

GENESIS 32, 33, 34, 35, and 36

MAN DEVELOPS his faculties in an orderly manner when he looks to Divine Mind as the one and only guide. But he does not always seek this inner wisdom, and the result is a disorderly development. Jacob represents the mind in man that directs the physical body (Esau) in all its acts. In divine order Jacob should be born first—we should think before we act—but we find that as a rule people do not reflect and then act, and especially is this true among people who are in the first stages of their race journey.

The natural man in his immature consciousness is moved by desire and not by rational thinking. He seeks to satisfy appetite regardless of higher law and sells his birthright for a mess of pottage. When understanding (Jacob) takes the ascendancy, there is an entire change. Jacob went toward Haran ("enlightened," "mountainous"). The significance of this sentence is that when we let our meditations and blessings fall on the "knowing" part of ourselves (Jacob instead of Esau) we go into a higher mental state or an exalted condition of mind, wherein we receive a higher and clearer conception of things spiritual.

Gen. 32:1, 2. And Jacob went on his way, and

the angels of God met him. And Jacob said when he saw them, This is God's host: and he called the name of the place Mahanaim.

The name *Mahanaim* means "two camps," "two hosts," "companies." In the individual consciousness Mahanaim represents spiritual ideas and the physical realm ("two hosts"). This idea is brought out very clearly in the naming of the place by Jacob. The "two hosts" are the angels of God (messengers of God: spiritual ideas) on the one hand, and Jacob and his company, his wives, children, and possessions (manifestations of ideas) on the other.

Gen. 32:3-28. And Jacob sent messengers before him to Esau his brother unto the land of Seir, the field of Edom. And he commanded them, saying, Thus shall ye say unto my lord Esau: Thus saith thy servant Jacob, I have sojourned with Laban, and stayed until now: and I have oxen, and asses, *and* flocks, and men-servants, and maid-servants: and I have sent to tell my lord, that I may find favor in thy sight. And the messengers returned to Jacob, saying, We came to thy brother Esau, and moreover he cometh to meet thee, and four hundred men with him. Then Jacob was greatly afraid and was distressed: and he divided the people that were with him, and the flocks, and the herds, and the camels, into two companies; and he said, If Esau come to the one company, and smite it, then the company which is left shall escape. And Jacob said, O God of my father Abraham, and God of my father Isaac, O Jehovah, who saidst unto me, Return unto thy country, and to thy kindred, and I will do thee good: I am not worthy of the least of all the lovingkindnesses, and of all the truth, which thou hast shown unto thy servant; for with my staff I passed over this Jordan; and now I am become two companies.

Deliver me, I pray thee, from the hand of my brother, from the hand of Esau: for I fear him, lest he come and smite me, the mother with the children. And thou saidst, I will surely do thee good, and make thy seed as the sand of the sea, which cannot be numbered for multitude.

And he lodged there that night, and took of that which he had with him a present for Esau his brother: two hundred she-goats and twenty he-goats, two hundred ewes and twenty rams, thirty milch camels and their colts, forty cows and ten bulls, twenty she-asses and ten foals. And he delivered them into the hand of his servants, every drove by itself, and said unto his servants, Pass over before me, and put a space betwixt drove and drove. And he commanded the foremost, saying, When Esau my brother meeteth thee, and asketh thee, saying, Whose art thou? and whither goeth thou? and whose are these before thee? then thou shalt say, *They are* thy servant Jacob's; it is a present sent unto my lord Esau: and, behold, he also is behind us. And he commanded also the second, and the third, and all that followed the droves, saying, On this manner shall ye speak unto Esau, when ye find him; and ye shall say, Moreover, behold, thy servant Jacob is behind us. For he said, I will appease him with the present that goeth before me, and afterward I will see his face; peradventure he will accept me. So the present passed over before him: and he himself lodged that night in the company.

· And he rose up that night, and took his two wives, and his two hand-maids, and his eleven children, and passed over the ford of the Jabbok. And he took them, and sent them over the stream, and sent over that which he had. And Jacob was left alone; and there wrestled a man with him until the breaking of the day. And when he saw that he prevailed not against him, he touched the hollow of his thigh; and the hollow of Jacob's thigh was strained, as he wrestled with him. And he said, Let me go, for the day breaketh. And he said, I will not let thee go, except thou bless me. And he said unto him, What is thy name? And he said, Jacob. And he said, Thy name shall be called no more Jacob, but Israel: for thou hast striven with God and with men, and hast prevailed.

Edom was the name of the country where Esau's descendants lived. It represents the outer man, the body, or the carnal, physical phase of man's consciousness and organism. The significance of Seir is virtually the same as that of Edom. Seir apparently designates especially the emotional and stormy yet deep-seated carnal tendencies in the physical.

The Jordan ("flowing of judgment") may be said to represent that place in consciousness where we are willing to meet the results of our thoughts face to face and understandingly and courageously to pass judgment on all thoughts.

In the soul's unfoldment the higher faculties forge ahead, establish states of consciousness, and gather possessions of substance that must afterward be distributed to the lower faculties. Jacob represents the soul that has become rich in ideas. A time comes when an equalizing process begins and the body (Esau) must be given some of the riches of the soul.

Until love has done its perfect work man is fearful. Jacob feared to meet Esau. We find it hard to face the full claims of the body (Esau) after we have cheated it of its birthright, unity of soul and body in spiritual thought. Divine courage must supplant this fear before we are equal to facing the consequences of our self-centered thoughts and to taking up the task of harmonizing all our forces. But the vital power of Spirit animates the body, and it responds readily to our true thought when we give it of our substance.

The soul does not like to enter into struggles to overcome material habits, but it is necessary that it do so. The name of the ford where Jacob wrestled with the angel means "wrestling," and the inference is that it was hard for Jacob to put aside the things that he loved and to enter alone into the invisible to wrestle with the forces of the subconsciousness or sense consciousness in darkness. This struggle with the physical is illustrated in the overcoming by Jesus in the garden of Gethsemane. The error is "pressed out" and the rich oil of reality saved.

The life in the subconsciousness has several planes of action. In the deep recesses of the nerves it sends its energy to and fro, coming to the surface here and there in flesh-and-blood sensation. There is a strong man down there about whom the average person knows little. He lives so far below the plane of common consciousness that the great majority of men go through their whole life without making his acquaintance. This man is pure nature, the foundation of the body. Without him man could not take form, and it is his tenacity that keeps our organism intact. He belongs to nature and is universal; hence when the individual attempts to control him and to lift him up, there is resistance, and a severe struggle with him is inevitable. "The flesh lusteth against the Spirit, and the Spirit against the flesh."

The mind controls the body through the thoughts acting on the nerves. The sciatic nerve runs down the leg through the hollow of the thigh, and the will acts directly through this nerve. When the intellect (Jacob) exercises its power in the effort to control the natural man within, there follows a letting go of human will—Jacob's thigh is out of joint. A great light of understanding breaks in on the struggling soul, of which the intellect is a part, when it discovers that there is a divine-natural body, and it clings to that inner life and strength until it brings to the surface the blessing of perpetual physical vigor. Jacob (intellect) said, "I will not let thee go, except thou bless me." The blessing carried with it a new name, Israel; one who has striven with God and with men and has prevailed. "Israel" is one who is a prince and has power as regards both God and man, the spiritual and the material.

We can appreciate why Jacob (the intellect) after this experience was willing to make amends to Esau (the body), whom he had cheated and neglected all these years. When the intellect or conscious mind realizes and exercises its superior ability there is an intuitive feeling of injustice and a fear of the results. An awareness of having disregarded divine law coupled with inability to recall the cause of this fear results in much mental concern. Persons who let the ambitious intellect override the demands and rights of the body (Esau) eventually find themselves afraid and anxious to make restitution to the body.

> *Gen. 32:29-32.* And Jacob asked him, and said, Tell me, I pray thee, thy name. And he said, Wherefore is it that thou dost ask after my name? And he blessed him there. And Jacob called the name of the place Peniel: for, *said he*, I have seen God face to face, and my life is preserved. And the sun rose

upon him as he passed over Penuel, and he limped
upon his thigh. Therefore the children of Israel
eat not the sinew of the hip which is upon the
hallow of the thigh, unto this day: because he touched
the hollow of Jacob's thigh in the sinew of the hip.

Instead of Jacob being weaker, as his limp would
indicate, he was stronger, because he had made a spiritual adjustment between the higher and the lower in
his body consciousness. One can change one's attitude
toward the body and thus change the body itself by
following the advise of Paul: "Be ye transformed by
the renewing of your mind." Do not judge by the
appearance, do not call your body temple evil or corruptible flesh; do not fall into the error of mortal
mind. See in the body what Jacob saw, the face of God;
for it is ever the temple of the living God.

The name *Peniel* means "turned toward God,"
"face of God," "within the presence of God." Peniel
symbolizes the inner realization of the divine presence,
the realization of having met God face to face and of
having succeeded through prayer in attaining the divine favor and blessing that have been sought.

(Penuel is the same name as Peniel and carries the
same meaning and symbology.)

The "children of Israel eat not the sinew of the
hip which is upon the hollow of the thigh, unto this
day," as a reminder of a spiritual truth that they may
not understand now but will eventually.

Gen. 33:1-11. And Jacob lifted up his eyes, and
looked, and, behold, Esau was coming, and with
him four hundred men. And he divided the children
unto Leah, and unto Rachel, and unto the two handmaids. And he put the handmaids and their children

foremost, and Leah and her children after, and
Rachel and Joseph hindermost. And he himself
passed over before them, and bowed himself to the
ground seven times, until he came near to his
brother. And Esau ran to meet him, and embraced
him, and fell on his neck, and kissed him: and
they wept. And he lifted up his eyes, and saw the
women and the children; and said, Whose are these
with thee? And he said, The children whom God
hath graciously given thy servant. Then the handmaids came near, they and their children, and they
bowed themselves. And Leah also and her children
came near, and bowed themselves: and after came
Joseph near and Rachel, and they bowed themselves,
And he said, What meanest thou by all this company
which I met? And he said, To find favor in the
sight of my lord. And Esau said, I have enough, my
brother; let that which thou hast be thine. And
Jacob said, Nay, I pray thee, if now I have found
favor in thy sight, then receive my present at my
hand; forasmuch as I have seen thy face, as one
seeth the face of God, and thou wast pleased with
me. Take, I pray thee, my gift that is brought to
thee; because God hath dealt graciously with me,
and because I have enough. And he urged him, and
he took it.

Jacob, now become Israel, was reunited with Esau
after he crossed the ford Jabbok ("wrestling"). The
universal law of the unity of all things was fulfilled.
The way in which the mind (Israel) projects its
thoughts toward the body (Esau) is symbolized by
the way in which Rachel and her children, Leah and
her children, and the handmaids with their children
were presented to Esau. The handmaids were presented
first because they represent physical thoughts. Leah and
her children, presented next, represent intellectual
thoughts. Rachel (most beloved) and her son Joseph

were presented last because they represent the more
spiritual thoughts. Then Jacob himself "passed over
before them, and bowed himself to the ground seven
times, until he came near to his brother." This means
that the intellect recognizes the body as its equal and
the body's well-being as necessary to harmonious existence. In his spiritual self man must give his body
place as a divine creation and co-operate with it in his
evolution.

The body always obeys the conscious or subconscious behests of the mind. "Esau ran to meet him, and
embraced him, and fell on his neck, and kissed him:
and they wept." He rufused at first to accept the
proffered gifts of Jacob. The body at first feels its own
completeness and resists the rich ideas that the mind has
developed in its unfoldment. Jacob (illumined intellect) said, "Receive my present at my hand; forasmuch
as I have seen thy face, as one seeth the face of God."

Job says, "In my flesh shall I see God." (A.V.)
Jesus said, "He that hath seen me hath seen the Father." The mind must ideate the body as God substance.
This will raise the body to the higher consciousness of
its innate divinity. The I AM does not make spiritual
union with the body until it sees it as the pure and
holy temple of God.

The gifts that Jacob gave to Esau represent the
innate abilities that are wrapped up in the body and that
can be expressed only through union with the mind.
Persons who are skilled in exercises of agility and
strength must have the will to win a contest before
they are victorious, and trainers are giving more and
more attention and assigning ever greater importance
to the mental state of their athletes.

Gen. 33:12-16. And he said, Let us take our journey, and let us go, and I will go before thee. And he said unto him, My lord knoweth that the children are tender, and that the flocks and herds with me have their young: and if they overdrive them one day, all the flocks will die. Let my lord, I pray thee, pass over before his servant: and I will lead on gently, according to the pace of the cattle that are before me and according to the pace of the children, until I come unto my lord unto Seir. And Esau said, Let me now leave with thee some of the folk that are with me. And he said, What needeth it? let me find favor in the sight of my lord. So Esau returned that day on his way unto Seir.

Here is a lesson in co-operation between mind and body. This unity is essential not only to the development of the mental and the physical but to the unfoldment of the spirit. The body is lifted up and the mind strengthened when they work in unison. The children of the mind are the new ideas ushering in the untried capacities of both mind and body. They were now penetrating into the body consciousness (Seir) or the home of the physical (Esau), where the mind will lay hold of the essential physical elements and lift them up to a higher plane.

Gen. 33:17. And Jacob journeyed to Succoth, and built him a house, and made booths for his cattle: therefore the name of the place is called Succoth.

The name *Succoth* means "interwoven," "booths," "tents." Booths or tents represent temporary abiding places as compared with permanent houses. Succoth represents the seeming temporary, carnal, material organism of man, which is the fruit or manifestation of the belief that the spiritually unawakened man holds concerning his physical body. The abiding, spiritual body will come into manifestation when man learns that he is wholly spiritual and that no part of him, not even his body, is material and subject to corruption. Spiritual, true thinking will transform the present material seeming and will bring forth immortality, eternal life, throughout the whole man's being.

> *Gen. 33:18-20.* And Jacob came in peace to the city of Shechem, which is in the land of Canaan, when he came from Paddan-aram; and encamped before the city. And he bought the parcel of ground where he had spread his tent, at the hand of the children of Hamor, Schechem's father, for a hundred pieces of money. And he erected there an altar, and called it El-Elohe-Israel.

Jacob again entered the land of Canaan, as the Lord had promised he should, and encamped there. His fears gone—he came in peace to Shechem—he was free to pitch his tent wherever he pleased. So we, studying his example, may overcome the self through the transforming power of love. We may have a vision of the power of God indwelling, and in the patience that this vision teaches us we may cease striving with the personal self and henceforth strive only for the possession of the eternal ideal. Thus we make a new name for ourselves, supplanting the former natural self with the divine self. We find our new name written on the white stone that no one else knows, for it is "I."

When love has preformed its work in his consciousness man ceases to struggle against the seeming evils in the world without and turns his attention to overcoming the inharmonies of the world within himself.

"Ye have heard that it is said, An eye for an eye, and a tooth for a tooth: but I say unto you, Resist not him that is evil . . . Ye have heard that it was said, Thou shalt love thy neighbor, and hate thine enemy: but I say unto you, Love your enemies, and pray for them that persecute you."

All through the Bible life is compared to a battle but not to war: "the battle is Jehovah's." The Lord does not fight ignorance and evil; the foundation of all existence being good, the law is constantly at work reducing error to its exact stature. As man develops in consciousness, both the soul and the body constantly become more refined under the law of Spirit. This causes a seeming struggle sometimes with adverse conditions, materiality, ignorance, and evil.

The city of Shechem in the land of Canaan is in the locality where Hamor and his son Shechem dwelt. This is the consciousness into which Jacob (illumined intellect) came. The children of Hamor ("stubborn," "dark," "ignorant") represent the earthly, carnal, state of mind. Shechem represents a burden-bearing attitude of mind ("bending down," "a burden"). The name *El-Elohe-Israel* means "Elohe [Elohim], God of Israel," "mighty God of Israel," "Elohim He of Israel." The altar symbolizes the giving up of the "mind of the flesh" in individual consciousness to make way for the spiritual so that the spiritual may prevail throughout and God alone may be recognized. Thus Israel (the true, spiritual thoughts, beliefs, and faculties) may indeed become a prince, prevailing and ruling with God, having power with both God and man; that is, having power for good in every phase of the consciousness, from the very highest to the most material plane.

> *Gen. 34:1-3.* And Dinah the daughter of Leah,
> whom she bare unto Jacob, went out to see the
> daughters of the land. And Shechem the son of
> Hamor the Hivite, the prince of the land, saw her;
> and he took her, and lay with her, and humbled her.
> And his soul clave unto Dinah the daughter of Jacob,
> and he loved the damsel, and spake kindly unto the
> damsel.

The name *Dinah* means "justified," "avenged."
Dinah represents the soul side of or the feminine element in the judgment faculty in man, which may be
called intuition, the intuition of the natural man. The
thought of vengeance that is suggested in the name
always comes to the natural man in the process of
judging; he is more likely to discern the error side of a
proposition than the true side. Dinah, representing this
feminine element, went out and mingled with the
daughters of the land, who were Hivites. The Hivites
were descended from Canaan, son of Ham, and
represent the physical and carnal qualities in the individual. Any unlawful relationship of thoughts or elements results in a heavy, burdensome, attitude of mind
(Shechem). Hamor represents a central or ruling
thought (he was a Hivite prince) in the carnal consciousness of man.

> *Gen. 34:4-7.* And Shechem spake unto his
> father Hamor, saying, Get me this damsel to wife.
> Now Jacob heard that he had defiled Dinah his
> daughter; and his sons were with his cattle in the
> field: and Jacob held his peace until they came.
> And Hamor the father of Shechem went out unto
> Jacob to commune with him. And the sons of Jacob
> came in from the field when they heard it: and the
> men were grieved, and they were very wroth, be-
> cause he had wrought folly in Israel in lying with

Jacob's daughter; which thing ought not to be done.

Shechem (burden-bearing thoughts), representing a belief in the reality of the material and physical, sought to make his relationship with Dinah (feminine, intuitional element) permanent. When Jacob's sons (the offspring of the illumined intellect) discovered the unholy state of affairs they were naturally grieved and angered.

Gen. 34:8-31. And Hamor communed with them, saying, The soul of my son Shechem longeth for your daughter: I pray you, give her unto him to wife. And make ye marriages with us; give your daughters unto us, and take our daughters unto you. And ye shall dwell with us: and the land shall be before you; dwell and trade ye therein, and get you possessions therein. And Shechem said unto her father and unto her brethren, Let me find favor in your eyes, and what ye shall say unto me I will give. Ask me never so much dowry and gift, and I will give according as ye shall say unto me: but give me the damsel to wife. And the sons of Jacob answered Shechem and Hamor his father with guile, and spake, because he had defiled Dinah their sister, and said unto them, We cannot do this thing, to give our sister to one that is uncircumcised; for that were a reproach unto us. Only on this condition will we consent unto you: if ye will be as we are, that every male of you be circumcised; then will we give our daughters unto you, and we will take your daughters to us, and we will dwell with you, and we will become one people. But if ye will not hearken unto us, to be circumcised; then will we take our daughter, and we will be gone.

And their words pleased Hamor, and Shechem Hamor's son. And the young man deferred not to do the thing, because he had delight in Jacob's daughter: and he was honored above all the house of his father. And Hamor and Shechem his son came unto the gate of their city, and communed with the men of their city, saying, These men are peaceable with us; therefore let them dwell in the land, and trade therein; for, behold, the land is large enough for them; let us take their daughters to us for wives, and let us give them our daughters. Only on this condition will the men consent unto us to dwell with us, to become one people, if every male among us be circumcised, as they are circumcised. Shall not their cattle and their substance and all their beasts be ours? only let us consent unto them, and they will dwell with us. And unto Hamor and unto Shechem his son hearkened all that went out of the gate of his city; and every male was circumcised, all that went out of the gate of his city. And it came to pass on the third day, when they were sore, that two of the sons of Jacob, Simeon and Levi, Dinah's brethren, took each man his sword, and came upon the city unawares, and slew all the males. And they slew Hamor and Shechem his son with the edge of the sword, and took Dinah out of Shechem's house, and went forth. The sons of Jacob came upon the slain, and plundered the city, because they had defiled their sister. They took their flocks and their herds and their asses, and that which was in the city, and that which was in the field; and all their wealth, and all their little ones and their wives, took they captive and made a prey, even all that was in the house. And Jacob said to Simeon and Levi, Ye have troubled me, to make me odious to the inhabitants of the land, among the Canaanites and the Perizzites: and, I bring few in number, they will gather themselves together against me and smite me; and I shall be destroyed, I and my house. And they said, Should he deal with our sister as with a harlot?

The whole purpose of Jacob (illumined intellect) in penetrating down into the city of Shechem (materiality) in the land of Canaan (the physical and carnal) was to lay hold of new vigor, vitality and substance. Dinah represents the intuitive natural judgment that determines virtue and law in the physical. When this intuitive natural judgment is united with sense it loses its protective integrity, which is resented by the related faculties on that plane of consciousness (Dinah's brothers). A strict law of chastity is often observed even among primitive people. They may be cannibals or head-hunters yet be concerned for the preservation of the purity of their women. "And they slew Hamor and Shechem his son with the edge of the sword, and took Dinah out of Shechem's house, and went forth."

The thought of judgment and punishment that is suggested in the name *Dinah* is carried out in the action of Simeon and Levi in taking vengeance for Dinah's disgrace on Shechem and his people. As man becomes more spiritual in his ideas of judgment, thoughts of revenge, punishment, and evil are eliminated from his mind and he sees the love, mercy, and goodness of God instead.

(On the subject of circumcision see interpretation of Gen. 17:9-14.)

The Canaanites represent the elemental life forces in the subconsciousness.

The Perizzites were inhabitants of Canaan and, like the Canaanites, represent the fundamental life element in the organism, only elevated to a more exalted plane by the outer, personal man and more strongly entrenched in the sense consciousness of the individual.

Gen. 35:1-7. And God said unto Jacob, Arise, go up to Beth-el, and dwell there: and make there an altar unto God, who appeared unto thee when thou fleddest from the face of Esau thy brother. Then Jacob said unto his household, and to all that were with him, Put away the foreign gods that are among you, and purify yourselves, and change your garments: and let us arise, and go up to Beth-el; and I will make there an altar unto God, who answered me in the day of my distress, and was with me in the way which I went. And they gave unto Jacob all the foreign gods which were in their hand, and the rings which were in their ears; and Jacob hid them under the oak which was by Shechem. And they journeyed: and a terror of God was upon the cities that were round about them, and they did not pursue after the sons of Jacob. So Jacob came to Luz, which is in the land of Canaan (the same is Beth-el), he and all the people that were with him. And he built there an altar, and called the place El-beth-el; because there God was revealed unto him, when he fled from the face of his brother.

God commanded Jacob to arise (lift up his thoughts) and go unto Beth-el ("house of God"). After a progressive soul has passed through such an experience as the one recorded in the preceding chapter, this soul feels the need of and affirms the cleansing, purifying, and uplifting power of the word and resolves to keep its face turned more steadfastly toward the light. The foreign gods here referred to supposedly are little images (made of a material substance such as clay or iron) representing ideas. The rings symbolize ornaments in which a vain and frivolous soul delights.

All these relics of the country they were leaving were now to be cast out of the conscious mind. The change of garments represents a change of thoughts.

The name *Luz* means "turning away," "departing," "a shrub bearing nuts." Luz indicates separation. It also carries with it the idea of substance and strength ("a shrub bearing nuts") of a more or less material character. When Jacob realized the omnipresence of God he changed the name of Luz to Beth-el ("house of God"). (See interpretation of Gen. 28:18-22.)

On the occasion of this, Jacob's second journey to Luz, he set up an altar and called the place El-beth-el, which means "toward Beth-el; strength of the house of God." It symbolizes the revelation from within that the true origin of man is spiritual, that God dwells in man and reveals Himself when man comes to the place in consciousness where he is willing to give up the lower for the higher (builds an altar to Jehovah). Man is the house (temple) of God, and he is greatly strengthened when he perceives this truth.

> *Gen. 35:8.* And Deborah Rebekah's nurse died, and she was buried below Beth-el under the oak; and the name of it was called Allon-bacuth.

Rebekah represents the soul's natural delight in the beautiful. The name of *Deborah* means "a bee." The name *Allon-bacuth* means "oak of weeping." Weeping is an expression of emotion, a negative condition, a letting go throughout the organism. Rebekah's nurse Deborah represents the quality of the soul by virtue of which it serves instinctively and is guided by discrimination and judgment. In mixed states of consciousness, where error seems strongest, Spirit can lead by following the guidance of instinct. Deborah was buried below Bethel ("house of God") under the oak (the protection of Spirit).

Allon-bacuth ("oak of weeping") represents the inner strengthening of the true man that comes when, in trying to serve, he lets go of the outer personal activities and goes within to the source of all strength and true energy (the oak) and rests there in God.

> *Gen. 35:9-15.* And God appeared unto Jacob again, when he came from Paddan-aram, and blessed him. And God said unto him, Thy name is Jacob: thy name shall not be called any more Jacob, but Israel shall be thy name: and he called his name Israel. And God said unto him, I am God Almighty: be fruitful and multiply; a nation and a company of nations shall be of thee, and kings shall come out of thy loins; and the land which I gave unto Abraham and Isaac, to thee I will give it, and to thy seed after thee will I give the land. And God went up from him in the place where he spake with him. And Jacob set up a pillar in the place where he spake with him, a pillar of stone: and he poured out a drink-offering thereon, and poured oil thereon. And Jacob called the name of the place where God spake with him, Beth-el.

The foregoing incident left an idelible impression on Jacob's mind, and he counted it as a great spiritual experience and set up a stone as a pillar in commemoration of it.

The name *Aram* means "high," "exalted," and Aram denotes the intellect. The name *Paddan* means "field," "tableland." Paddan-aram represents substance lifted to a broad, level place in the intellectual thought of the individual. This incident in the life of Jacob has much in common with an earlier one. (See interpretation of Gen. 28:18-22).

> *Gen. 35:16-21.* And they journeyed from Beth-el; and there was still some distance to come to

> Ephrath: and Rachel travailed, and she had hard
> labor. And it came to pass, when she was in hard
> labor, that the midwife said unto her, Fear not;
> for now thou shalt have another son. And it came to
> pass, as her soul was departing (for she died), that
> she called his name Ben-oni: but his father called
> him Benjamin. And Rachel died, and was buried in
> the way to Ephrath (the same is Beth-lehem). And
> Jacob set up a pillar upon her grave: the same is
> the Pillar of Rachel's grave unto this day. And Israel
> journeyed, and spread his tent beyond the tower of
> Eder.

Ephrath is the original name of the town of Bethlehem. Ephrath represents a realization of abundant substance, this increase of substance ideas in consciousness bringing about a corresponding fruitfulness, abundance, throughout one's life and affairs.

The last of the sons of Jacob was born after his return to Canaan. The death of Rachel and birth of Benjamin represent the transition of a potential soul quality from the subjective to the objective plane of consciousness. Rachel ("ewe," "lamb") represents the pure, innocent, potentially spiritual soul that is a composite of faith, love, power, and the like. It is through Jacob (the intellect) that these qualities are made objective, and when this comes to pass there is temporary sorrow ("son of my sorrow"), followed by rejoicing at the realization of the birth of the new power that has come through the transition ("son of my right hand"). "A woman when she is in travail hath sorrow, because her hour is come: but when she is delivered of the child, she remembereth no more the anguish, for the joy that a man is born into the world."

The name *Eder* means "troop," "flock." The tower called Eder, beyond which Israel (Jacob) journeyed and spread his tent, symbolizes the gathering of thoughts of dominion and rulership (Israel means "rulership with God") and the raising of them to a higher degree of understanding; lifting them to a ·spiritual level by realizing that power and dominion come from God.

> *Gen. 35:22.* And it came to pass, while Israel dwelt in that land, that Reuben went and lay with Bilhah his father's concubine: and Israel heard of it.

All these illustrations show that the divine law must be observed in developing the faculties. Reuben's laying with Bilhah evidently symbolizes an abortive attempt of man's perception of Truth (Reuben) to develop them through an illegitimate union with a negative element (Bilhah: "bashfulness," "timidity"). That there is no record of any progeny from this union indicates that it was not in divine order.

> *Gen. 35:23-26.* Now the sons of Jacob were twelve: the sons of Leah: Reuben, Jacob's first-born, and Simeon, and Levi, and Judah, and Issachar, and Zebulun; the sons of Rachel: Joseph and Benjamin; and the sons of Bilhah, Rachel's handmaid: Dan and Naphtali; and the sons of Zilpah, Leah's handmaind: Gad and Asher: these are the sons of Jacob, that were born to him in Paddan-aram.

Leah ("weary," "exhausted") represents the human soul. She became the mother of six sons:

Reuben, whose name means "behold a son," "vision of the son," represents faith in its aspect of discernment, of sight in the outer. Reuben like Simeon bespeaks understanding.

Simeon, whose name means "hearkening," "obeying," represents the bringing forth of hearing; receptivity.

Levi, whose name signifies "joining," "clinging," represents the love faculty in human consciousness.

The name *Judah* means "praise Jehovah." Judah symbolizes the prayer and praise faculty in consciousness.

The name *Issachar* means "he will bring reward," "who brings recompense." Issachar represents active zeal.

The name *Zebulun* means "habitation," "dwelling." Zebulun represents the order faculty.

Rachel ("ewe," "lamb") symbolizes the spiritual soul. She became the mother of Joseph and Benjamin.

The name *Joseph* means "Jehovah shall increase." Joseph represents the imagination.

The name *Benjamin* means "son of good fortune." Benjamin represents an active, accomplishing faith.

Bilhah ("bashfulness," "timidity") represents a tendency toward self-abasement. She bore Jacob two sons, Dan and Naphtali:

Dan ("a judge") symbolizes the faculty of judgment.

Naphtali ("my wrestling") represents the power of elimination.

Zilpah ("distilling," "dropping," "leaking") represents the unfolding soul of man in the phase of its awakening to spiritual thought, marked by hesitation and lack of perseverance; too much of the human is expressed and much of the good is dissipated (leaking). Zipah's two sons were Gad and Asher.

Gad ("fortunate," "good fortune") represents the

faculty of power, but still mostly on the personal plane.

Asher ("straightforward") symbolizes the faculty of understanding.

> *Gen. 35:27, 28.* And Jacob came unto Isaac his father to Mamre, to Kiriath-arba (the same is Hebron), where Abraham and Isaac sojourned.

And the days of Isaac were a hundred and fourscore years. And Isaac gave of the ghost, and died, and was gathered unto his people, old and full of days: and Esau and Jacob his sons buried him.

Kiriath-arba ("city of Arba") represents the tendency of the sense mind to attribute strength, power, knowledge, and greatness to the outer formed world rather than to Spirit. Kiriath-arba was the old name of Hebron, which represents an association of ideas.

Mamre signifies a consciousness of substance and riches.

The death of Isaac represents the passing or giving up of that phase of the individual consciousness which has to do with the pleasures of the natural man; or its sinking back into the subconsciousness (giving up of the ghost).

> *Gen. 36:1-5.* Now these are the generations of Esau (the same is Edom). Esau took his wives of the daughters of Canaan: Adah the daughter of Elon the Hittite, and Oholibamah the daughter of Anah, the daughter of Zibeon the Hivite, and Basemath Ishmael's daughter, sister of Nebaioth. And Adah bare to Esau Eliphaz; and Basemath bare Reuel; and Oholibamah bare Jeush, and Jalam, and Korah: these are the sons of Esau, that were born unto him in the land of Canaan.

Metaphysically Esau symbolizes the body or physical vigor. He took wives from among the daughters of

Canaan ("lowland"), which represents the body consciousness.

His first wife was Adah ("beauty," "comeliness," "adornment," "ornament," "pleasure"), who represents a phase of the human soul or love nature. Love, even in its limited expression in personal consciousness, adorns a person with a certain beauty of character and a grace and comeliness not found in those lacking in love.

Another of Esau's wives was Oholibamah, whose name means "tent of the high place," "my tabernacle is exalted." Oholibamah was the granddaughter of Zibeon the Hivite.

The name *Zibeon* means "wild robber," and the Hivites represent thoughts belonging to the carnal consciousness in man. Oholibamah signifies the lifting up and exalting of materiality by the carnal phase of the soul.

Another of his wives was Basemath, whose name means "fragrant," "sweet," "pleasant." Basemath represents the soul or feminine element in man in the fineness of its ability to perceive or receive intuitively.

Adah bore to Esau a son, Eliphaz, whose name means "God is purification," "God is dispenser," "God of strength."

Basemath bore Reuel, whose name signifies "led of God," "shepherded of God," "companion of God." Reuel denotes a thought of divine guidance and care; also a sense of mutual understanding, comradeship, fellowship existing between God and man.

Oholibamah bore Jeush and Jalam and Korah.

The name *Jeush* means "he will bring together." Jeush represents strong, unifying, attracting, accumu-

lifting thoughts in consciousness; also the final lifting
up and unifying of the entire man in spiritual life and
wholeness. The name *Jalam* means "whom God hides."

The name *Korah* means "ice," "bald." Korah denotes the coldness, the crystallization ("ice"), and the
barrenness (baldness) of consciousness that result from
dominance of the "mind of the flesh" (Esau) in the
individual.

> *Gen. 36:6-12.* And Esau took his wives, and his
> sons, and his daughters, and all the souls of his
> house, and his cattle, and all his beasts, and all his
> possessions, which he had gathered in the land of
> Canaan; and went into a land away from his brother
> Jacob. For their substance was too great for them to
> dwell together; and the land of their sojournings
> could not bear them because of their cattle. And Esau
> dwelt in mount Seir: Esau is Edom.
>
> And these are the generations of Esau the father
> of the Edomites in mount Seir: these are the names
> of Esau's sons: Eliphaz the son of Adah the wife of
> Esau, Reuel the son of Basemath the wife of Esau.
> And the sons of Eliphaz were Teman, Omar, Zepho,
> and Gatam, and Kenaz. And Timna was concubine
> to Eliphaz Esau's son; and she bare to Eliphaz
> Amalek: these are the sons of Adah, Esau's wife.

The original separation between mind (Jacob) and
body (Esau) was caused by the cunning mind taking
advantage of the stupid body; also the lusts and weak-
nesses of the body appetite played their part. Here is
illustrated a further separation because of the physical
possessions of Esau. Those who cultivate the physical
grow physically and require so much room that the
mental is crowded out, and they exalt the things of the
flesh. Esau dwelt in Mount Seir. The name *Seir* means
"shaggy," "rough," "tempestuous," "hairy," pointing

to the deep-seated emotions in carnal consciousness. Eventually the two states of consciousness represented by Jacob and Esau must be merged.

(For Eliphaz and Basemath see the interpretation of Gen. 36:3, 4.)

The sons of Eliphaz were Teman, Omar, Zepho, Gatam, and Kenaz.

The name *Teman* means "prosperity," "abundance," "good faith." Teman denotes the realm of the subconsciousness, with its inherently rich stores of substance and good. Here this realm is under the influence of the Esau-Edom state of mind in the individual; in other words, under the influence of material thought. Omar represents the ability of the outer man to receive the higher Truth ideals ("mountaineer," "summit") and to express them ("bringing forth," "bearing into the light"). The name *Zepho* (Zephi) means "outlook," "watchtower." Zepho represents an expectant state of mind that seemingly belongs to the outer or physical man but whose desire is toward Spirit.

The name *Gatam* means "puny," "exhausted," and the like. (Eliphaz, father of Gatam, represents an active thought of strength.) Strength is from God, while that represented by Eliphaz is of the physical consciousness and does not lay hold of the truth about strength. The meanings attributed to Gatam's name —"puny," "greatest fatigue," "burned field"—clearly indicate the results of believing in material strength. Until man realizes that his strength is spiritual it cannot become abiding, unfailing, and enduring.

The name *Kenaz* means "spear thrower," "lancer," "archer," "hunter." A "hunter," in the sense of a

Kenaz, denotes a thought that is connected with the animal forces of the organism. Kenaz symbolizes the thought of man engrossed in the animal phase of his nature, in animal strength and activity ("spear thrower," "lancer," "archer").

Timna was Eliphaz's concubine. Timna represents a restricting, curbing influence ("withheld," "restrained," "forbidden") that is ever at work in the soul of man and in his body consciousness. If there were no restraint on the carnal mind in man and its activities, man would destroy himself utterly.

Timna bore Amalek, whose name means "warlike," "dweller in the vale," "that licks up or consumes." Amalek symbolizes lust, the base desire that, once established in the animal forces of the subconscious mind of man, is the begetter of destructive, rebellious, perverted appetites and passions. Amalek's father was Eliphaz, whose name means "God of strength," "God is purification." Thus desire at its origin is good and is of God; but when it is misinterpreted by the carnal man it becomes lust (Amalek).

> *Gen. 36:13.* And these are the sons of Reuel: Nahath, and Zerah, Shammah, and Mizzah: these were the sons of Basemath, Esau's wife.

(For Reuel see interpretation of Gen. 36:4.)

Reuel's first son was Nahath, who represents one of the prevailing beliefs of the outer man at a certain period of his unfoldment: restful, lulling, contentment ("resting," "quieting") in his seemingly material type of expression ("lowness"). However higher thoughts must be introduced into even the outer consciousness of man if he is to be aroused out of the false lethargy of the carnal and to be quickened throughout his whole spirit, soul, and body to the Truth of his being.

The name of another son, Zerah, means "sunrise," "germination of a seed." "splendor." Zerah denotes the rise of new light or understanding in the consciousness; the first conscious awakening to the presence of this new inner light or understanding. (The sun rises in the east; and the east signifies the within.)

Shammah, a third son, represents a destructive, fearful tendency in consciousness that leads to inharmonies of mind and body. The outer man, apart from the dominion of Spirit, is very likely to swing from one extreme to the other, from the height of noble thinking and feeling ("fame," "renown") to the depths of fear, desolation, emptiness, and error. By consciously laying hold of the Christ Truth and making it practical in his life, this outer man must come into a better balance, greater stability and poise.

Mizzah, the fourth son, represents a steady tearing down and wearing away of the consciousness and organism ("flowing down," "disintegration," "exhaustion") as the result of fear, fear being one of the most subtle and destructive errors that the carnal mind in man contains. The destructive element is redeemed through divine love, which knows only the good.

> *Gen. 36:14.* And these were the sons of Oholibamah the daughter of Anah, the daughter of Zibeon, Esau's wife: and she bare to Esau Jeush, and Jalam, and Korah.

(For Oholibamah see interpretation of Gen. 36:2. For Oholibamah's sons, Jeush, Jalam, and Korah, see interpretation of Gen. 36:1-5.)

Gen. 36:15-19. These are the chiefs of the
sons of Esau: the sons of Eliphaz the first-born of
Esau: chief Teman, chief Omar, chief Zepho, chief
Kenaz, chief Korah, chief Gatam, chief Amalek:
these are the chiefs that came of Eliphaz in the
land of Edom; these are the sons of Adah. And
these are the sons of Reuel, Esau's son: chief
Nahath, chief Zerah, chief Shammah, chief Mizzah:
these are the chiefs that came of Reuel in the land
of Edom: these are the sons of Basemath, Esau's wife.
And these are the sons of Oholibamah, Esau's wife:
chief Jeush, chief Jalam, chief Korah: these are
the chiefs that came of Oholibamah the daughter of
Anah, Esau's wife. These are the sons of Esau, and
these are their chiefs: the same is Edom.

(See interpretation of Gen. 36:9-12 for the sons of
Eliphaz: Teman, Omar, Zepho, Kenaz, Gatam, and
Amalek. For Korah, see interpretation of Gen. 36:5.)

(See interpretation of Gen. 36:13 for the sons of
Reuel: Nahath, Zerah, Shammah, Mizzah.)

(See interpretation of Gen. 36:1-5 for the sons of
Oholibamah: Jeush and Korah.)

(See interpretation of Gen. 36:1-5 for Jalam.)

Gen. 36:20-30. These are the sons of Seir the
Horite, the inhabitants of the land: Lotan and Shobal
and Zibeon and Anah, and Dishon and Ezer and
Dishan: these are the chiefs that came of the Horites,
the children of Seir in the land of Edom. And the
children of Lotan were Hori and Heman; and Lotan's
sister was Timna. And these are the children of
Shobal: Alvan and Manahath and Ebal, Shepho and
Onam. And these are the children of Zibeon: Aiah
and Anah; this is Anah who found the hot springs
in the wilderness, as he fed the asses of Zibeon his
father. And these are the children of Anah: Dishon
and Oholibamah the daughter of Anah. And these
are the children of Dishon: Hemdan and Eshban

and Ithran and Cheran. These are the children of Ezer: Bilhan and Zaavan and Akan. These are the children of Dishan: Uz and Aran. These are the chiefs that came of the Horites: chief Lotan, chief Shobal, chief Zibeon, chief Anah, chief Dishon, chief Ezer, chief Dishan: these are the chiefs that came of the Horites, according to their chiefs in the land of Seir.

The Horites were very closely connected with the Edomites, the descendants of Esau. They were inhabitants of the land of Mount Seir before they were overcome by Esau. After that they lived in the land with the Edomites.

Metaphysically the Horites, like the Edomites, represent forces having their seat of action in the physical organism. The Horites denote more especially the deep-seated, subconscious errors (cave dwellers) and fleshly tendencies and activities of the physical in man, while the Edomites designate forces in the outer or body consciousness.

The name of Lotan, the son of Seir the Horite, means "covered," "secret," "dark." Metaphysically Lotan represents a secret, hidden, ignorant ruling thought in the realm in man symbolized by the Horites.

Shobal, the name of another son, means "way," "traveling." Each individual is "traveling" the pathway of life. To a great extent the race has been and still is "wandering" about in ignorance and darkness as to the true source of man's being. The "way" that each takes in his thoughts, beliefs, and expressions determines whether that which he brings forth shall be the fruit of the "mind of the flesh" or the fruit of the Spirit ("growing," "producing ears," "rain").

The name *Zibeon* means "immersed," "ravenous

preyer," "wild robber," "dyed." Metaphysically Zibeon
symbolizes a wild, lawless sense thought that has the
capacity of adapting itself to the varying ideas and
moods of the individual, and that thus remains in his
consciousness (until it is cast forth by Truth), robbing
his body of its energy and substance.

The name *Anah* means "answering." Metaphysically Anah denotes error tendencies or strongly in-
fluencing thoughts deep within the subjective life forces
in the individual consciousness that cause these life
forces to respond to the desires of the flesh or sense
man ("answering") instead of listening to Spirit. (The
Hivites and the Horites were descendants of Canaan,
son of Ham; they were hostile to the Israelites in the
Promised Land, and they had to be destroyed.)

The name *Dishon* means "fatness," "opulence,"
"fertile," "ashes." Metaphysically Dishon symbolizes
richness and seeming fertility on the physical plane.

The name *Ezer* means "envelop," "help," "unite,"
"treasure." Metaphysically Ezer symbolizes man's innate belief in a substance, a wisdom ("treasure"), an
established oneness with All-Good (unity), and a power
to aid and to protect ("envelop," "help") that comes
from something higher, stronger, and more real and
lasting than sense consciousness can give.

The name *Dishan* means virtually the same thing as
Dishon. Metaphysically Dishan represents a very active,
rich, or fertile controlling thought belonging to the
Horite consciousness in the individual.

The children of Lotan were Hori and Heman.

The name *Hori* means "cave dweller," "imprisoned," "black." Metaphysically Hori denotes thoughts
belonging to the depths of the subconsciousness ("cave

dweller"), or a person wholly given over to the error beliefs signified by the Horites.

The name *Heman* means "lasting," "faithful," "trustworthy." Heman represents thoughts full of faith and trust in God. Great wisdom and harmony are the result of these thoughts.

The children of Shobal were Alvan and Manahath and Ebal, Shepho and Onam.

The name *Alvan* means "tall," "sublime." Metaphysically Alvan denotes a lofty concept on the part of man in regard to the sensual or physical phase of his organism, whereby he glimpses the truth that even the outer man has his origin in Spirit.

The name *Manahath* means "resting," "restoring," "forsaking." Metaphysically Manahath designates a peaceful, restful thought and place in consciousness; a ceasing from outer activity, wherein both soul and body are renewed, and wherein something of error is forsaken and a degree of Truth is realized.

The name *Ebal* means "stripped of all," "bare," "barren," "stone." Metaphysically Ebal represents the adverse activity of the law in those who think and act out of harmony with divine principle; that in us which takes cognizance of the working out of error resulting from ignorance and disobedience. This phase of the activity of the law always seems hard ("stone") to the sense consciousness upon which it falls, and it surely exposes ("bares") the nothingness of all that does not measure up to the spiritual.

The name *Shepho* means "nakedness," "barren," "wasted away," "unconcerned." Metaphysically Shepho denotes a mental activity in the body consciousness that is wholly "unconcerned" with the things of Spirit, hence is unfruitful and "naked" in so far as real life, strength, wholeness, substance, and good are concerned ("nakedness," "barren" "wasted away").

The name *Onam* means "vigorous," "powerful," "wealthy," "substantial." Metaphysically Onam denotes thoughts pertaining to strength and vigor; also to understanding and substance. He represents a belief in purely physical strength and power, outer possessions, and the carnal thought of understanding.

The children of Zibeon were Aiah and Anah.

The name *Aiah* means "a cry," "a clamor," "a vulture." Metaphysically Aiah denotes destructive, devouring thoughts pertaining to the animal consciousness and to what should be the higher thought realm in the individual ("a cry," "a clamor," and so on).

The name *Anah* means "answering." (For further comment see interpretation of Gen. 36:20).

The children of Anah were Dishon and Oholibamah. (For Dishon see interpretation of Gen. 36:21; for Oholibamah, Gen. 36:2.)

The children of Dishon were Hemdan, Eshban, Ithran, Cheran.

The name *Hemdan* means "desirable," "pleasant," "precious." Metaphysically Hemdan represents the seemingly "desirable" and "pleasant" sense beliefs and activities of one who is not awakened spiritually. These beliefs and activities however are but transitory and soon turn to dust and ashes, to vanity and vexation of spirit.

The name *Eshban* means "man of wisdom," "man of understanding," "son of fire." Metaphysically Eshban represents the belief held by the outer man that wisdom and understanding come through the perceptions of the senses, and through reasoning.

The name *Ithran* means "abundant," "excellent," "plenty," Metaphysically Ithran represents ideas of great "excellence" and of great value; thoughts that are superior to their fellows, being active both in the deep-seated sense consciousness (Horites) in the individual and on the more spiritual level of his mind (the Israelites). These are ideas that have taken on abundant substance, they involve belief in bountiful supply, and they lead to "plenty."

The name *Cheran* means "lyre," "united," "a joyous shout." Metaphysically Cheran denotes a harmonious, unifying thought that is active in the depths of the physical being of man ("united," "lyre"). Since this thought is not consciously united with Spirit, though its origin and tendency are good, it cannot bring about the perfect union of man with God and the true spiritual harmony implied by the meaning of the name.

The children of Ezer were Bilhan, Zaavan, and Akan.

The name *Bilhan* means "confused," "weak," "tender." Metaphysically Bilhan represents a "confused" state of mind and a lack of self-assertion ("weak") that are the result of a giving way to the fulfillment of the thoughts and desires of the unredeemed subconsciousness.

The name *Zaavan* means "disquieted," "trembling," "terrified." Metaphysically Zaavan denotes a confused, fearful, unstable thought tendency in the outer or body consciousness of the individual.

The name *Akan* means "warped," "keen of vision." Metaphysically Akan represents a ruling thought, or at least a very strong influential thought, in the sense consciousness. This thought aids in diverting the individual from Truth and causes much trouble in the flesh. It is quick to perceive ("keen") on the sense plane but is blind ("warped") to the real truth of man's being.

The children of Dishan were Uz and Aran.

The name *Uz* means "substantiation," "formative power," "purpose," "fertility." Metaphysically Uz denotes the process of thought by which man arrives at a conclusion (be it Truth or error) and establishes it in consciousness ("substantiation," and so forth).

The name *Aran* means "active," "a wild goat," "firmness." Metaphysically Aran represents aggressiveness and a firmness or obstinacy of thought that is untrained and undisciplined and is guided not by understanding but by outer desires ("a wild goat," "firmness"). This makes a place of refuge for many of the sense ideas of man that should be overcome.

(For the names of the chiefs that came of the Horites—Lotan, Shobal, Zibeon, Anah, Dishon, Ezer, and Dishan—see interpretation of Gen. 36:20, 21.)

> *Gen. 36:31-39.* And these are the kings that reigned in the land of Edom, before there reigned any king over the children of Israel. And Bela the son of Beor reigned in Edom; and the name of his city was Dinhabah. And Bela died, and Jobab the son of Zerah of Bozrah reigned in his stead. And Jobab died, and Husham of the land of Temanites reigned in his stead. And Husham died, and Hadad the son of Bedad, who smote Midian in the field of Moab, reigned in his stead: and the name of his city was Avith. And Hadad died, and Samlah of Masrekah reigned in his stead. And Samlah died,

and Shaul of Rehoboth by the River reigned in his stead. And Shaul died, and Baalhanan the son of Achbor reigned in his stead. And Baalhanan the son of Achbor died, and Hadar reigned in his stead: and the name of his city was Pau; and his wife's name was Mehetabel, the daughter of Matred, the daughter of Me-zahab.

The name *Bela* means "destroy," "utterly consume." Metaphysically Bela represents destructive tendencies in consciousness.

The name *Dinhabah* means "robbers' den," "place of plundering." Metphysically Dinhabah signifies an aggregation of thoughts belonging to man's outer, carnal consciousness. These thoughts are error; they build up and sustain destructive sense tendencies that rob the real inner man of the substance that is rightly his. The name *Jobab* means "howling of wild beasts," "wail of tribulation." Metaphysically Jobab denotes the noisy, contentious tumultuousness of the outer personal man while under the dominion of the "mind of the flesh."

The name *Husham* means "hasting," "vehement," "passionate." Metaphysically Husham represents the hurried attitude of mind as related to satisfying physical desire. This attitude belongs to the outer consciousness and tends to confusion and disorder.

The name *Hadad* means "quick," "might," "majesty." Metaphysically Hadad represents the setting up as all-powerful of the intellect in its spiritually unawakened state.

The name *Samlah* means "outer garment," "mantle," "clothed." Metaphysically Samlah represents the general ruling characteristics of the outer, mortal phase of consciousness in man represented also by Edom.

The name *Shaul* means "desired," "demanded," "inquiring," "excavating." Shaul is a form of the name Saul, and its meaning is the same. Shaul symbolizes the will in individual consciousness, the presonal will.

The name *Baalhanan* means "Baal is gracious," "possessor of compassion," "lord of mercy." Metaphysically Baalhanan represents grace, mercy, and kindliness as belonging to and being expressed by the outer man ("Baal is gracious," and so forth). All these God qualities are expressed in a measure by the outer physical and mental man even before their true origin is understood to be spiritual. Until man learns the Truth, he usually takes to himself all the honor and glory resulting from any good that he does, instead of ascribing all honor and glory to God, Divine Mind.

The name *Hadar*, a form of the name Hadad, means "where one returns for rest," "concealed inner chamber," "hidden principle." While Hadad represents the setting up as all-powerful of the intellect in its spiritually unawakened state, Hadar, in addition to that, represents the "hidden principle" of all light, all wisdom, all knowledge (God, Spirit) that exists back of the intellect, back of every expression of intelligence or understanding.

Matred ("a short spear") and Mehetabel ("God benefits"), women of Edom, represent activities in the soul's progress toward spiritual perfection. Even the phase of the soul represented by Edom, the outer physical man, has impulses that are uplifting and that are ever moving toward the more perfect understanding and expression of Being.

Me-zahab, the name of Matred's father, means "water of gold," "emanations of the shining one." Me-zahab represents a wisdom that is of the one light or sun, Spirit, though it may be somewhat negative, as suggested by "water," "water of gold." Matred represents a pushing or urging forward of the soul ("thrusting forward"), by means of the wisdom symbolized by Me-zahab, to still higher and clearer light and dominion ("a scepter"). Mehetabel, the daughter of Matred ("to whom God does good," "God is the greatest good") represents the further awakening of the human soul to the goodness of God.

> *Gen. 36:40-43.* And these are the names of the chiefs that came to Esau, according to their families, after their places, by their names: chief Timna, chief Alvah, chief Jetheth, chief Oholibamah, chief Elah, chief Pinon, chief Kenaz, chief Teman, chief Mibzar, chief Magdiel, chief Iram: these are the chiefs of Edom, according to their habitations in the land of their possession. This is Esau, the father of the Edomites.

(For Timna see the interpretation of Gen. 36:12.)

The name *Alvah* means "sublimation (of evil)," "sublimity," "wicked." Metaphysically Alvah represents the animal nature exalting itself—"sublimation (of evil)." This is evil in the sight of Truth, since true sublimity and exaltation come only from the unifying of the entire being with the spiritual or Christ consciousness.

The name *Jetheth* means "securing," "stability," "subjection," Metaphysically Jetheth represents in the outer, material consciousness of man a ruling belief in the use of force to compel, drive, suppress in order to keep the individual steadfast. This of course is error and leads to bondage instead of true freedom.

The name *Elah* means "terebinth," "oak," a name implying strength, hardiness, and size. Metaphysically Elah represents the consciousness of strength and protection that is based on material beliefs; hence a limited consciousness, one likely to fail at the very time when most needed.

The name *Pinon* means "darkness," "perplexity," "hopelessness." Metaphysically Pinon represents the great anxiety, confusion, and hopelessness that often come over the purely mortal, darkened consciousness of man in times of error reaping.

The name *Kenaz* means "possessor," "lancer," "hunter," "flank." The name *Teman* means "abundance," "good faith," "firm." (For further comment see interpretation of Gen. 36:11.)

The name *Mibzar* means "inaccessible," "lofty," "impervious." Metaphysically Mibzar represents ruling belief of the carnal mind in man that the things of Spirit, of God, are hard to understand, that they are so far removed from the apparently finite mind of man that they are unattainable.

The name *Magdiel* means "most precious fruits of God," "praise of God," "God is renowned." Metaphysically Magdiel represents the truth about the outer and seemingly material phase of man's being Esau and Edom). This truth is that even man's physical body is the precious fruit of God. It has its origin in Spirit and is innately spiritual. It must eventually express and manifest God, Spirit, thus giving all praise, honor, and glory to the Father-Mind, through which it came into existence ("God is renowned").

Chapter XI

Joseph a Type of the Christ

GENESIS 37, 38, 39, 40, and 41

MAN, AN IDEA in Divine Mind, is manifested in various states of consciousness. These appear outwardly as personalities and take form as bodies. In describing states of consciousness the Bible uses the personality in a representative sense, with the meaning of the name as a key to the state of being explained.

The meaning of the name *Joseph* is "whom Jehovah will add to." He represents the "increasing" faculty of the mind, that state of consciousness in which we increase in all phases of our character. This is especially true of substance; for Joseph as imagination molds mind substance in the realm of forms. He had a coat of many colors; his dreams were always of forms and shapes—the sheaves of wheat, the stars and moon. An interpreter of dreams, the phenomenal was his field of action. This formative power is characteristic of the imagination, and among the twelve primal faculties of mind we find that this faculty of the imagination is represented by Joseph.

The Joseph faculty is the dreamer of dreams and the seer of visions, which are expressed always in forms and symbols. If you are a vivid dreamer and can correctly interpret your own dreams, you may know that you are developing your Joseph faculty. However, it is one thing to dream and quite another to interpret dreams correctly. All people dream more or less, but few can interpret dreams. Visions come under the same head, for dreams are not necessarily the sole concomitant of sleep.

> *Gen. 37:1-8.* And Jacob dwelt in the land of his father's sojournings, in the land of Canaan. These are the generations of Jacob. Joseph, being seventeen years old, was feeding the flock with his brethren; and he was a lad with the sons of Bilhah, and with the sons of Zilpah, his father's wives: and Joseph brought the evil report of them unto his father. Now Israel loved Joseph more than all his children, because he was the son of his old age: and he made him a coat of many colors. And his brethren saw that their father loved him more than all his brethren; and they hated him, and could not speak peaceably unto him.
>
> And Joseph dreamed a dream, and he told it to his brethren: and they hated him yet the more. And he said unto them, Hear, I pray you, this dream which I have dreamed: for, behold, we were binding sheaves in the field, and, lo, my sheaf arose, and also stood upright; and, behold, your sheaves came round about, and made obeisance to my sheaf. And his brethren said to him, Shalt thou indeed reign over us? or shalt thou indeed have dominion over us? And they hated him yet the more for his dreams, and for his words.

Joseph represents the faculty of imagination. This faculty produces the pictures or images that make visible every idea that the mind can conceive and reveals to the illumined intellect (Jacob) the activities of the other faculties (Joseph's brothers; in this case the sons of Bilhah and Zilpah).

Joseph was the proud owner of a coat of many colors, a gift from his father. The coat is the symbol of the Truth given to us by the Father. Truth in its entirety is symbolized by the seamless garment that Jesus wore, for it cannot be separated into divisions or parts. All truth is one Truth. Joseph's coat being of many colors indicates that when we open up this new realm of consciousness and begin to use the imagination, our conception of Truth is colored by the many previous mental states that have so long herded our flocks of thoughts. At this stage we have not yet come into the understanding, into the pure white light of unqualified Truth, that is symbolized by the seamless robe of unity.

The home of the imagination is in the realm of ideas, where another dimension of mind is opened to it, even the kingdom of the heavens. The imaging faculty gives man the ability to project himself through time and space and thus rise above these limitations as well as all other limitations. Even when the conscious mind is asleep the imagination continues its activity and we have dreams.

As we have learned, we cannot take our dreams literally but must interpret them by means of the symbols given us. For instance, Joseph's dream about the sheaves was a dream about substance and a prophecy of his attainment of a superior consciousness of universal substance. That consciousness of substance afterward brought forth fruit when he supervised the storage of grain in Egypt, and this grain furnished needed supply to his father and brothers and brought them to him. Imagination uses ideas to increase its store of universal substance and clothes ideas in form; for it is both a formative and an increasing faculty.

An uncontrolled imagination will often exaggerate

and increase one's consciousness of trivial or even
unreal things until both mind and body are affected.
(Joseph carried tales about his brothers to his father.)
The imagination is a very powerful faculty, and we
must learn to discipline it if we would make it practical
in serving our highest good. By following the inspiration of the supermind or Jehovah consciousness we can
control the imagination and direct its work to practical
ends.

Gen. 37:9-22. And he dreamed yet another
dream, and told it to his brethren, and said, Behold,
I have dreamed yet a dream; and, behold, the sun
and the moon and eleven stars made obeisance to me.
And he told it to his father, and to his brethren;
and his father rebuked him, and said unto him,
What is this dream that thou hast dreamed? Shall
I and thy mother and thy brethren indeed come to
bow down ourselves to thee to the earth? And his
brethren envied him; but his father kept the saying
in mind.
   And his brethren went to feed their father's flock
in Shechem. And Israel said unto Joseph, Are not
thy brethren feeding the flock in Shechem? come,
and I will send thee unto them. And he said to him,
Here am I. And he said to him, Go now, see whether
it is well with thy brethren, and well with the flock;
and bring me word again. So he sent him out of the
vale of Hebron, and he came to Shechem. And a certain man found him, and behold, he was wandering in the field: and the man asked him, saying,
What seekest thou? And he said, I am seeking my
brethren: tell me, I pray thee, where they are feeding *the flock.* And the man said, They are departed
hence; for I heard them say, Let us go to Dothan.
And Joseph went after his brethren, and found
them in Dothan.
   And they saw him afar off, and before he came

near unto them, they conspired against him to slay
him. And they said one to another, Behold, this
dreamer cometh. Come now therefore, and let us
slay him, and cast him into one of the pits, and we
will say, An evil beast hath devoured him: and we
shall see what will become of his dreams. And
Reuben heard it, and delivered him out of their
hand, and said, Let us not take his life. And Reuben
said unto them, Shed no blood; cast him into this
pit that is in the wilderness, but lay no hand upon
him: that he might deliver him out of their hand, to
restore him to his father.

In the foregoing Scripture Joseph's dream is very
significant. Jacob's words "Shall I and thy mother
and thy brethren indeed come to bow down ourselves
to thee to the earth?" are self-explanatory.

Shechem denotes a thought of burdens, which reveals that the brothers took to heart Joseph's superior
attitude. Joseph's talebearing propensity and the fact
that their father loved Joseph better than he did his
brothers served to stir up the antagonism of the other
sons toward Joseph. Jacob (the I AM) (functioning in
Hebron, which means "united," "bound by a common
bond") sent Joseph (the imagination) down into
Shechem ("bending down," "a burden") to see how
his brothers (the other faculties) fared. Jacob (the I
AM) operating in the consciousness of friendship and
unity did not take seriously the contention that Joseph
(the boasting imagination) had brought about.

The name *Dothan* means "two wells," "edicts,"
"customs." Dothan symbolizes the double standard of
thought that man holds regarding his life and substance, the law of Being on the one hand, custom on the
other. His customary beliefs lead to limited, warped

experiences, while an understanding of the true law of Being increases the activity of the power of God in his life and also makes him conscious of that activity. (Dothan is the place where Joseph found his brethren.)

Reuben, symbolizing the faculty of discernment in the outer, suggested the pit (which represents a pitfall or trap), intending later to deliver Joseph and thus restore him to the arms of his father.

> *Gen. 37:23-28.* And it came to pass, when Joseph was come unto his brethren, that they stripped Joseph of his coat, the coat of many colors that was on him; and they took him, and cast him into the pit: and the pit was empty, there was no water in it.
>
> And they sat down to eat bread: and they lifted up their eyes and looked, and, behold, a caravan of Ishmaelites was coming from Gilead, with their camels bearing spicery and balm and myrrh, going to carry it down to Egypt. And Judah said unto his brethren, What profit is it if we slay our brother and conceal his blood? Come, and let us sell him to the Ishmaelites, and let not our hand be upon him; for he is our brother, our flesh. And his brethren hearkened unto him. And there passed by Midianites, merchantmen; and they drew and lifted up Joseph out of the pit, and sold Joseph to the Ishmaelites for twenty pieces of silver. And they brought Joseph into Egypt.

Gilead represents the high place in consciousness where Spirit discerns and witnesses to what is true and to all man's thoughts and acts so that an adjustment may be made throughout mind and body. The Ishmaelites represent the fruit of the thought of the natural man at work in the flesh; also the consciousness that recognizes God but that, because of the seeming opposition of the outer world, does not find expression according to the highest standard.

The Midianites were enemies of the Israelites. The Midianites represent discrimination or judgment employed according to human standards. Judging according to outer appearances produces discordant thoughts and jealousies and their kin.

The fact that Joseph was sold as a slave into Egypt by his brothers signifies that at a certain stage of his unfoldment man will barter away his high ideals of Truth in order to go on living in sense consciousness. He will even debase his imagination (Joseph) and send it down into his body consciousness to stir up his emotions and get the thrill of sensation. However the faculty of imagination, if it has been trained and disciplined, will work for the good of man even in the darkened realm of sense (Egypt). Though the purpose in selling Joseph into Egypt was error, the result proved to be good. This shows the outworking of the law stated in Romans 8:28: "To them that love God all things work together for good." Even when error seems to be in the ascendancy there is that in us which remains true to God and finally brings about our deliverance. "The wrath of man shall praise thee."

The great point in the story is that Joseph, even when overcome by error from without and sold into Egyptian slavery, still remained true to the divine ideas of his Father. In any department of life the imagination will work for the development and perfection of the individual or for the direct opposite of this, depending on how it has been trained. It is a powerful faculty, for it forms ideas in substance and brings desire into manifestation. If the desires are allowed to run riot on the sense plane, the imagination will proceed di-

rectly to bring them into manifestation as inharmony or
disease. On the other hand, when the imagination is
kept busy with high ideas, ideas originally inspired in it
by the I AM, it is the most effective of all the faculties
for the work of spiritual development. Faithfulness to
high ideas, when coupled with an unshaken confidence
in the I AM, cannot be wholly overcome by error, nor
can anyone who exercises these faculties be kept for
long in the background.

Judah (representing prayer and praise), the fourth
son of Jacob and Leah, suggested the idea of selling
Joseph into Egypt rather than taking his life.

> *Gen. 37:29-36.* And Reuben returned unto the
> pit; and, behold, Joseph was not in the pit; and he
> rent his clothes. And he returned unto his brethren,
> and said, The child is not; and I, whither shall I go?
> And they took Joseph's coat, and killed a he-goat,
> and dipped the coat in the blood; and they sent
> the coat of many colors, and they brought it to their
> father, and said, This have we found: know now
> whether it is thy son's coat or not. And he knew it,
> and said, It is my son's coat; an evil beast hath de-
> voured him; Joseph is without doubt torn in
> pieces. And Jacob rent his garments, and put sack-
> cloth upon his loins, and mourned for his son many
> days. And all his sons and all his daughters rose up
> to comfort him; but he refused to be comforted; and
> he said, For I will go down to Sheol to my son
> mourning. And his father wept for him. And the
> Midianites sold him into Egypt unto Potiphar, an
> officer of Pharaoh's, the captain of the guard.

Jacob represents intellectual illumination. However
illumination on the intellectual plane often lacks discernment; it has not attained the power to express the
sure, steady, revealing light of Spirit. Jacob was in the

dark as regards the fate of his son Joseph (symbolical of the imagination). Hence Jacob was deceived by blood on the coat and mourned with the crowd.

Among the twelve faculties the imagination is least understood in its evolution from sense to soul consciousness. To this day those who function in sense echo the brothers of Joseph in their slighting exclamation, "Here comes that dreamer." Yet in art, science, literature, religion, and even business the cry is "Give us men of imagination!" The fact is there is no progress of man or the race without expansion of the imagination. The history of Joseph, the attempts of those nearest and dearest to him to thwart the unfoldment of his innate ability, and his final victory in attaining the exalted office of prime minister of Egypt, shows us in symbols how the whole man will eventually be glorified in Spirit.

However in the early stages of the Joseph quickening all the other faculties combine to destroy it; they think it visionary and impractical.

The blood-drenched coat represents the futile attempt of the outer realm of sense to kill out the inner Spirit life. Life marches on and the vision of the soul finds new expression in other states of consciousness.

Pharaoh represents the ego or will that rules the body under the natural law. Potiphar symbolizes the executive arm of the will.

Sheol is the abode of the dead conceived by the Hebrews as a subterranean region clothed in thick darkness. It represents the mental gloom into which the personal man is plunged when he gives himself over to thoughts of death and grief.

Gen. 38:1-11. And it came to pass at that time, that Judah went down from his brethren, and turned in to a certain Adullamite, whose name was Hirah. And Judah saw there a daughter of a certain Canaanite whose name was Shua; and he took her, and went in unto her. And she conceived, and bare a son; and he called his name Er. And she conceived again, and bare a son; and she called his name Onan. And she yet again bare a son, and called his name Shelah: and he was at Chezib, when she bare him. And Judah took a wife for Er his first-born, and her name was Tamar. And Er, Judah's first-born, was wicked in the sight of Jehovah; and Jehovah slew him. And Judah said unto Onan, Go in unto thy brother's wife, and perform the duty of a husbands' brother unto her, and raise up seed to thy brother. And Onan knew that the seed would not be his; and it came to pass, when he went in unto his brother's wife, that he spilled it on the ground, lest he should give seed to his brother. And the thing which he did was evil in the sight of Jehovah: and he slew him also. Then said Judah to Tamar his daughter-in-law, Remain a widow in thy father's house, till Shelah my son be grown up; for he said, Lest he also die, like his brethren. And Tamar went and dwelt in her father's house.

The predominant thought in the minds of the people at that time was to produce progeny (seed), and they restored to every device in order to attain their end.

Hirah was an Adullamite, a friend of Judah. The name Hirah means "splendid," "noble," "pure," "liberty." An Adullamite was a native of the city of Adullam, which represents a state of poise in prayer in which spiritual ideas flow into consciousness without obstruction. Being in the valley, it would not refer to a high, exalted state of mind in prayer but rather to an established equilibrium and adjustment in the body consciousness. But even if at first it seems to be only in the material consciousness, it imparts a "splendid," "noble" quality to the man and leads toward true "liberty." Such a state of consciousness is represented by Hirah.

Shua ("broad," "ample," "riches") represents the broad, rich thoughts of abundant substance in the depths of the subconscious mind. Judah united with a daughter of Shua, who symbolizes the feminine element in the rich subconsciousness. Three sons were born to this union:

Er represents observant, vigilant thoughts. It matters a great deal what one watches or gives attention to. If one persists in recognizing that which appears to be evil, one cannot obtain abiding life and good. (Er was wicked in the sight of Jehovah.)

Onan symbolizes thoughts pertaining to strength and vigor, yet thoughts that are not spiritual but of the intellect. They are influenced too by the lower emotions and tendencies of the carnal soul (Onan's mother was a Canaanitish woman); therefore they are likely to bring about inharmony and error because of the misdirection of energy. Yet in themselves these thoughts are good and if directed by spiritual understanding yield great blessings.

Shelah represents a sense of peace, harmony, and security that has come about through prayer, affirmation, and desire. However Shelah was born in Chezib, which symbolizes a deceptive state of mind that lies deep within the elemental life forces of the individual. This deceptive state of consciousness must be cleansed thoroughly of its error, its double-minded, idolatrous belief in a power of evil as well as a power of good, so that the truth of the one life and the one God, good, may be established within its depths.

> *Gen. 38:12-30.* And in process of time Shua's daughter, the wife of Judah, died; and Judah was comforted, and went up unto his sheep-shearers to Timnah, he and his friend Hirah the Adullamite. And it was told Tamar, saying, Behold, thy father-in-law goeth up to Timnah to shear his sheep. And she put off from her the garments of her widowhood, and covered herself with her veil, and wrapped herself, and sat in the gate of Enaim, which is by the way to Timnah; for she saw that Shelah was grown up, and she was not given unto him to wife. When Judah saw her, he thought her to be a harlot; for she had covered her face. And he turned unto her by the way, and said, Come, I pray thee, let me come in unto thee: for he knew not that she was his daughter-in-law. And she said, What wilt thou give me, that thou mayest come in unto me? And he said, I will send thee a kid of the goats from the flock. And she said, Wilt thou give me a pledge, till thou send it? And he said, What pledge shall I give thee? And she said, Thy signet and thy cord, and thy staff that is in thy hand. And he gave them to her, and came in unto her, and she conceived by him. And she arose, and went away, and put off her veil from her, and put on the garments of her widowhood. And Judah sent the kid of the goats by the hand of his friend the Adullamite, to receive the pledge from the woman's hand: but he found her not. Then he asked the men of her place, saying, Where is the prostitute, that was at Enaim by the wayside? And they said, There hath been no prostitute here. And he returned to Judah, and said, I have not found her; and also the men of the place said, There hath

been no prostitute here. And Judah said, Let her take it to her, lest we be put to shame: behold, I sent this kid, and thou hast not found her.

And it came to pass about three months after, that it was told Judah, saying, Tamar thy daughter-in-law hath played the harlot; and moreover, behold, she is with child by whoredom. And Judah said, Bring her forth, and let her be burnt. When she was brought forth, she sent to her father-in-law, saying, By the man, whose these are, am I with child: and she said; Discern, I pray thee, whose are these, the signet, and the cords, and the staff. And Judah acknowledged them, and said, She is more righteous than I, forasmuch as I gave her not to Shelah my son. And he knew her again no more. And it came to pass in the time of her travail, that, behold, twins were in her womb. And it came to pass, when she travailed, that one put out a hand: and the midwife took and bound upon his hand a scarlet thread, saying, This came out first. And it came to pass, as he drew back his hand, that, behold, his brother came out: and she said, Wherefore hast thou made a breach for thyself? therefore his name was called Perez. And afterward came out his brother, that had the scarlet thread upon his hand: and his name was called Zerah.

The name *Judah* means "praise Jehovah." Praise is closely related to prayer; under the law of mind, whatever we praise we increase. Praise is the key to the increase of life activity. If you depreciate your life you decrease your consciousness of life. Thus we find that, besides symbolizing the place in consciousness where we come in contact with the highest activities of Divine Mind, Judah also represents the central faculty of consciousness.

This faculty operates in the body consciousness

through the spinal cord, as well as in the top head, and finds its outer expression through the life center, which, unregenerated, is Judas, who hath a devil. When life is separated from the inner faculties and endeavors to find expression without their co-operation, man gives himself over to his animal nature and inclinations.

The name *Tamar* means "palm," "erect," "upright." Tamar represents victory and conquest through uprightness. "And Judah . . . said, She is more righteous than I, forasmuch as I gave her not to Shelah my son." This consciousness of victory or conquest and overcoming power is of the soul in the individual.

Timnah symbolizes the error race belief that a share of the life forces in man rightly belongs to the purely animal, physical, and sense part of his being. Judah kept his sheep in this Canaanitish city. Sheep represent the pure, natural life of the organism and Canaanites the elemental life forces in man.

Enaim, in whose gate Tamar sat, is supposed to be one with the city of Enam. The name means "two eyes," "double springs." It signifies the fountain of understanding in man, which because of his belief in good and evil, in materiality as well as spirituality, is dedicated to both generation and regeneration, both sense and Spirit. Double-mindedness causes instability. Stability is needed if one is to grow and develop spiritually. One establishes stability of character by giving oneself up wholly, with singleness of purpose, to the regenerative law.

The name *Perez* means "broken through," "torn asunder." Perez represents victory through praise, or making a way out of apparent limitation and error and prevailing over them by means of prayer and praise.

(Tamar said, "Wherefore hast thou made a breach for thyself? therefore his name was called Perez.")

Zerah ("sunrise," "birth of a child," "germination of a seed") represents awakening to new light, new understanding, in consciousness; the first conscious awakening to the presence of this new inner light or understanding. (The sun rises in the east, and the east denotes the within.)

In the journey from sense to Spirit the soul passes through many phases, misdirects its faculties, and practices multitudinous forms of dissipation or waste. (These verses in Genesis illustrate this fact.) But as man follows the light as it is given him to see the light, he gradually learns to understand himself and his soul activities. Then he begins to conform to spiritual law and to conserve his energies, forces, and substance, which in turn results in lifting up the whole man, spirit, soul, and body, out of the mire of materiality and sense into the new estate of the regenerate man, the Jesus Christ man.

> *Gen. 39:1-3.* And Joseph was brought down to Egypt; and Potiphar, an Officer of Pharaoh's, the captain of the guard, an Egyptian, bought him of the hand of the Ishmaelites, that had brought him down thither. And Jehovah was with Joseph, and he was a prosperous man; and he was in the house of his master the Egyptian. And his master saw that Jehovah was with him, and that Jehovah made all that he did to prosper in his hand.

Joseph's being brought down into Egypt signifies the imagination's becoming active in the body consciousness and in the subconsciousness. Imagination usually reaches out into the unseen world about us and forms substance according to the pattern of our thoughts. But its first duty is to go down into the Egyptian darkness of our material and sense thoughts and, under the law, lift the body consciousness to a higher plane. Body, soul, and spirit are unified as one, and the Truth student cannot afford to lose sight of the fact that all three are to be lifted up. Unless he is careful in this regard, the body consciousness may be left far behind the soul and spirit and some unfavorable reaction become manifest in the body or affairs.

The word *Pharaoh* means "the sun," "the Ra." Joseph was sold to Potiphar, an executive officer of Pharaoh's court, who represents one of the ruling ideas in the state of consciousness symbolized by Pharaoh, "the sun." Egypt symbolizes the material body consciousness ruled by the "sun" or solar plexus, which is the center in the subconsciousness. Pharaoh rules in obscurity or darkness because the great sun of the body, the solar plexus, is obscured or unknown to the conscious mind. The light of the sun of righteousness is veiled by our conscious living on the low plane of sense.

God prospers us when we give the best that is in us and do all things unto Him, acknowledging Him in all our affairs. This is a sure way to success, and when success does come we should realize that it resulted from the work of Spirit in us, because we made ourselves channels through which the Christ Mind could bring its ideas into manifestation. The true Christian never boasts that he is a self-made man, for he well knows that all that he is and has, together with all that he can ever hope to be or to have, is but God finding expression through him as life.

Gen. 39:4-6. And Joseph found favor in his sight, and he ministered unto him: and he made him overseer over his house, and all that he had he put into his hand. And it came to pass from the time that he made him overseer in his house, and over all that he had, that Jehovah blessed the Egyptian's house for Joseph's sake; and the blessing of Jehovah was upon all that he had, in the house and in the field. And he left all that he had in Joseph's hand; and he knew not aught *that was* with him, save the bread which he did eat. And Joseph was comely, and well favored.

Joseph was a spiritual character and worked from principle, hence he found favor in Potiphar's house and brought added blessings to it. This Scripture proves the simple outworking of the law. "And Joseph was comely, and well favored."

Gen. 39:7-23. And it came to pass after these things, that his master's wife cast her eyes upon Joseph; and she said, Lie with me. But he refused, and said unto his master's wife, Behold, my master knoweth not what is with me in the house, and he hath put all that he hath into my hand: he is not greater in this house than I; neither hath he kept back anything from me but thee, because thou art his wife: how then can I do this great wickedness, and sin against God? And it came to pass, as she spake to Joseph day by day, that he hearkened not unto her, to lie with her, *or* to be with her. And it came to pass about this time, that he went into the house to do his work; and there was none of the men of the house there within. And she caught him by his garment, saying, Lie with me: and he left his garment in her hand, and fled, and got him out. And it came to pass, when she saw that he had left his garment in her hand, and was fled forth, that she called unto the men of her house, and spake

unto them, saying, See, he hath brought in a Hebrew
unto us to mock us: he came in unto me to lie
with me, and I cried with a loud voice: and it came
to pass, when he heard that I lifted up my voice
and cried, that he left his garment by me, and fled,
and got him out. And she laid up his garment by
her, until his master came home. And she spake
unto him according to these words, saying, The
Hebrew servant, whom thou hast brought unto us,
came in unto me to mock me: and it came to pass,
as I lifted up my voice and cried, that he left his
garment by me, and fled out.

And it came to pass, when his master heard
the words of his wife, which she spake unto him,
saying, After this manner did thy servant to me;
that his wrath was kindled. And Joseph's master
took him, and put him into the prison, the place
where the king's prisoners were bound: and he was
there in the prison. But Jehovah was with Joseph,
and showed kindness unto him, and gave him favor
in the sight of the keeper of the prison. And the
keeper of the prison committed to Joseph's hand
all the prisoners that were in the prison; and
whatsoever they did there, he was the doer of it.
The keeper of the prison looked not to anything
that was under his hand, because Jehovah was
with him; and that which he did, Jehovah made
it to prosper.

The imagination is liable to get into trouble because it is so little understood. The sense consciousness
of the animal soul (Potiphar's wife) tempts us
through the imagination to gratify its sense desires.
When we refuse it expression there is a reaction, and
we seem for a time to be imprisoned or limited in
making progress. But if we patiently bide our time,
knowing that only good can come to us, the seemingly
imprisoned faculty (Joseph) will prove its God-given

power. Although physically imprisoned, Joseph (the imagination) expresses himself spiritually, for the Lord (law) is with him, and in due time he will come into his rightful place as one of the important faculties in the consciousness. (Jehovah, the law, was with Joseph.)

By faithfully performing the routine duties intrusted to one, even in a prison, one is certain to be advanced to a better and more remunerative position. However faithfulness has an even greater reward than this, for all the while the faithful one is building a firmer, truer, and more Godlike character in himself, which is an enduring recompense; for thus he enters into the possession of the true riches, the spiritual consciousness. Joseph was made the overseer of all the prisoners and later was released and given the highest position in the land as prime minister or adviser to Pharaoh.

> *Gen. 40:1-23.* And it came to pass after these things, that the butler of the king of Egypt and his baker offended their lord the king of Egypt. And Pharaoh was wroth against his two officers, against the chief of the butlers, and against the chief of the bakers. And he put them in ward in the house of the captain of the guard, into the prison, the place where Joseph was bound. And the captain of the guard charged Joseph with them, and he ministered unto them: and they continued a season in ward. And they dreamed a dream both of them, each man his dream, in one night, each man according to the interpretation of his dream, the butler and the baker of the king of Egypt, who were bound in the prison. And Joseph came in unto them in the morning, and saw them, and, behold, they were sad. And he asked Pharaoh's officers that were with

him in ward in his master's house, saying, Wherefore look ye so sad today? And they said unto him, We have dreamed a dream, and there is none that can interpret it. And Joseph said unto them, Do not interpretations belong to God? tell it me, I pray you.

And the chief butler told his dream to Joseph, and said to him, In my dream, behold, a vine was before me; and in the vine were three branches: and it was as though it budded, *and* its blossoms shot forth; *and* the clusters thereof brought forth ripe grapes: and Pharaoh's cup was in my hand; and I took the grapes, and pressed them into Pharaoh's cup, and I gave the cup into Pharaoh's hand. And Joseph said unto him, This is the interpretation of it: the three branches are three days; within yet three days shall Pharaoh lift up thy head, and restore thee unto thine office: and thou shalt give Pharaoh's cup into his hand, after the former manner when thou wast his butler. But have me in thy remembrance when it shall be well with thee, and show kindness, I pray thee, unto me, and make mention of me unto Pharaoh, and bring me out of this house: for indeed I was stolen away out of the land of the Hebrews: and here also have I done nothing that they should put me into the dungeon.

When the chief baker saw that the interpretation was good, he said unto Joseph, I also was in my dream, and, behold, three baskets of white bread were on my head: and in the uppermost basket there was of all manner of baked food for Pharaoh; and the birds did eat them out of the basket upon my head. And Joseph answered and said, This is the interpretation thereof: the three baskets are three days; within yet three days shall Pharaoh life up thy head from off thee, and shall hang thee on a tree; and the birds shall eat thy flesh from off thee. And it came to pass the third day, which was Pharaoh's birthday, that he made a feast unto all his servants:

and he lifted up the head of the chief butler and the head of the chief baker among his servants. And he restored the chief butler unto his butlership again; and he gave the cup into Pharaoh's hand: but he hanged the chief baker: as Joseph had interpreted to them. Yet did not the chief butler remember Joseph, but forgat him.

The chief butler and the chief baker were also in prison (the subconsciousness). This shows how we put the Spirit of life (the butler's wine) and of substance (the baker's bread) in bondage to or under the dominion of the sense man. By this time Joseph had become the warden in charge of all the prisoners, so that life and substance were under his control. When imagination controls these it exercises a powerful influence in the subconsciousness, bringing into manifestation many things that are so foreign and strange to us that they seem to come from without.

Joseph's interpretation of the dreams and the coming to pass of events exactly as he had predicted them gave him prestige as an interpreter of dreams and later brought him to the attention of the king.

What is the significance of dreams? The time of dreaming is either when we are losing consciousness in the process of going to sleep or when we are regaining it during awakening. When we are in deep sleep we live in the subconsciousness, a life of which the conscious mind knows nothing. This mind catches glimpses of it when we are making the transition from one state to the other. However we are in close touch with the superconscious, the mind of Spirit, when we are in the borderland state between sleeping and waking. At such times one who is spiritual-minded and

who at all times seeks to know what infinite wisdom
has to reveal, receives his message. Spirit speaks in
symbols such as the butler's cup of wine and the baker's
loaf of bread, and the trained faculty of imagination
(Joseph) interprets the symbols to the conscious mind.

> *Gen. 41:1-44.* And it came to pass at the end
> of two full years, that Pharaoh dreamed: and, behold,
> he stood by the river. And, behold, there came up
> out of the river seven kine, well-favored and fat-
> fleshed: and they fed in the reed-grass. And, behold,
> seven other kine came up after them out of the
> river, ill-favored and lean-fleshed, and stood by the
> other kine upon the brink of the river. And the ill-
> favored and lean-fleshed kine did eat up the seven
> well-favored and fat kine. So Pharaoh awoke. And
> he slept and dreamed a second time: and, behold,
> seven ears of grain came up upon one stalk, rank
> and good. And, behold, seven ears, thin and blasted
> with the east wind, sprang up after them. And the
> thin ears swallowed up the seven rank and full
> ears. And Pharaoh awoke, and, behold, it was a
> dream. And it came to pass in the morning that his
> spirit was troubled; and he sent and called for all
> the magicians of Egypt, and all the wise men there-
> of: and Pharaoh told them his dream; but there was
> none that could interpret them unto Pharaoh.
>
> Then spake the chief butler unto Pharaoh, saying,
> I do remember my faults this day: Pharaoh was
> wroth with his servants, and put me in ward in the
> house of the captain of the guard, me and the
> chief baker: and we dreamed a dream in one night,
> I and he; we dreamed each man according to the
> interpretation of his dream. And there was with us
> there a young man, a Hebrew, servant to the captain
> of the guard; and we told him, and he interpreted to
> us our dreams; to each man according to his dream
> he did interpret. And it came to pass, as he inter-

preted to us, so it was; me he restored unto mine office, and him he hanged.

Then Pharaoh sent and called Joseph, and they brought him hastily out of the dungeon: and he shaved himself, and changed his raiment, and came in unto Pharaoh. And Pharaoh said unto Joseph, I have dreamed a dream, and there is none that can interpret it: and I have heard say of thee, that when thou hearest a dream thou canst interpret it. And Joseph answered Pharaoh, saying, It is not in me: God will give Pharaoh an answer of peace. And Pharaoh spake unto Joseph, In my dream, behold, I stood upon the brink of the river: and, behold, there came up out of the river seven kine, fat-fleshed and well-favored; and they fed in the reed-grass: and, behold, seven other kine came up after them, poor and very ill-favored and lean-fleshed, such as I never saw in all the land of Egypt for badness: and the lean and ill-favored kine did eat up the first seven fat kine: and when they had eaten them up, it could not be known that they had eaten them; but they were still ill-favored, as at the beginning. So I awoke. And I saw in my dream, and, behold, seven ears came up upon one stalk, full and good: and, behold, seven ears, withered, thin, *and* blasted with the east wind, sprung up after them: and the thin ears swallowed up the seven good ears: and I told it unto the magicians; but there was none that could declare it to me.

And Joseph said unto Pharaoh, The dream of Pharaoh is one: what God is about to do he hath declared unto Pharaoh. The seven good kine are seven years; and the seven good ears are seven years: the dream is one. And the seven lean and ill-favored kine that came up after them are seven years, and also the seven empty ears blasted with the east wind; they shall be seven years of famine. That is the thing which I spake unto Pharaoh: what God is about to do he hath showed unto Pharaoh. Behold, there

come seven years of great plenty throughout all the
land of Egypt: and there shall arise after them
seven years of famine; and all the plenty shall be
forgotten in the land of Egypt; and the famine shall
consume the land; and the plenty shall not be known
in the land by reason of that famine which follow-
eth; for it shall be very grievous. And for that the
dream was doubled unto Pharaoh, it is because the
thing is established by God, and God will shortly
bring it to pass. Now therefore let Pharaoh look out
a man discreet and wise, and set him over the land
of Egypt. Let Pharaoh do *this,* and let him appoint
overseers over the land, and take up the fifth part of
the land of Egypt in the seven plenteous years. And
let them gather all the food of these good years that
come, and lay up grain under the hand of Pharaoh
for food in the cities, and let them keep it. And
the food shall be for a store to the land against the
seven years of famine, which shall be in the land
of Egypt; that the land perish not through the
famine.

And the thing was good in the eyes of Pharaoh,
and in the eyes of all his servants. And Pharaoh said
unto his servants, Can we find such a one as this, a
man in whom the spirit of God is? And Pharaoh
said unto Joseph, Forasmuch as God hath showed
thee all this, there is none so discreet and wise as
thou: thou shalt be over my house, and according
unto thy word shall all my people be ruled: only in
the throne will I be greater than thou. And Pharaoh
said unto Joseph, See, I have set thee over all the
land of Egypt. And Pharaoh took off his signet ring
from his hand, and put it upon Joseph's hand, and
arrayed him in vestures of fine linen, and put a gold
chain about his neck; and he made him to ride in
the second chariot which he had; and they cried
before him, Bow the knee: and he set him over all
the land of Egypt. And Pharaoh said unto Joseph,
I am Pharaoh, and without thee shall no man lift

up his hand or his foot in all the land of Egypt.

When a person has developed the Joseph state of consciousness and can give vivid form to his ideas by using his imaginative faculty, he does not take his dreams or visions in a literal sense. He rather unclothes the dream of its form by using the same power that he has of clothing ideas with form. Then he clearly sees the idea hidden behind the forms and symbols of his dream. He knows that all forms represent ideas and is able to resolve the form back into the primal idea of Divine Mind. Thus he is taught by Spirit more directly than is the ordinary individual. Spiritual Truth comes to him directly through an always open channel.

One of the surest proofs that you have opened yourself to Spirit is that you have symbolical dreams and can spiritually interpret them. Divine ideas are imaged in your placid soul like shadows on a quiet pool. You see them mentally and you may catch their import if you meditate patiently and persistently on the relation that each image or symbol bears to thought. Things are first ideas, then thoughts reduced in radiation to the plane of sense perception. When you still the senses you will begin to perceive the thoughts that are back of things. This may be a slow way, but it is a sure way to learn the language of mind, and in time it will enable you to translate all the shapes and forms you see on any plane of consciousness, into their corresponding thoughts. When this is accomplished you have become a Joseph and stand next to Jesus.

Joseph correctly interpreted the dreams of Pharaoh that later came to pass. The name *Pharaoh* means "the sun," "the king"; he is the king of the subconscious

realm whose throne is located in the solar plexus. This
brain of the body, plays an important role in directing
the circulation, the digestion and assimilation of food,
and so forth. Students of mind have discovered that
the solar plexus is but the organ through which the
ruling ego, Pharaoh, acts.

The signet ring that Pharaoh placed upon Joseph's
hand represents authority, and the fine raiment with
which he clothed Joseph symbolizes approval; that is,
the ruling power of the body gives to the imagination
authority and approval in both the within and the
without.

Gen. 41:45-57. And Pharaoh called Joseph's
name Zaphenath-paneah; and he gave him to wife
Asenath, the daughter of Potiphera priest of On.
And Joseph went out over the land of Egypt.

And Joseph was thirty years old when he stood
before Pharaoh king of Egypt. And Joseph went out
from the presence of Pharaoh, and went throughout
all the land of Egypt. And in the seven plenteous
years the earth brought forth by handfuls. And he
gathered up all the food of the seven years which
were in the land of Egypt, and laid up the food in
the cities: the food of the field, which was round
about every city, laid he up in the same. And Joseph
laid up grain as the sand of the sea, very much, until
he left off numbering; for it was without number.
And unto Joseph were born two sons before the year
of famine came, whom Asenath, the daughter of
Poti-phera priest of On, bare unto him. And Joseph called the name of the first-born Manasseh:
For, *said he,* God hath made me forget all my toil,
and all my father's house. And the name of the second called he Ephraim: For God hath made me
fruitful in the land of my affliction. And the seven
years of plenty, that was in the land of Egypt,

came to an end. And the seven years of famine began to come, according as Joseph had said: and there
was famine in all the lands; but in all the land of
Egypt there was bread. And when all the land of
Egypt was famished, the people cried to Pharaoh
for bread: and Pharaoh said unto all the Egyptians,
Go unto Joseph; what he saith to you, do. And the
famine was over all the face of the earth: and
Joseph opened all the storehouses, and sold unto
the Egyptians; and the famine was sore in the land
of Egypt. And all countries came into Egypt to
Joseph to buy grain, because the famine was sore in
all the earth.

In lower Egypt during the time of Joseph was the
city of On, one of the world's oldest cities. Here was
located one of the great temples of Egypt, whose
high priest was Potiphera. The daughter of the high
priest was Asenath, who became Joseph's wife.

Asenath represents the feminine or love side of the
natural man. Two sons were born of this union, Manasseh (understanding) and Ephraim (will), and they inherited Joseph's allotment in the Promised Land (regenerated perfect body). Understanding and will are
dominant forces in the race because they are necessary
in the development of the soul. If the imagination
(Joseph) were wholly free (unmarried or without responsibility), it would indulge in daydreams and
fanciful schemes that could not be worked out in a
practical world governed by inexorable law. If in this
dreamy state the mind is given a definite thought of
Truth (such as monotheism, taught at the school of
On) and is joined with the natural soul (Asenath), it
brings forth the two stabilizing mental qualities will
and understanding, symbolized by Joseph's sons

Ephraim and Manasseh.

The name *Manasseh* means "who makes to forget."
Manasseh was the first son born to Joseph, who had a
great deal to forget. Joseph needed to forget the wrong
done him by his brothers, the temptation of Potiphar's
wife, and the error of long imprisonment. Thus Manasseh represents the understanding of how to use one's
ability to forget or deny that which is no longer profitable to the man.

The name *Ephraim* means "very fruitful." Ephraim
represents the ability of man to add to his consciousness through the action of his will whatever he may
choose to affirm and to become fruitful in his thoughts
even in the land of affliction.

The first step for the beginner in Truth is to set up
a new and better state of consciousness based on the
absolute. He must develop the Manasseh quality of
forgetting the not-good by denial and the Ephraim
quality of increasing the good by affirming it to be the
real. The understanding and the will must be especially
active in one who would overcome and master the
sensations of the body, which is one of the first steps
in its regeneration.

Joseph was thirty years old when he began his
great work in Egypt. At about that age a man completes a natural cycle in the evolution of his soul and
is ready for an adventure into the spiritual. When
the spiritually awakening man has reached this stage
of development there is an increase of energy throughout the body. As we have previously noted, the imagination is the "increasing faculty" as well as the
formative faculty. The Hebrew meaning of the name
Joseph is "Jehovah shall increase." The great increase

that comes at this period in his unfoldment lasts about seven years, or passes through seven stages of activity, symbolized in Pharaoh's dream by the seven fat kine and the seven full ears of corn.

Those who are wise will conserve this energy in the storehouse of subconsciousness, because there is certain to be a reaction proportionate to action. The law holds good for every form of energy. When this generated force is properly conserved, the reaction is not felt. When we exalt the Joseph state of consciousness (as did Pharaoh) and let it rule in our body, Spirit will show us how to handle the situation. Then we shall make storage batteries of our "cities," which are the ganglionic centers of the body (Egypt). When Pharaoh gave Joseph the power and authority to do this conserving work, he changed his name to Zaphenath-paneah, a compound word meaning "savior of the universe," "sustainer of the life of the world," "governor of the district or place of stored-up life." This would clearly indicate that the body should be ruled over by the spiritualized imaginative faculty working under the direction and by the power of Spirit.

The word *famine* implies extreme scarcity of food, reducing people to an extremity of hunger, of starvation. Here Egypt (the subconsciousness), the storehouse of plenty, is the source from which all the surrounding countries (states of consciousness) come for sustenance when the outer man has exhausted his resources.

The seven years of plenty followed by seven years of famine show that the unregenerate man lives in a consciousness of duality, seeing good and evil, heat and cold, plenty and poverty, feast and famine; the spirit-

ualized imagination (Joseph) sees the whole of life
as one. He sees no lack but recognizes a coming consciousness of lack and relates it to the present consciousness of plenty, and by this unifying work he lays
up a store of substance for future use. The imagination
should rank high among all the faculties of man, for
without its magic touch life would become flat, stale,
and meaningless; but once imagination is awakened,
man is filled with health, life, substance, and abundance.

Chapter XII

The I AM and Its Faculties in the Body

GENESIS 42, 43, 44, 45, and 46

THE BIRTH of Jacob, son of Isaac and Rebekah, is described in the 25th chapter of Genesis, and the remainder of the book, or exactly half of its fifty chapters, tells of the activities of Jacob and his twelve sons. Such emphasis shows the importance of Jacob as a symbol of the I AM, that spiritual man whose creation, manifestation, and development is the theme of Genesis. This ideal man does not fully develop in the Jacob symbol but continues to unfold all through the Bible, coming into full expression as Christ Jesus. As Jacob however we find man developing his spiritual faculties (twelve sons) and then taking them down into Egypt (body consciousness) to begin the great work of redemption.

Involution always precedes evolution. The I AM and its spiritual faculties must be sent down into the body consciousness before the evolution of the spiritual man can begin. Spirit does not direct the work of regeneration from a distant heaven, but from its center in the crown of the head directs and transforms the very heart of each atom of the body.

> *Gen. 42:1-5.* Now Jacob saw that there was grain in Egypt, and Jacob said unto his sons, Why do ye look one upon another? And he said, Behold, I have heard that there is grain in Egypt: get you down thither, and buy for us from thence; that we

may live, and not die. And Joseph's ten brethren
went down to buy grain from Egypt. But Benjamin,
Joseph's brother, Jacob sent not with his brethren;
for he said, Lest peradventure harm befall him. And
the sons of Israel came to buy among those that
came: for the famine was in the land of Canaan.

Many workers in Truth think it is useless to go
down into this obscure kingdom of Egypt within each
man. They are not willing for Joseph to spend a part
of his time in that country making ready the storehouses and filling them with the vitality that will be
needed when the outer man has used up his resources.
These persons will find that they cannot have that joyous reunion of mind and body with all the faculties unless they are willing to let the higher thought go
consciously down into the body (Egypt) and rule
there, as Joseph ruled second only to Pharaoh himself.

We must not forget that it is down in Egypt (the
body) that we find the "grain" or substance that is required to sustain the whole man. The several visits
of Joseph's brothers to Egypt for grain and their final
reconciliation with him are a symbolical representation
of the manner in which we make connection with the
obscured vitality center within the organism, eventually bringing all our faculties into conjunction with
it, that it may in due course be lifted up to a spiritual
manifestation.

Canaan, from which Jacob and his sons migrated,
means "lowland," while Egypt means "tribulation."
To the metaphysician these names represent the two
phases of substance. Canaan represents the invisible
substance that surrounds and interpenetrates all bodies,
while Egypt represents substance that has been formed

as material and is perceived by the senses. The faculties of mind, represented by Jacob's sons, first inhabit the realm of invisible substance and are sustained by it; then they pass into the realm of the visible or formed substance—from Canaan to Egypt. This is the way in which the mind forms the soul and its vehicle, the physical body. Thoughts are first expressed as ideas in the invisible substance, then they enter into visibility as things.

When man is ignorant of the creative power of his mind, he gravitates to a material basis in all his thinking and acting. Among the sons of Jacob only Joseph (imagination) had knowledge of the reality of the invisible. The others scoffed at him as a visionary. They refused to plant their seed thoughts in the soil of the invisible substance, and the result was a famine —there was no grain in Canaan.

When we refuse to observe the law of creative mind, we oppose the working out of life's problems in the divine way, according to principle, and are compelled to work them out in a harder way. This is why the "way of the transgressor is hard." Thousands go down into Egypt and suffer the trials and limitations of materiality when, if they were more observant of the law and obedient to their spiritual leadings, they might remain in the joy and freedom of Christ. Yet even in the world of materiality (Egypt) the chosen of the Lord (Israelites) prosper and multiply. The children of Jacob increased from a few score to over two million during their sojourn in Egypt. No matter how great your trials or how dark your way may seem, if you hold to your belief in the omnipresence, omnipotence, and goodness of God, you will succeed, and no material oppression can hold you down.

> *Gen. 42:6-24.* And Joseph was the governor
> over the land; he it was that sold to all the people of
> the land. And Joseph's brethren came, and bowed
> down themselves to him with their faces to the
> earth. And Joseph saw his brethren, and he knew
> them, but made himself strange unto them, and spake
> roughly with them; and he said unto them, Whence
> came ye? And they said, From the land of Canaan
> to buy food. And Joseph knew his brethren, but
> they knew not him. And Joseph remembered the
> dreams which he dreamed of them, and said unto
> them, Ye are spies; to see the nakedness of the
> land ye are come. And they said unto him, Nay, my
> lord, but to buy food are thy servants come. We are
> all one man's sons; we are true men, thy servants
> are no spies. And he said unto them, Nay, but to see
> the nakedness of the land ye are come. And they said,
> We thy servants are twelve brethren, the sons of
> one man in the land of Canaan; and, behold, the
> youngest is this day with our father, and one is not.
> And Joseph said unto them, That is it that I spake
> unto you, saying, Ye are spies: hereby ye shall be
> proved: by the life of Pharaoh ye shall not go forth
> hence, except your youngest brother come hither.
> Send one of you, and let him fetch your brother,
> and ye shall be bound, that your words may be
> proved, whether there be truth in you: or else by
> the life of Pharaoh surely ye are spies. And he put
> them all together into ward three days.
>
> And Joseph said unto them the third day, This
> do, and live; for I fear God: if ye be true men, let
> one of your brethren be bound in your prisonhouse;
> but go ye, carry grain for the famine of your houses:
> and bring your youngest brother unto me; so shall
> your words be verified, and ye shall not die. And
> they did so. And they said one to another, We are
> verily guilty concerning our brother, in that we saw

the distress of his soul, when he besought us, and we would not hear; therefore is this distress come upon us. And Reuben answered them, saying, Spake I not unto you, saying, Do not sin against the child; and ye would not hear? therefore also, behold, his blood is required. And they knew not that Joseph understood them; for there was an interpreter between them. And he turned himself about from them, and wept; and he returned to them, and spake to them, and took Simeon from among them, and bound him before their eyes.

A spy is one who seeks to discover certain facts by stealthy observation. Joseph was testing out his brothers in his endeavor to ascertain where they stood in consciousness; also whether his beloved father Jacob (the I AM) was still alive (functioning in the conscious mind) and how it was with him. He also desired to see again his own brother Benjamin (faith). All in all Joseph was yearning to see his kindred and to be reunited with them.

The brothers were greatly troubled when Joseph insisted that they bring Benjamin, their youngest brother, down into Egypt. Benjamin, among the twelve faculties, represents faith. Imagination (Joseph) needs faith (Benjamin) to complete its work and to hold fast the gains it has made. Like Joseph's brothers, we think that faith is too pure, too lofty and holy to risk contaminating it with the things of material sense. We like to hold it on the high plane of spiritual consciousness rather than send it down into the body consciousness. Yet this we must do if we are to save the other faculties and the whole man. The brothers were in grave danger of being held prisoners, or so it seemed to them, unless Benjamin were brought down into

Egypt. They remembered their father's great grief over
the loss of Joseph and they felt that the sacrifice of
parting with Benjamin, the other son of his beloved
Rachel, would be too much for him.

During these trying moments their minds recalled
Joseph and his cries for mercy, to which they had turned
a deaf ear when they sold him into slavery. Joseph's
immediate presence may have had something to do
with suggesting this memory even though they did not
recognize him. Conscience stricken, they said one to
another, "We are verily guilty concerning our brother,
in that we saw the distress of his soul, when he besought
us, and we would not hear; therefore is this distress
come upon us." They evidently understood something
of the law of sowing and reaping in those days, for
at least they did not lay their troubles to charge of
Providence, as is done so much now. They thought they
were about to reap what they had sown years before.

Simeon ("one who listens and obeys") was held in
bondage by Joseph, which reveals that soul receptivity
and obedience are necessary adjuncts to the imagination.

> *Gen. 42:25-38.* Then Joseph commanded to fill
> their vessels with grain, and to restore every man's
> money into his sack, and to give them provision for
> the way: and thus was it done unto them.
>
> And they laded their asses with their grain,
> and departed thence. And as one of them opened
> his sack to give his ass provender in the lodging-
> place, he espied his money; and, behold, it was in
> the mouth of his sack. And he said unto his brethren,
> My money is restored; and, lo, it is even in my
> sack: and their heart failed them, and they turned
> trembling one to another, saying, What is this that
> God hath done unto us? And they came unto Jacob

their father unto the land of Canaan, and told him all that had befallen them, saying, The man, the lord of the land, spake roughly with us, and took us for spies of the country. And we said unto him, We are true men; we are no spies; we are twelve brethren, sons of our father; one is not, and the youngest is this day with our father in the land of Canaan. And the man, the lord of the land, said unto us, Hereby shall I know ye are true men: leave one of your brethren with me, and take *grain for* the famine of your houses, and go your way; and bring your youngest brother unto me: then shall I know that ye are no spies, but that ye are true men: so will I deliver you your brother, and ye shall traffic in the land.

And it came to pass as they emptied their sacks, that, behold, every man's bundle of money was in his sack: and when they and their father saw their bundles of money, they were afraid. And Jacob their father said unto them, Me have ye bereaved of my children: Joseph is not, and Simeon is not, and ye will take Benjamin away: all these things are against me. And Reuben spake unto his father, saying, Slay my two sons, if I bring him not to thee: deliver him into my hand, and I will bring him to thee again. And he said, My son shall not go down with you; for his brother is dead, and he only is left: if harm befall him by the way in which ye go, then will ye bring down my gray hairs with sorrow to Sheol.

Joseph (the imaging power of the mind) has access to unlimited supply (all the substance in Egypt). Joseph knew that his brothers possessed the same capacities that he himself did, but they were not consciously aware of this. Through Joseph they (the other faculties) are being educated; the famine in their land means that they lack understanding of their spiritual resources. Joseph (imagination) is the avenue through which these resources are brought to them, and one of the lessons here presented under the guise of restoring to them their purchase money is "Give, and it shall be given unto you." They are treated as spies or aliens in this land of omnipresent divine resources because they are ignorant of the fact that they belong in the family of God and that Joseph is their kin.

Jacob, grieving over the loss of two sons and fearful at the prospect of losing the third and dearest son next to Joseph (Benjamin), represents the personal man who is still in bondage to personal thoughts. But Reuben (spiritual perception) is launching out and is beginning to realize that all is well (in divine order) and is willing to offer up his most valuable possessions as surety for the safe return of his brother Benjamin: "Slay my two sons, if I bring him not to thee."

"If harm befall him by the way in which ye go, then will ye bring down my gray hairs with sorrow to Sheol" is indicative of the grief, sorrow, and darkened state of mind that result when the human consciousness sees death or the loss of loved ones as reality.

> *Gen. 43:1-15.* And the famine was sore in the land. And it came to pass, when they had eaten up the grain which they had brought out of Egypt, their father said unto them, Go again, buy us a little food. And Judah spake unto him, saying, The man did solemnly protest unto us, saying, Ye shall not see my face, except your brother be with you. If thou wilt send our brother with us, we will go down and buy thee food: but if thou wilt not send him, we will not go down; for the man said unto us, Ye shall not see my face, except your brother be

with you. And Israel said, Wherefore dealt ye
so ill with me, as to tell the man whether ye had
yet a brother? And they said, The man asked
straitly concerning ourselves, and concerning our
kindred, saying, Is your father yet alive? have ye
another brother? and we told him according to the
tenor of these words: could we in any wise know
that he would say, Bring your brother down? And
Judah said unto Israel his father, Send the lad with
me, and we will arise and go; that we may live, and
not die, both we, and thou, and also our little ones.
I will be surety for him; of my hand shalt thou
require him: if I bring him not unto thee, and set
him before thee, then let me bear the blame for
ever: for except we had lingered, surely we had now
returned a second time. And their father Israel said
unto them, If it be so now, do this: take the choice
fruits of the land in your vessels, and carry down
the man a present, a little balm, and a little honey,
spicery and myrrh, nuts, and almonds; and take
double money in your hand; and the money that was
returned in the mouth of your sacks carry again
in your hand; peradventure it was an oversight: take
also your brother, and arise, go again unto the man:
and God Almighty give you mercy before the man,
that he may release unto you your other brother
and Benjamin. And if I be bereaved of my children,
I am bereaved. And the man took that present, and
they took double money in their hand, and Benjamin; and rose up, and went down to Egypt, and
stood before Joseph.

Here again the outer man has appropriated all his
substance and must go down into Egypt to replenish
his store. Judah (the prayer faculty) calls the attention
of Jacob (the I AM) to the fact that the journey
would be fruitless unless they were accompanied by
Benjamin (awakening faith). It really requires awaken-

ing faith to open the door into the storehouse of substance over which the imagination (Joseph) rules.

With great bitterness of heart Jacob finally consents. He directs his sons (the faculties) to take with them presents—"a little balm, and a little honey, spicery and myrrh, nuts, and almonds; and take double money in your hand; and the money that was returned in the mouth of your sacks carry again in your hand"—which represent the limited substance ideas of the personal man. His sons go forth into Egypt with Jacob's blessing, which Jacob has poured out upon his idea of substance, though it be meager. By so doing he has opened the way for a larger spiritual inflow. "The blessing of Jehovah, it maketh rich."

Gen. 43:16-34. And when Joseph saw Benjamin with them, he said to the steward of his house, Bring the men into the house, and slay, and make ready; for the men shall dine with me at noon. And the man did as Joseph bade; and the man brought the men to Joseph's house. And the men were afraid, because they were brought to Joseph's house; and they said, Because of the money that was returned in our sacks at the first time are we brought in; that he may seek occasion against us, and fall upon us, and take us for bondmen, and our asses. And they came near to the steward of Joseph's house, and they spake unto him at the door of the house, and said, Oh, my lord, we came indeed down at the first time to buy food: and it came to pass, when we came to the lodging-place, that we opened our sacks, and, behold, every man's money was in the mouth of his sack, our money in full weight: and we have brought it again in our hand. And other money have we brought down in our hand to buy food: we know not who put our money in our sacks. And he said, Peace be to you, fear not: your God, and the God of your father, hath given you treasure in your sacks: I had your money. And he brought Simeon out unto them. And the man brought the men into Joseph's house, and gave them water, and they washed their feet; and he gave their asses provender. And they made ready the present against Joseph's coming at noon: for they heard that they should eat bread there.

And when Joseph came home, they brought him the present which was in their hand into the house, and bowed down themselves to him to the earth. And he asked them of their welfare, and said, Is your father well, the old man of whom ye spake? Is he yet alive? And they said, Thy servant our father is well, he is yet alive. And they bowed the head, and made obeisance. And he lifted his eyes, and saw Benjamin his brother, his mother's son, and said, Is this your youngest brother, of whom ye spake unto me? And he said, God be gracious unto thee, my son. And Joseph made haste; for his heart yearned over his brother: and he sought where to weep; and he entered into his chamber, and wept there. And he washed his face, and came out; and he refrained himself, and said, Set on bread. And they set on for him by himself, and for them by themselves, and for the Egyptians, that did eat with him, by themselves: because the Egyptians might not eat bread with the Hebrews; for that is an abomination unto the Egyptians. And they sat before him, the first-born according to his birthright, and the youngest according to his youth: and the men marveled one with another. And he took *and sent* messes unto them from before him: but Benjamin's mess was five times so much as any of theirs. And they drank, and were merry with him.

It seems almost sacrilegious to give an interpretation of this Scripture, because it is so beautiful as literature and so true on the natural plane. However it

is symbolical of the consummation or final union of the
imagination (Joseph) with its brother faculty faith
(Benjamin). Substance (represented by the feast set
before them) also plays an important part. This is the
fulfillment of the law through faith and imagination
and their auxiliary powers.

The Egyptians and Hebrews sat apart from Joseph.
The Egyptians represent substance on the formed or
physical plane, and the Hebrews represent substance in
the spiritual or invisible realm. Joseph represents the
directive or molding power of Spirit.

The movements of mind just described also presage
a new cycle or round in soul unfoldment.

Gen. 44:1-13. And he commanded the steward
of his house, saying, Fill the men's sacks with food,
as much as they can carry, and put every man's money
in his sack's mouth. And put my cup, the silver cup,
in the sack's mouth of the youngest, and his grain
money. And he did according to the word that
Joseph had spoken. As soon as the morning was light,
the men were sent away, they and their asses. *And*
when they were gone out of the city, and were not
yet far off, Joseph said unto his steward, Up, follow
after the men; and when thou dost overtake them,
say unto them, Wherefore have ye rewarded evil
for good? Is not this that in which my lord drinketh,
and whereby he indeed divineth? ye have done evil
in so doing. And he overtook them, and he spake unto
them these words. And they said unto him, Wherefore speaketh my lord such words as these? Far be it
from thy servants that they should do such a thing.
Behold, the money, which we found in our sacks'
mouths, we brought again unto thee out of the land
of Canaan: how then should we steal out of thy lord's
house silver or gold? With whomsoever of thy
servants it be found, let him die, and we also will be

my lord's bondmen. And he said, Now also let it be according unto your words: he with whom it is found shall be my bondman; and ye shall be blameless. Then they hasted, and took down every man his sack to the ground, and opened every man his sack. And he searched, *and* began at the eldest, and left off at the youngest: and the cup was found in Benjamin's sack. Then they rent their clothes, and laded every man his ass, and returned to the city.

Joseph in Egypt symbolizes the word of the imagination in subconsciousness, or the involution of a high spiritual idea. In this Scripture the imagination is given the opportunity to try out the strength of the other faculties (Joseph's brothers) in an endeavor to discover if they have come to that place in consciousness where they can work from the viewpoint of Truth, regardless of all else.

Joseph's having the cup put into Benjamin's sack represents one of the subtle ways in which the Lord imparts Truth to man's consciousness. The cup symbolizes the word or measure in which Truth is realized, and although the recipient is not aware of it, it does its work and finally comes to consciousness in the presence of Jehovah's representative (Joseph) and all the other faculties (brothers).

This cup, the Scripture relates, was used by Joseph to "divine" with, which shows its mystical quality. It is also related to the cup that Jesus used at the Last Supper.

Gen. 44:14-34. And Judah and his brethren came to Joseph's house; and he was yet there: and they fell before him on the ground. And Joseph said unto them, What deed is this that ye have done? know ye not that such a man as I can indeed divine? And

Judah said, What shall we say unto my lord? what
shall we speak? or how shall we clear ourselves? God
hath found out the iniquity of thy servants: behold,
we are my lord's bondmen, both we, and he also
in whose hand the cup is found. And he said, Far
be it from me that I should do so: the man in whose
hand the cup is found, he shall be my bondman;
but as for you, get you up in peace unto your father.

Then Judah came near unto him, and said, Oh,
my lord, let thy servant, I pray thee, speak a word in
my lord's ears, and let not thine anger burn against
thy servant: for thou are even as Pharaoh. My lord
asked his servants, saying, Have ye a father, or a
brother? And we said unto my lord, We have a
father, an old man, and a child of his old age, a little
one; and his brother is dead, and he alone is left of
his mother; and his father loveth him. And thou
saidst unto thy servants, Bring him down unto me,
that I may set mine eyes upon him. And we said unto
my lord, The lad cannot leave his father: for if he
should leave his father, his father would die. And
thou saidst unto thy servants, Except your youngest
brother come down with you, ye shall see my face
no more. And it came to pass when we came up unto
thy servant my father, we told him the words of my
lord. And our father said, Go again, buy us a little
food. And we said, We cannot go down: if our
youngest brother be with us, then will we go down;
for we may not see the man's face, except our youngest brother be with us. And thy servant my father said
unto us, Ye know that my wife bare me two sons:
and the one went out from me, and I said, Surely he
is torn in pieces; and I have not seen him since: and
if ye take this one also from me, and harm befall him,
ye will bring down my gray hairs with sorrow to
Sheol. Now therefore when I come to thy servant my
father, and the lad is not with us; seeing that his life
is bound up in the lad's life; it will come to pass,
when he seeth that the lad is not *with us*, that he

will die: and thy servants will bring down the gray hairs of thy servant our father with sorrow to Sheol. For thy servant became surety for the lad unto my father, saying, If I bring him not unto thee, then shall I bear the blame to my father for ever. Now therefore, let thy servant, I pray thee, abide instead of the lad a bondman to my lord; and let the lad go up with his brethren. For how shall I go up to my father, if the lad be not with me? lest I see the evil that shall come on my father.

Judah made an effective plea for Benjamin and his father. This is one of the most excellent things of its kind in all literature. It shows a complete change of mind and heart, which is true repentance. Judah had proposed to sell Joseph into slavery. The praise faculty represented by Judah had been on a low plane of expression at that time. But Judah had grown with the years (as the praise faculty grows with use) and had become most unselfish, even to the point of offering himself as a hostage for his youngest brother. Where selfishness, jealousy, and hardness had ruled him before, there was now unselfish love, humility, devotion to principle, and willingness to serve even to the extent of giving up his liberty or his life, if need be, for the sake of his father (the I AM).

True repentance is always followed by forgiveness, which is a complete wiping out of the error thought from consciousness and a full deliverance from the inharmony that the error thought has produced.

Gen. 45:1-15. Then Joseph could not refrain himself before all them that stood by him; and he cried, Cause every man to go out from me. And there stood no man with him, while Joseph made himself known unto his brethren. And he wept aloud: and the Egyptians heard, and the house of Pharaoh heard. And Joseph said unto his brethren, I am Joseph; doth my father yet live? And his brethren could not answer him; for they were troubled at his presence. And Joseph said unto his brethren, Come near to me, I pray you. And they came near. And he said, I am Joseph your brother, whom ye sold unto Egypt. And now be not grieved, nor angry with yourselves, that ye sold me hither: for God did send me before you to preserve life. For these two years hath the famine been in the land: and there are yet five years, in which there shall be neither plowing nor harvest. And God sent me before you to preserve you a remnant in the earth, and to save you alive by a great deliverance. So now it was not you that sent me hither, but God: and he hath made me a father to Pharaoh, and lord of all his house, and ruler over all the land of Egypt. Haste ye, and go up to my father, and say unto him, Thus saith thy son Joseph, God hath made me lord of all Egypt: come down unto me, tarry not; and thou shalt dwell in the land of Goshen, and thou shalt be near unto me, thou, and thy children, and thy children's children, and thy flocks, and thy herds, and all that thou hast: and there will I nourish thee; for there are yet five years of famine; lest thou come to poverty, thou, and thy household, and all that thou hast. And, behold, your eyes see, and the eyes of my brother Benjamin, that it is my mouth that speaketh unto you. And ye shall tell my father of all my glory in Egypt, and of all that ye have seen: and ye shall haste and bring down my father hither. And he fell upon his brother Benjamin's neck, and wept; and Benjamin wept upon his neck. And he kissed all his brethren, and wept upon them: and after that his brethren talked with him.

After hearing Judah's plea Joseph could restrain himself no longer. He made himself known to his brothers, and there was a happy reunion. This whole

Scripture proves that back of all the Spirit of the Lord is working to bring forth the perfect world. "To them that love God all things work together for good."

Joseph was the chosen servant of the Lord to preserve not only the Egyptians but also those who dwelt in the surrounding countries. Out of a seemingly unbearable jealous condition the lives of thousands were preserved, and most important, a wonderful soul unfoldment took place in the whole Israelitish race. Joseph symbolizes the sublime idea of Truth's going down into the darkened sense consciousness and under the law raising it up and out of sense into Spirit. Joseph was seemingly forced to go to Egypt by his brothers, yet he was sent by the Lord to prepare for the maintenance of Jacob's family through the period of dearth that later came to Canaan. The Truth idea he represents, when taken down into the sense consciousness, establishes there a new realization of life that results in the regeneration of the entire man. We must often go consciously into every part of our body and build it up in Truth with new ideas of life and substance.

The name *Goshen* means "drawing near." Metaphysically it represents a state of unity.

Gen. 45:16-28. And the report thereof was heard in Pharaoh's house, saying, Joseph's brethren are come: and it pleased Pharaoh well, and his servants. And Pharaoh said unto Joseph, Say unto thy brethren, This do ye: lade your beasts, and go, get you unto the land of Canaan; and take your father and your households, and come unto me: and I will give you the good of the land of Egypt, and ye shall eat the fat of the land. Now thou art commanded, this do ye: take you wagons out of the land of Egypt for your little ones, and for your wives, and bring your

father, and come. Also regard not your stuff; for the
good of all the land of Egypt is yours.

And the sons of Israel did so: and Joseph gave
them wagons, according to the commandment of
Pharaoh, and gave them provisions for the way. To
all of them he gave each man changes of raiment;
but to Benjamin he gave three hundred pieces of
silver, and five changes of raiment. And to his
father he sent after this manner: ten asses laden
with the good things of Egypt, and ten she-asses
laden with grain and bread and provision for his
father by the way. So he sent his brethren away, and
they departed: and he said unto them, See that ye
fall not out by the way. And they went up out of
Egypt, and came into the land of Canaan unto Jacob
their father. And they told him, saying, Joseph is yet
alive, and he is ruler over all the land of Egypt.
And his heart fainted, for he believed them not. And
they told him all the words of Joseph, which he had
said unto them: and when he saw the wagons which
Joseph had sent to carry him, the spirit of Jacob
their father revived: and Israel said, It is enough;
Joseph my son is yet alive: I will go and see him be-
for I die.

Joseph sent his brothers home rejoicing, laden with
presents for their father, and there was no longer any
regret that they had brought Benjamin down into
Egypt. True repentance means the changing of the
mind and all its contents of error belief. When we have
done this we can unify ourselves with Truth, and then
we are blessed in both mind and body with the true
riches of Spirit.

Pharaoh, the ruling ego of the subconsciousness,
joyfully welcomes Joseph's kindred. This reveals that
the constructive imagination (Joseph) not only mirrors
forth plenty that becomes manifest as substantial supply

but also brings peace and harmony to the whole man. Every form and thing, whether in the ether or on the earth, represents some idea or mental attitude. The idea is first projected into mind substance and afterward formed in consciousness through the imagining faculty of the mind.

> *Gen. 46:1-7.* And Israel took his journey with all that he had, and came to Beer-sheba, and offered sacrifices unto the God of his father Isaac. And God spake unto Israel in the visions of the night, and said, Jacob, Jacob. And he said, Here am I. And he said, I am God, the God of thy father: fear not to go down into Egypt; for I will there make of thee a great nation: I will go down with thee into Egypt; and I will also surely bring thee up again: and Joseph shall put his hand upon thine eyes. And Jacob rose up from Beer-sheba: and the sons of Israel carried Jacob their father, and their little ones, and their wives, in the wagons which Pharaoh had sent to carry him. And they took their cattle, and their goods, which they had gotten in the land of Canaan, and came into Egypt, Jacob, and all his seed with him: his sons, and his sons' sons with him, his daughters, and his sons' daughters, and all his seed brought he with him into Egypt.

Beer-sheba here represents spiritual inspiration (wells of water, reservoir) within man's consciousness that he has received and is acting on. The amazing activity and success of the imagination has opened up a larger substance source in body, and the whole thought family (Jacob's) is moving in and taking conscious possession of it.

God spoke to Jacob and told him not to fear to go down into Egypt, because He (God) would go with him and bring him out again after he had become a

great nation. The descent into the land of Egypt of
Jacob and his sons, together with the possessions that
they had accumulated in Canaan, their wives, children,
goods, flocks, and herds, symbolizes to us the unification of the I AM with all the faculties of the mind and
of the life energy and substance of the whole man
with the body. This happy result is brought about by
the action of the faculty of imagination (all dwelt
together "in the land of Goshen," which signifies
unity). This new state of mind becomes a part of the
permanent consciousness in the new land.

"And Joseph shall put his hand upon thine eyes"
means that through the faculty of imagination the
perception of the other faculties is quickened and
increased.

Gen. 46:8-27. And these are the names of the
children of Israel, who come into Egypt, Jacob and
his sons: Reuben, Jacob's first-born. And the sons
of Reuben: Hanoch, and Pallu, and Hezron, and
Carmi. And the sons of Simeon: Jemuel, and Jamin,
and Ohad, and Jachin, and Zohar, and Shaul the
son of a Canaanitish woman. And the sons of Levi:
Gershon, Kohath, and Merari. And the sons of Judah:
Er, and Onan, and Shelah, and Perez, and Zerah; but
Er and Onan died in the land of Canaan. And the
sons of Perez were Hezron and Hamul. And the sons
of Issachar: Tola, and Puvah, and Iob, and Shimron.
And the sons of Zebulun: Sered, and Elon, and
Jahleel. These are the sons of Leah, whom she bare
unto Jacob in Paddan-aram, with his daughter Dinah:
all the souls of his sons and his daughters were thirty
and three. And the sons of Gad: Ziphion, and Haggi,
Shuni, and Ezbon, Eri, and Arodi, and Areli. And the
sons of Asher: Imnah, and Ishvah, and Ishvi, and
Beriah, and Serah their sister; and the sons of
Beriah: Heber, and Malchiel. These are the sons of

Zilpah whom Laban gave to Leah his daughter; and these she bare unto Jacob, even sixteen souls. The sons of Rachel Jacob's wife: Joseph and Benjamin. And unto Joseph in the land of Egypt were born Manasseh and Ephraim, whom Asenath, the daughter of Poti-phera priest of On, bare unto him. And the sons of Benjamin: Bela, and Becher, and Ashbel, Gera, and Naaman, Ehi, and Rosh, Muppim, and Huppim, and Ard. These are the sons of Rachel, who were born to Jacob: All the souls were fourteen. And the sons of Dan: Hushim. And the sons of Naphtali: Jahzeel, and Guni, and Jezer, and Shillem. These are the sons of Bilhah, whom Laban gave unto Rachel his daughter, and these she bare unto Jacob: all the souls were seven. All the souls that came with Jacob into Egypt, that came out of his loins, besides Jacob's sons' wives, all the souls were threescore and six; and the sons of Joseph, who were born to him in Egypt, were two souls: all the souls of the house of Jacob, that came into Egypt, were threescore and ten.

(For the symbology of Jacob's twelve sons, his wives Leah and Rachel, and the two handmaids Bilhah and Zilpah see the interpretation of Gen. 35: 23-26.)

Hanoch ("instructed," "dedicated") represents entrance into a higher consciousness than has been known and experienced before.

Pallu ("marvelous," "extraordinary") represents the great general uplift that comes to the consciousness that has begun to awaken out of the purely animal phase of thought to a higher and truer conception of God and of life.

Hezron ("inclosed," "green pasture") represents thoughts that belong to the perceiving faculty (Reuben) and the praise of life in its activity (Judah).

Mysteries of Genesis

These thoughts are not yet free in their expression in the consciousness and the organism. They are "inclosed" by the subconscious limiting error belief of man that all his faculties and powers are material and transient instead of spiritual and abiding. (There were two men named Hezron, one the son of Reuben and the other the grandson of Judah.)

Carmi ("fruitful," "generous") symbolizes a vital, prosperous, and fruitful attitude of mind.

Jemuel ("God is light," "day of God") represents the stage of individual unfoldment when the light of Truth is accepted into consciousness and realized.

Jamin ("right hand," "right place") represents thoughts pertaining to divine order.

The name *Ohad* means "one," "unity." Ohad was the son of Simeon. The name *Simeon* means "one who listens and obeys." Simeon represents the spiritually receptive and obedient attitude in man. Ohad symbolizes unity with God and the conscious increase of the Christly attributes that is the result of this union between the divine and the individual.

Jachin ("whom He [God] makes firm") represents the firmness, steadfastness, and strength of character that result from the establishment of the consciousness in Truth.

Zohar ("whiteness," "nobility") represents thoughts of a pure, lofty, discriminating character.

Shaul is a form of the name *Saul*, and its meaning is the same as that of Saul ("desired," "demanded"). Shaul represents the personal will in individual consciousness. He was the son of a Canaanitish woman (body consciousness).

Gershon was a son of Levi. The name means "expulsion," "exile." The natural law of love is to express itself, but there are conditions under which the love thought (Gershon) is exiled from its native element and for a time retarded or unexpressed.

Kohath ("called together," "assembly") represents the attracting, unifying element in love, and the power of love.

Merari ("galling," "rebellious") symbolizes love directed by the ignorance and selfishness of the personal man.

Er ("awake," "watchful") represents observant, attentive, vigilant thoughts.

Onan ("able-bodied," "strong") represents thoughts pertaining to strength and vigor yet with a tendency toward materiality. (Onan's mother was a Canaanitish woman.)

Shelah ("security," "rest," "peace") represents a sense of peace, harmony, and security that has come about through prayer.

Perez ("breached," "torn asunder") represents victory gained through praise or by making one's way out of apparent limitation and error by means of prayer and praise.

The name *Zerah* means "rising of light." Zerah represents the rise of new light, new understanding, in the consciousness.

The name *Hamul* means "spared," "gentleness," "compassion"; it also signifies "forgiveness." The attitudes of mind thus implied are Godlike, and they have to do with the salvation of the individual who entertains them.

The name *Tola* means "crimson," "scarlet," "coccus worm." Tola represents life activity on a seemingly low plane but in process of unfoldment to higher and greater expressions.

Puvah is the same name as Puah, which means "mouth," "blast," "utterance." Puvah symbolizes the giving of one's true thoughts, one's zeal, to establishing the activity of Truth throughout the consciousness so that it may be declared aloud and expressed. (Puvah was the son of Issachar, zeal.)

Shimron ("watch," "careful keeping") represents a watchful, observant, attentive attitude, which raises to a high plane the faculties of mind represented by Issachar (zeal) and Zebulun (order).

Sered ("fear," "trembling," "flight," "escape") represents fearfulness, extreme unrest, in the order faculty in the individual consciousness.

Elon ("strong man," "an oak") represents thoughts of strength and power.

The name *Jahleel* means "waiting on God," "hoping in God." Jahleel represents waiting in the silence upon God in an expectant attitude of mind.

"My soul, wait thou in silence for God only;
For my expectation is from him."

Dinah ("judged," "justified") symbolizes the soul or feminine side of the judgment faculty, which may be called intuition, the intuition of the natural man.

Ziphion is the same name as Zephon, which means "watchman," "observer," "keeper of the high watch." Ziphion represents the realization of power (Gad symbolizes power) that is the result of a desire for and a seeking after power. This suggests prayer and an earnest desire for and expectation of something higher and better than the purely mental and physical aspects of power and might.

The name *Haggi* means "feast," "rejoicing," "festival." Haggi symbolizes a realization of good as taking the place of seeming evil.

Shuni ("rest," "quiet," "calm," "peace") represents a tranquil, poised, peaceful state of thought.

Ezbon ("hastening to understand," "splendor," "bright") represents thoughts that come into the light, into the brightness and glory of Truth, because they are concerned with the things of Spirit.

Eri ("my watcher," "worshiping Jah") represents an unfolding of the power faculty.

Arodi is the same name as Arod and means "fleeing," "a wild ass." Arod and his descendants represent those traits of the animal nature in man which are characteristic of the ass: meekness, stubbornness, persistence, and endurance. These qualities are good when directed by the true I AM but are destructive when given over to sense rule.

Areli ("lionlike," "valiant," "heroic") represents the courage to abide by that which one believes to be right and best; also boldness and fearlessness in applying one's ideas practically.

Imnah ("good fortune," "prosperity") represents a strong belief in and realization of prosperity as being man's inheritance and the Father's will for him.

Asher had three sons. The first two, Imnah and Ishvah, represent thoughts of the higher order, but the name of the third son, *Beriah,* means "evil," "calamity," "misfortune," indicating a negative tendency to evil that sometimes runs parallel with the good in human consciousness. However the good tendencies are so much in the ascendant that they overcome the weaker evil thoughts that belittle man and cause him to develop an inferiority complex.

Ishvah means "equality," "even," "smooth," "resembling (another)," "self-answering." On the highest plane Ishvah represents that true poise, peace, and equableness that come from within man's own true spiritual self when he realizes that he is made in the likeness of God and is certain that he will manifest this in the outer in due time. The thought of "self-satisfying" is also brought out in this name. This suggests the truth that as we become conscious of the source of all understanding within us, namely Spirit, we find within ourselves the answer to all our questionings, the satisfaction of all our desires.

Serah ("extension," "abundance," "poured forth," "diffused") represents a rich, broad, extensive group of soul qualities, but there is also a strong suggestion of waste of substance; lack of conservation.

The name *Heber* means "a passing over" from the purely sensate, physical, earthly thought to a higher conception of religious Truth.

Malchiel ("rule of God," "God is king") symbolizes man's acknowledgment of the supremacy of divine power and rulership; in other words, the exalting of God in consciousness, giving Him dominion; bowing to and obeying Truth.

Manasseh ("who makes to forget") represents understanding; understanding here denoting denial, the negative activity of mind. (See Gen. 41:45-47.)

Ephraim ("doubly fruitful") symbolizes the will, which is the positive or affirmative quality of mind.

The name *Asenath* means "dedicated to Neith," "favorite of Neith." Asenath represents the feminine or love side of the natural man.

The name *Poti-phera* means "belonging to Ra." Poti-phera represents a natural religious tendency in the individual that gives the force of its influence to the worship and building up of that for which On stands.

The name *On* means "city of the sun." In its purity On is a symbol of Spirit and of true spiritual understanding, substance, and power. As it appears in our Bible, however, it represents the worship of the outer sun, and the truth back of the symbol has been lost sight of to a great degree.

The name *Bela* means "swallow up," "destroy." Bela, the eldest son of Benjamin, represents the destroying or letting go of error by denial, an absorption (swallowing up) of error by Truth.

The name *Becher* means "early," "first fruits," "first-born." Becher represents the first-born or first fruits of faith, or the first bringing forth of positive, upbuilding thoughts. (Benjamin represents faith.)

The name *Ashbel* means "reproof of God," "man of Baal," "judgment of God." Ashbel denotes the admonition of Spirit ("reproof of God") in consciousness against man's looking upon as real the material thought about formed things ("man of Baal"). The inharmonious result of looking upon the outer world as real and as the source of life, understanding, and existence, instead of seeing formless Spirit (Divine Mind) as the true God and as the one reality standing back of all manifestation—this is what is suggested in the phrase "judgment of God."

Gera ("grain," "kernel") symbolizes faith's taking on of, or working in, substance.

Naaman ("sweet," "pleasant," "good") denotes

the joy, and pleasant, agreeable, harmonious, unifying result that ensues in consciousness when one's faith and will act in accord with one's highest Truth ideals.

Ehi is the name of a son of Benjamin also called Aharah, which means "brother." Ehi represents that in man's spiritually awakening consciousness which follows after lofty, kindly, brotherly, constructive ideals. The name *Ehi* also carries with it the thought of unity.

The name *Rosh* means "inclination," "will," "head." Rosh represents the will. Since Rosh was a son of Benjamin (faith) the significance is that the will, having been given first place in the consciousness of the individual, is acting through faith or in conjunction with it.

The name *Muppim* means "serpents," "glidings," "obscurities," "darkenings." Muppim represents human or sense knowledge that is very subtle but that is unsteady and unsettled in its reasonings and deductions. Muppim represents that knowledge which does not reveal the true light, and therefore it does not lead the individual into spiritual understanding.

The name *Huppim* is the same as that of Hupham, which means "coastman," "seashore," "bank." In all likelihood a coastman is a fisherman. Huppim thus symbolizes a gatherer of ideas, especially ideas of increase.

The name *Ard* means "fugitive," "to flee," "wild ass." The thought that Ard represents belongs to the outer or animal phase of consciousness, where fear enters and one runs away from seeming evil or resists it wildly and stubbornly, as the case may be, because one fears it. In this phase of consciousness one does not understand that evil is unreal and has no power of itself. When one realizes the truth about seeming evil, one no longer fears it, and it is dissolved from one's world.

The name *Hushim* means "people of haste," "vehement people." Hushim represents an acceleration of activity in connection with thoughts of judgment in man (one Hushim was the son of Dan, who represents judgment) and in connection with thoughts of active faith (another Hushim was a Benjamite).

Jahzeel, the name of a son of Naphtali (strength), means "whom God apportions." Jahzeel represents the realization that strength is from God and that one receives it according to one's need or to the extent that one makes use of it.

The name *Guni* means "colored," "tinted," "painted," which suggests the taking on of some foreign idea or substance. In this case Naphtali (strength) and Gad (power) are involved. These qualities represented by Naphtali and Gad are inherently spiritual, divine, but in coming into expression in the outer, physical, sense man they become tinged with and colored by material ideas.

Jazer ("formation") represents the formative faculty of mind, the imagination, established in strength (Naphtali).

The name *Shillem* means "restoration," "salvation," "peace." Shillem represents the thought that restoration, salvation, peace, and perfection are the result of sowing to Spirit. This restorative, peace-giving thought force is particularly active in connection with strength and thus gives its substance to the working out of the law of cause and effect in consciousness.

Gen. 46:28-34. And he sent Judah before him

unto Joseph, to show the way before him unto
Goshen; and they came into the land of Goshen. And
Joseph made ready his chariot, and went up to meet
Israel his father, to Goshen; and he presented himself unto him, and fell on his neck, and wept on his
neck a good while. And Israel said unto Joseph, Now
let me die, since I have seen thy face, that thou art
yet alive. And Joseph said unto his brethren, and
unto his father's house, I will go up, and tell Pharaoh,
and will say unto him, My brethren, and my father's
house, who were in the land of Canaan, are come
unto me; and the men are shepherds, for they have
been keepers of cattle; and they have brought their
flocks, and their herds, and all that they have. And
it shall come to pass, when Pharaoh shall call you,
and shall say, What is your occupation? that ye shall
say, Thy servants have been keepers of cattle from
our youth even until now, both we, and our fathers:
that ye may dwell in the land of Goshen; for every
shepherd is an abomination unto the Egyptians.

The Israelites represent radiant or unformed substance and life, and the Egyptians represent conservators
of formed substance. Jacob (I AM) sent Judah (praise)
before him unto Joseph (imagination) so that the
Israelites might be guided to Goshen, thus forming a
perfect union of life (Israel) and substance (Egypt).
The sheep represent the uncontaminated animal or life
forces that are to be expressed more fully through union
with materiality (the Egyptians). The conservators of
formed substance (Egyptians) have no appreciation of
this life ("for every shepherd is an abomination unto
the Egyptians").

Chapter XIII

The Blessing of the Faculties

GENESIS 47, 48, 49, and 50

J OSEPH IS A SUBLIME IDEA of Truth that goes
down into the darkened sense consciousness, and
under the law finally raises it up and out of sense
and into Spirit. He was seemingly forced there by his
brothers, yet he was sent by the Lord to prepare for the
maintenance of Jacob's family through the period of
dearth that later came to Canaan. The Truth he represents, when taken down into the sense consciousness,
establishes there a new realization of life that will
result in the regeneration of the entire man. We must
often go consciously into every part of our body and
build it up in Truth with new ideas of life and substance.

> *Gen. 47:1-12.* Then Joseph went in and told
> Pharaoh, and said, My father and my brethren, and
> their flocks, and their herds, and all that they have,
> are come out of the land of Canaan; and, behold,
> they are in the land of Goshen. And from among his
> brethren he took five men, and presented them unto
> Pharaoh. And Pharaoh said unto his brethren, What
> is your occupation? And they said unto Pharaoh, Thy
> servants are shepherds, both we, and our fathers.
> And they said unto Pharaoh, To sojourn in the land
> are we come; for there is no pasture for thy servants'
> flocks; for the famine is sore in the land of Canaan:
> now therefore, we pray thee, let thy servants dwell
> in the land of Goshen. And Pharaoh spake unto
> Joseph, saying, Thy father and thy brethren are come

unto thee: the land of Egypt is before thee; in the
best of the land make thy father and thy brethren
to dwell; in the land of Goshen let them dwell: and
if thou knowest any able men among them, then
make them rulers over my cattle. And Joseph brought
in Jacob his father, and set him before Pharaoh: and
Jacob blessed Pharaoh. And Pharaoh said unto Jacob,
How many are the days of the years of thy life?
And Jacob said unto Pharaoh, The days of the years
of my pilgrimage are a hundred and thirty years:
few and evil have been the days of the years of my
life, and they have not attained unto the days of the
years of the life of my fathers in the days of their
pilgrimage. And Jacob blessed Pharaoh, and went
out from the presence of Pharaoh. And Joseph
placed his father and his brethren, and gave them a
possession in the land of Egypt, in the best of the
land, in the land of Rameses, as Pharaoh had commanded. And Joseph nourished his father, and his
brethren, and all his father's household, with bread,
according to their families.

Joseph's brothers had been shepherds in Canaan.
It is the business of our mind faculties (Jacob's sons)
to tend those thought aggregations (flocks, herds)
that pertain to our vitality. There were no sheep
in Egypt, but Pharaoh made them "rulers" over his
cattle. Cattle represent physical strength, which like all
the powers of man on the natural plane, must be
spiritualized. The faculties, having come down into a
more material state of consciousness (Egypt), take
dominion over and lift up the animal thoughts and
tendencies in the body and unify them with Spirit. This
is done by a transmutation of quality and is attained
by right thinking, by putting the "cattle" under the
control of the thoughts of reality or Spirit, represented
by the Israelites.

Joseph brought his father to the ruler, and Jacob blessed Pharaoh. This shows that the power that rules the body, under the material regime, rules in obscurity or is without spiritual understanding. When imagination (Joseph) brings the higher understanding (Jacob) to the body consciousness (Pharaoh), the higher blesses the lower.

Thus, the father and the brothers of Joseph took up their abode in the land of Egypt, and Joseph nourished them there. The imagination, which is our faculty of increase, when established in Truth, prepares the way for us. It inspires, encourages, and sustains the other faculties in us when they fall into a seemingly material phase of being, and ultimately brings about the spiritualization of the whole organism, mind, soul, and body.

It is thought that Rameses is the same name as Raamses, which means "son of Ra," "son of the sun," "sun's emanation." Rameses represents a consciousness of substance in the domain of the physical ego (Pharaoh). This "sun" or "light" consciousness, which in Pharaoh and Egypt is obscured or veiled by the life on the lower sense plane, works in conjunction with the higher religious thoughts (Hebrews) that are in servitude to the darkened sense consciousness symbolized by Egypt, and so this reserve substance (Rameses) is built up in Egypt.

> *Gen. 47:13-26.* And there was no bread in all the land; for the famine was very sore, so that the land of Egypt and the land of Canaan fainted by reason of the famine. And Joseph gathered up all the money that was found in the land of Egypt, and in the land of Canaan, for the grain which they

bought: and Joseph brought the money into Pharaoh's house. And when the money was all spent in the land of Egypt, and in the land of Canaan, all the Egyptians came unto Joseph, and said, Give us bread: for why should we die in thy presence? for *our* money faileth. And Joseph said, Give your cattle; and I will give you for your cattle, if money fail. And they brought their cattle unto Joseph; and Joseph gave them bread in exchange for the horses, and for the flocks, and for the herds, and for the asses: and he fed them with bread in exchange for all their cattle for that year. And when that year was ended, they came unto him the second year, and said unto him, We will not hide from my lord, how that our money is all spent; and the herds of cattle are my lord's; there is nought left in the sight of my lord, but our bodies, and our lands: wherefore should we die before thine eyes, both we and our land? buy us and our land for bread, and we and our land will be servants unto Pharaoh: and give us seed, that we may live, and not die, and that the land be not desolate.

So Joseph bought all the land of Egypt for Pharaoh; for the Egyptians sold every man his field, because the famine was sore upon them: and the land became Pharaoh's. And as for the people, he removed them to the cities from one end of the border of Egypt even to the other end thereof. Only the land of the priests bought he not: for the priests had a portion from Pharaoh, and did eat their portion which Pharaoh gave them; wherefore they sold not their land. Then Joseph said unto the people, Behold, I have bought you this day and your land for Pharaoh: lo, here is seed for you, and ye shall sow the land. And it shall come to pass at the ingatherings, that ye shall give a fifth unto Pharaoh, and four parts shall be your own, for seed of the field, and for your food, and for them of your households, and for food for your little ones. And they said, Thou hast saved our lives: let us find favor in the sight of my lord, and we will be, Pharaoh's servants. And Joseph made it a statute concerning the land of Egypt unto this day, that Pharaoh should have the fifth; only the land of the priests alone became not Pharaoh's.

In the early stages of regeneration there are times when the developing soul has exhausted its resources and the outer world no longer satisfies. When it reaches this point man has to turn within and appropriate from the higher principles that which they have to give. The center of the great solar plexus (Pharaoh) is also the conservator of substance and life in the organism. When man is spiritually famished and feels the lack he is eager regardless of cost to go to the inner reservoirs of stored-up substance for sustenance. First he gives up to the higher principles the power and strength of the natural man (symbolized by money and cattle), then he draws on the fixed forces, the land (representing the body), until it is finally realized that the higher principles really are in authority. In the last analysis the "sun" (solar plexus) consciousness is actually the great distributor. The men (thought forces) were given seed to sow the land, and Pharaoh (the great distributing ego) permitted them to have four fifths of the harvest for sustenance, while retaining one fifth (in the subconscious) to meet any usual demands. The man now becomes aware of the presence of this subconscious ego that, when spiritually instructed by the imagination (Joseph), will handle all the processes of rebuilding the body. Finally this becomes an established law. The priests, representing the higher spiritual life, are not subject to this law.

Gen. 47:27-31. And Israel dwelt in the land of Egypt,. in the land of Goshen; and they gat them possessions therein, and were fruitful, and multiplied exceedingly. And Jacob lived in the land of Egypt seventeen years: so the days of Jacob, the years of his life, were a hundred forty and seven years. And the time drew near that Israel must die: and he called his son Joseph, and said unto him, If now I have found favor in thy sight, put, I pray thee, thy hand under my thigh, and deal kindly and truly with me: bury me not, I pray thee, in Egypt; but when I sleep with my fathers, thou shalt carry me out of Egypt, and bury me in their burying-place. And he said, I will do as thou hast said. And he said, Swear unto me: and he sware unto him. And Israel bowed himself upon the bed's head.

The central thought in this Scripture is that Jacob is giving up old ideas and taking on new. The life of Jacob in a certain unfoldment was drawing to a close, and his desire was that his body be buried with his fathers in the cave of Machpelah. This indicates that a certain phase of the illumined intellect is sinking back into the subconsciousness (Macpelah). All experiences in life that have spiritual qualities and all realities gained in the land of unity (Goshen) are preserved in the subconsciousness. Joseph's placing his hand under the thigh of Jacob symbolizes the truth that the illumined intellect needs the encouragement and support and power of the imagination in order to effect spiritually the change that is about to take place. When this is granted, Jacob bows down in gratitude and thanksgiving to the Holy One and rests in the realization that all is well. "And Israel bowed himself upon the bed's head."

Jacob's age is significant. The number seven symbolizes fullness in the world of phenomena. It is so universally used as a mystical number that its basis must be in some fundamental arrangement of the natural world.

(For significance of the oath see interpretation of Gen. 24:9.)

> *Gen. 48:1-4.* And it came to pass after these things, that one said to Joseph, Behold, thy father is sick: and he took with him his two sons, Manasseh and Ephraim. And one told Jacob, and said, Behold, thy son Joseph cometh unto thee: and Israel strengthened himself, and sat upon the bed. And Jacob said unto Joseph, God Almighty appeared unto me at Luz in the land of Canaan, and blessed me, and said unto me, Behold, I will make thee fruitful, and multiply thee, and I will make of thee a company of peoples, and will give this land to thy seed after thee for an everlasting possession.

In this Scripture the I AM functioning in the illumined intellect (Jacob) is taking cognizance of its abilities and possessions before it sinks back into the subconsciousness for a season of rest. The I AM faculty of imagination (Joseph) is quick to discern what is taking place and brings the will and the understanding, the yes and the no of the mind (Ephraim and Manasseh), to the I AM for a final blessing. (The will and the understanding are the powers that say yes and no to your thoughts.)

The Lord had blessed Jacob (the I AM) at Luz. One interpretation of Luz is "separation," but under the light of Spirit we find that that which we conceive to be apart from God (Luz) is in truth His abode (Bethel, house of God). Therefore this Luz state of consciousness belongs eternally to the I AM and its

faculties will (Ephraim) and understanding (Manasseh), which faculties are to multiply and bring forth
fruit exceedingly.

> *Gen. 48:5, 6.* And now thy two sons, who were
> born unto thee in the land of Egypt before I came
> unto thee into Egypt, are mine; Ephraim and Manas-
> seh, even as Reuben and Simeon, shall be mine. And
> thy issue, that thou begettest after them, shall be
> thine; they shall be called after the name of their
> brethren in their inheritance.

The I AM (Jacob) here claims Joseph's two sons
Ephraim and Manasseh (fruit of the imagination) as
his own. The primal faculties of will (Ephraim) and
understanding (Manasseh) or of affirmation and denial now come under the dominion of the I AM, symbolized by Jacob. The secondary issues come under the
imagination (Joseph).

> *Gen. 48:7.* And as for me, when I came from
> Paddan, Rachel died by me in the land of Canaan in
> the way, when there was still some distance to come
> unto Ephrath: and I buried her there in the way
> to Ephrath (the same is Bethlehem).

When an important ego is about to change its
plane of expression, a memory of past experiences,
especially of those which are dear to the heart, flashes
into the mind. Spiritually that which is good in the
experiences is retained and that which is not good is
cast aside. In soul consciousness the soul intuitively
rejects the error and claims the good. It is an occasion
where denial and affirmation play an important part.

Jacob had been on his way from Paddan (a place of
substance in the consciousness and body organism of
the individual) and was yet some distance from Eph-

rath (realization of abundance.); that is, the illumined I AM (Jacob) had been passing from a lower plane of substance to a higher plane. During this period of transition the consciousness of love for material substance (Rachel) died, or sank back into the subconscious, there to become the foundation of a more spiritual love. Now through introspection Jacob was eliminating the error and affirming the good.

> *Gen. 48:8-22.* And Israel beheld Joseph's sons, and said, Who are these? And Joseph said unto his father, They are my sons, whom God hath given me here. And he said, Bring them, I pray thee, unto me, and I will bless them. Now the eyes of Israel were dim for age, so that he could not see. And he brought them near unto him; and he kissed them, and embraced them. And Israel said unto Joseph, I had not thought to see thy face: and, lo, God hath let me see thy seed also. And Joseph brought them out from between his knees; and he bowed himself with his face to the earth. And Joseph took them both, Ephraim in his right hand toward Israel's left hand, and Manasseh in his left hand toward Israel's right hand, and brought them near unto him. And Israel stretched out his right hand, and laid it upon Ephraim's head, who was the younger, and his left hand upon Manasseh's head, guiding his hands wittingly; for Manasseh was the first-born. And he blessed Joseph, and said, The God before whom my fathers Abraham and Isaac did walk, the God who hath fed me all my life long unto this day, the angel who hath redeemed me from all evil, bless the lads; and let my name be named on them, and the name of my fathers Abraham and Isaac; and let them grow into a multitude in the midst of the earth. And when Joseph saw that his father laid his right hand upon the head of Ephraim, it displeased him: and he held up his father's hand, to remove it from

Ephraim's head unto Manasseh's head. And Joseph
said unto his father, Not so, my father; for this
is the first-born; put thy right hand upon his head.
And his father refused, and said, I know *it*, my son,
I know *it;* he also shall become a people, and he also
shall be great; howbeit his younger brother shall be
greater than he, and his seed shall become a multitude of nations. And he blessed them that day, saying, In thee will Israel bless, saying, God make thee
as Ephraim and as Manasseh: and he set Ephraim before Manasseh. And Israel said unto Joseph, Behold,
I die: but God will be with you, and bring you again
unto the land of your fathers. Moreover I have given
to thee one portion above thy brethren, which I took
out of the hand of the Amorite with my sword and
with my bow.

When Joseph came to visit his father in the land
of Goshen, he brought his two sons with him. Hearing
that they were coming, "Israel strengthened himself,
and sat upon the bed." Thus understanding (Manasseh) and will (Ephraim) bring strength when weakness
appears. Job says, "When they cast *thee* down, thou
shalt say, *There is* lifting up."

Jacob blessed his grandsons, and his blessing is significant. Manasseh, being the first-born (under divine
law understanding precedes will), would be entitled to
the chief blessing, but Jacob laid his right hand upon
the head of Ephraim and his left hand upon the head
of Manasseh instead of the reverse, which was the
customary way of blessing. Joseph, thinking his aged
father's dim eyesight responsible for this seeming error,
called his attention to it. Jacob replied that he knew
what he was doing and that although the older son
was to become great and important, Ephraim (will)
would take precedence under the natural law to which

they were both to be subjected.

That certain laws in race evolution are involved in the blessing by Jacob of Joseph's two sons, also that a special spiritual dispensation to the Hebrews, to Abraham, Isaac, Jacob, and Joseph, was instituted must be admitted by those who believe that this Scripture is inspired. But this dependence on the Lord for guidance could not go on forever; the highest test of character is the self-made man. Man must develop from within, and the time comes to every soul when it must glow with its own inner light, regardless of the mistakes it may make.

Jacob saw that the time had come for Ephraim and Manasseh to act on their own initiative, and he knew what he was doing when he gave Ephraim (the will) first place. In the free, full development of man the will and ambition to achieve leap ahead of the understanding. This has been and still is the experience of the human race, and it will continue to be until man in his freedom willingly accepts divine guidance. Then Manasseh (the understanding) will come into his own and assume first place in consciousness. The blunders of man will then be corrected and a mutual understanding be restored to the whole world.

Up to this time the faculties symbolized by Ephraim and Manasseh had been under the inspiration of the imagination (Joseph). Joseph's taking his sons from between his knees and handing them over to Jacob for the final blessing symbolizes the restoration of the faculties to their natural estate. The dying of Jacob represents the withdrawal of the activity of this special spiritual inspiration imparted through the I AM.

The final blessing of the I AM on the imagination (Joseph) promised that it would be taken back or "reincarnated" in the land of the fathers. The one extra portion that Jacob gave to Joseph, which he "took out of the hand of the Amorite" (a race inheritance) with his sword (power of the word) and bow (directive power), is an amorous force that finds expression on the generative plane but which eventually must be elevated to spiritual consciousness. The exercise of any faculty to the best of one's ability is appreciated by the Lord (law), and we get an extra portion, a "free gift of God." We receive a certain return for our mental effort although we may not always directly recognize God as the source.

> *Gen. 49:1, 2.* And Jacob called unto his sons, and said: Gather yourselves together, that I may tell you that which shall befall you in the latter days.
> Assemble yourselves, and hear, ye sons of Jacob;
> And hearken unto Israel your father.

A blessing signifies the imparting of spiritual good, which the recipient may receive or reject according to his mental attitude. The blessing by Jacob of his twelve sons symbolizes the sowing of seed in consciousness for a future harvest. Through the power of his word Jacob was raising the consciousness of his primal ideas. In effect he was proclaiming: "You represent the A B C of man's life, and I am revealing to you in symbols the foundation you have laid, what you will have to contend with in the future, and what you can attain. You stand for the foundation faculties that constitute the coming ideal man. The true seed idea of this ideal man is implanted within each of you and will eventually become manifest. This process of manifestation covers your history up to the time of the appearance of the man that God imaged in the beginning, even Jesus Christ."

> *Gen. 49:3, 4.*
> Reuben, thou art my first-born, my might, and the
>   beginning of my strength;
> The pre-eminence of dignity, and the pre-eminence
>   of power.
> Boiling over as water, thou shalt not have the pre-
>   eminence;
> Because thou wentest up to thy father's bed;
> Then defilest thou it; he went up to my couch.

Reuben, the first-born, symbolizes the faith of man in his ability as expressed through his animal nature. Here we see the vigor and vitality of the functioning of man's elemental life, which boils over "as water," loses command. Reuben is represented as the natural man giving way to his passions and appetites before he has developed spiritual mastery.

> *Gen. 49:5, 7.*
> Simeon and Levi are brethren;
> Weapons of violence are their swords.
> O my soul, come not thou into their council;
> Unto their assembly, my glory, be not thou united;
> For in their anger they slew a man,
> And in their self-will they hocked an ox.
> Cursed be their anger, for it was fierce;
> And their wrath, for it was cruel:
> I will divide them in Jacob,
> And scatter them in Israel.

Simeon represents receptivity (feeling) and Levi love (sensation). The faculties of feeling and sensation in human consciousness have been debased on the mortal plane. Simeon, the obedient one, one who is easily influenced, falls under the sway of physical sensation.

In Simeon and Levi we also have an exhibition of animal love and of its vengefulness as exemplified in their treacherous attempt to right the wrong committed against their sister Dinah.

> *Gen. 49:8-12.*
> Judah, thee shall thy brethren praise:
> Thy hand shall be on the neck of thine enemies;
> Thy father's sons shall bow down before thee.
> Judah is a lion's whelp;
> From the prey, my son, thou art gone up:
> He stooped down, he couched as a lion,
> And as a lioness; who shall rouse him up?
> The sceptre shall not depart from Judah,
> Until Shiloh come;
> And unto him shall the obedience of the peoples be.
> Binding his foal unto the vine,
> And his ass's colt unto the choice vine;
> He hath washed his garments in wine,
> And his vesture in the blood of the grapes:
> His eyes shall be red with wine,
> And his teeth white with milk.

Jacob's blessing on Judah was the most significant. Judah was to conquer all his enemies:

> The sceptre shall not depart from Judah,
> Nor the ruler's staff from between his feet,
> Until Shiloh come;
> And unto him shall the obedience of the peoples be.

Shiloh signifies peace of mind, wholeness, completion or fullness, and represents the Prince of Peace, the Messiah or Savior. Jesus was a direct descendant of Judah, as is shown in the 1st chapter of Matthew. The name *Judah* applies to only one of the twelve tribes, but is often used to designate the Jewish nation as a whole. This would indicate that praise is such an active principle in spiritual thought that it is deserving of first place. The power of the word of praise shall be felt until the coming of the Prince of Peace.

> *Gen. 49:13.*
> Zebulun shall dwell at the haven of the sea;
> And he shall be for a haven of ships;
> And his border shall be upon Sidon.

Zebulun represents the law that relates man to the universal cosmos. He dwells under the law of protection and safety (refuge), yet has a realization of the universal Mind (sea). Zebulun is that in us which is concerned with the maintenance of our individual importance regardless of the immensity of the universal. Those who are in personality will find refuge in this state of consciousness. We lose consciousness of our spiritual importance by looking out into the universe but can retain our identity as children of God through realizing that Spirit is individualized in us.

> *Gen. 49:14, 15.*
> Issachar is a strong ass,
> Couching down between the sheepfolds:
> And he saw a resting-place that it was good,
> And the land that it was pleasant;
> And he bowed his shoulder to bear,
> And became a servant under taskwork.

Issachar symbolizes the inner latent powers in man. He represents that side of the natural man which accepts conditions as they appear to be and bears the burdens of life without question, as exemplified by the patient ass.

Gen. 49:16-18.
Dan shall judge his people,
As one of the tribes of Israel.
Dan shall be a serpent in the way,
An adder in the path,
That biteth the horse's heels,
So that his rider falleth backward.
I have waited for thy salvation, O Jehovah.

Dan represents discrimination or judgment, a choosing between good and evil. The serpent is used as a symbol of subtlety. "Now the serpent was more subtle than any beast of the field." Jesus advised His followers to be "wise as serpents, and harmless as doves." Sensation rushes through the organism like a race horse, but judgment "bites at the heels" to restrain the headlong flight.

Gen. 49:19.
Gad, a troop shall press upon him;
But he shall press upon their heel.

Gad represents latent spiritual power, which like an army is always ready to do a mighty work. Science tells of an omnipresent ether that presses upon us in the invisible from every direction. One scientist says that the atomic energy in a pea would propel a large seagoing vessel from America to England and return. This ether has its analogy in Spirit, which continually inspires us when we give it our attention. Our mind is in direct contact with this spiritual power, and our word puts it into action.

Gen. 49:20.
Out of Asher his bread shall be fat,
And he shall yield royal dainties.

Asher represents the understanding mind and its ability to manipulate universal substance (bread) and make it manifest richly. The bread or divine substance is susceptible of infinite adaptation. Those who think about it as limited in its expression manifest limited supply, while those who follow Jesus and realize the richness of this substance manifest it abundantly, being able even to transform it into loaves and fishes to feed the multitude.

> *Gen. 49:21.*
>> Naphtali is a hind let loose:
>> He giveth goodly words.

The Hebrew meaning of the name *Naphtali* is "my wrestling," "wrestling of Jehovah." Naphtali represents the activity of strength in man's consciousness. Jacob's blessing on Naphtali was that he might have the strength and speed of the deer and the power of the word to increase strength.

> *Gen. 49:22-26.*
> Joseph is a fruitful bough,
> A fruitful bough by a fountain;
> His branches run over the wall.
> The archers have sorely grieved him,
> And shot at him, and persecuted him:
> But his bow abode in strength,
> And the arms of his hands were made strong,
> By the hands of the Mighty One of Jacob
> (From thence is the shepherd, the stone of Israel),
> Even by the God of thy father, who shall help thee,
> And by the Almighty, who shall bless thee,
> With blessings of heaven above,
> Blessings of the deep that coucheth beneath,
> Blessings of the breasts, and of the womb.
> The blessings of thy father
> Have prevailed above the blessings of my progenitors

Unto the utmost bound of the everlasting hills:
They shall be on the head of Joseph,
And on the crown of the head of him that was sep-
arated from his brethren.

Joseph, representing the imagination, is at all times
very close to divine inspiration. If man would curb
his will and keep it in abeyance he would not "imagine
vain things." Notwithstanding the destructive power of
the personal will ("archers") with which he is associated his directive power is victorious. Joseph's perse-
cution and sale into Egypt by his willful brothers and
his demonstration of superiority to his fate illustrate
the victory of an inspired imagination. The whole story
of Joseph is an example of the successful functioning of
man's imaging faculty when he keeps contact with
Jehovah.

> *Gen. 49:27, 28.*
> Benjamin is a wolf that raveneth:
> In the morning he shall devour the prey,
> And at even he shall divide the spoil.
> All these are the twelve tribes of Israel: and this
> is it that their father spake unto them and blessed
> them; every one according to his blessing he blessed
> them.

Benjamin (faith) in his hunger after righteousness
is compared to a famished wolf. In the morning or
beginning he appropriates understanding to the full,
which he divides or imparts freely at the evening or
end of the period.

> *Gen. 49:29-33.* And he charged them, and said
> unto them, I am to be gathered unto my people: bury
> me with my fathers in the cave that is in the field of
> Ephron the Hittite, in the cave that is in the field of
> Machpelah, which is before Mamre, in the land of

Canaan, which Abraham bought with the field from Ephron the Hittite for a possession of a burying-place. There they buried Abraham and Sarah his wife; there they buried Isaac and Rebekah his wife; and there I buried Leah—the field and the cave that is therein, which was purchased from the children of Heth. And when Jacob made an end of charging his sons, he gathered up his feet into the bed, and yielded up the ghost, and was gathered unto his people.

In the Scripture allegories the various individuals represent the different phases of character through which one man passes in his spiritual unfoldment. As these follow in a series, gradually reaching greater heights, the old phases of character are left behind to be replaced by new ones. Thus the Biblical characters are said to "die" and to be "gathered unto their fathers." Tennyson was inspired to express a great truth, as poets often are, when he wrote,

"Men may rise on steppingstones
Of their dead selves to higher things."

So each of the great Bible personalities is gradually replaced in the mind of him who is in the narrow way. When a great change takes place, some old phase of consciousness has lost its hold, and we read that Jacob or Joseph or another character "dies." This does not mean that there has been any loss or that anything has "gone away" but that certain states of mind have fulfilled their regenerative work and have been succeeded by others.

(For Ephron, Machpelah, and Mamre see interpretation of Gen. 23:3-20.)

Gen. 50:1-13. And Joseph fell upon his father's face, and wept upon him, and kissed him. And

Joseph commanded his servants the physicians to embalm his father: and the physicians embalmed Israel. And forty days were fulfilled for him, for so are fulfilled the days of embalming: and the Egyptians wept for him threescore and ten days.

And when the days of weeping for him were past, Joseph spake unto the house of Pharaoh, saying, If now I have found favor in your eyes, speak, I pray you, in the ears of Pharaoh, saying, My father made me swear, saying, Lo, I die: in my grave which I have digged for me in the land of Canaan, there shalt thou bury me. Now therefore let me go up, I pray thee, and bury my father, and I will come again. And Pharaoh said, Go up, and bury thy father, according as he made thee swear. And Joseph went up to bury his father; and with him went up all the servants of Pharaoh, the elders of his house, and all the elders of the land of Egypt, and all the house of Joseph, and his brethren, and his father's house: only their little ones, and their flocks, and their herds, they left in the land of Goshen. And there went up with him both chariots and horsemen: and it was a very great company. And they came to the threshing-floor of Atad, which is beyond the Jordan, and there they lamented with a very great and sore lamentation: and he made a mourning for his father seven days. And when the inhabitants of the land, the Canaanites, saw the mourning in the floor of Atad, they said, This is a grievous mourning to the Egyptians: wherefore the name of it was called Abel-mizraim, which is beyond the Jordan. And his sons did unto him according as he commanded them: for his sons carried him into the land of Canaan, and buried him in the cave of the field of Machpelah, which Abraham bought with the field, for a possession of a burying place, of Ephron the Hittite, before Mamre.

Whenever the I AM withdraws, no matter in what state of consciousness it has been functioning, there is a great shock to the soul, and all the forces of the natural man are filled with grief and consternation. "And he made a mourning for his father seven days." The imagination (Joseph), favorite faculty (son) of the illumined intellect (Jacob), mourned greatly, not fully understanding that the withdrawal of the I AM eventually would culminate in good.

The name *Atad* means "bramble," "thornbush," "a thorn." It was on the threshing floor of Atad that Joseph and his brethren mourned seven days for their father Jacob. A threshing floor may be thought of as a place of judgment or separation, of letting go of that which is no longer needful to be expressed in consciousness. Atad represents the belief that vexations, trials, and sorrows are real. It is this unredeemed thought or belief in man that causes him to experience deep grief and tribulation at giving up his personal hold on old ideas and objects which are due to be released from his mind and affairs. This unredeemed belief is concerned with and dwells on the trial side of the process rather than on the blessing side of it.

The Canaanites symbolize the semispiritual in man. They changed the name (or character) of Atad. "And when the inhabitants of the land, the Canaanites, saw the mourning on the floor of Atad, they said, This is a grievous mourning to the Egyptians: wherefore the name of it was called Abel-mizraim." The Egyptians symbolize materiality.

Abel-mizraim ("mourning of Egypt or Egyptians," "mourning or meadow of distress") represents the feeling of sorrow and loss in the sense man that often accompanies the letting go of some good idea in consciousness after it has finished its work. Man's tendency

is to cling to the old ideas that have been helpful to
him. But when their work is done in the individual for
the time being, these old ideas, no matter how well
they have served, must be released from consciousness
so that other and higher ideas may take their place. This
is a process of judgment, a sifting of ideas and
thoughts, a letting go of the chaff and a laying hold
of the wheat (on the threshing floor).

The Jordan represents a stream of thought, good,
bad, and indifferent, flowing through the subconscious.

Machpelah refers to the subconscious body substance.

Ephron the Hittite symbolizes a phase of thought
that is quick to change its thinking base. The word
Hittite denotes thoughts belonging to the carnal consciousness of man.

Mamre suggests strength, vigor; it also represents
the seat of the conscious mind.

(For further discussion of these names see interpretation of Gen. 23:3-20.)

This closing chapter of Genesis is an allegorical
account of the end of the work of Jacob and his family
in Egypt. The descent of Joseph (the illumined imagination) into Egypt paved the way for Jacob (the
spiritually illumined ego) and his kin to make contact
with subconscious substance. These pioneers of Jehovah accomplished their work, and their leader Jacob
"died" or withdrew from consciousness. That the whole
man, including the physical, was helped by Jacob is
evidenced by the interest the Egyptians took in the
funeral of Jacob and the great company that went up to
Canaan with the Children of Israel.

Gen. 50:14-21. And Joseph returned into Egypt,

he, and his brethren, and all that went up with him
to bury his father, after he had buried his father.

And when Joseph's brethren saw that their father
was dead, they said, It may be that Joseph will hate
us, and will fully requite us all the evil which we did
unto him. And they sent a message unto Joseph,
saying, Thy father did command before he died,
saying, So shall ye say unto Joseph, Forgive, I pray
thee now, the transgression of thy brethren, and
their sin, for that they did unto thee evil. And now,
we pray thee, forgive the transgression of the servants of the God of thy father. And Joseph wept
when they spake unto him. And his brethren also
went and fell down before his face; and they said,
Behold, we are thy servants. And Joseph said unto
them, Fear not: for am I in the place of God? And
as for you, ye meant evil against me; but God
meant it for good, to bring to pass, as it is this day,
to save much people alive. Now therefore fear
ye not: I will nourish you, and your little ones. And
he comforted them, and spake kindly unto them.

The imagination returning to the body consciousness (Egypt) again takes up the work of redeeming it.

The confession of the brothers of Joseph to their
crime against him and his loving forgiveness both point
to the spiritual uplift that has taken place in soul
evolution.

"Now therefore fear ye not: I will nourish you, and
your little ones" signifies that the imagination in its
divine purity and holiness is one of the sources of good
to the whole man. What you mold in your mind under
the spiritual law is formed in your affairs and thus
is the source of prosperity.

Gen. 50:22-26. And Joseph dwelt in Egypt, he,
and his father's house: and Joseph lived a hundred
and ten years. And Joseph saw Ephraim's children

of the third generation: the children also of Machir
the son of Manasseh were born upon Joseph's knees.
And Joseph said unto his brethren, I die; but God
will surely visit you, and bring you up out of this
land unto the land which he sware to Abraham, to
Isaac, and to Jacob. And Joseph took an oath of the
children of Israel, saying, God will surely visit you,
and ye shall carry up my bones from hence. And
Joseph died, being a hundred and ten years old:
and they embalmed him, and he was put in a coffin
in Egypt.

Joseph also died in Egypt but not until he had
lived among the children of Ephraim unto "the third
generation." This means that the Joseph qualities of
mind are developing a deeper understanding of spiritual things. Machir, the name of a son of Manasseh
(understanding), means "acquired," "purchased." The
children of Machir that were "born upon Joseph's
knees" represent the balance and poise that must actively exist in us if we are abidingly to possess true
understanding. The Joseph characteristics gradually
become a part of the whole body consciousness.

The insistence by all these patriarchs that their
bones be taken to Canaan for burial is emblematic of
the truth that the substance of them and what they
represent is to be restored to its source, Spirit. Although
Joseph died and was embalmed and put in a coffin in
Egypt, his bones were finally brought to Canaan, as
stated in the last chapter of the Book of Joshua.

Question Helps

For Students of

Mysteries of Genesis

Chapter I

Spiritual Man

1. Give the metaphysical interpretation of the name *Genesis*.
2. What is the one and only logical key to the beginning of man and the universe?
3. Why has the Bible been preserved and prized beyond all other books?
4. Explain the threefold character and purpose of the Bible.
5. With what three phases of man's development do the Bible allegories deal?
6. What is the key to an interpretation of these allegories?
7. Explain the real purpose of these allegories.
8. What is a "day," as the term is used in Genesis 1?
9. How are numbers or figures used in allegories?
10. What is the "heaven" mentioned in the first creation? The "earth"?
11. Describe the nature and character of the first man God created.
12. Explain God as Divine Mind.
13. How does Divine Mind create?
14. What is the first step in the awakening of man to spiritual consciousness?
15. Did God create man and the earth as they appear today?
16. What is meant by "The Spirit of God moved upon the face of the waters"?
17. What, in terms of mind, is "darkness"? "Light"?
18. What is the central idea in the second day's creation?
19. Why is the word *heaven* capitalized in Genesis 1:8?
20. What is the third step in the creative process?
21. Does Divine Mind deal directly with things or ideas? Explain.
22. How does man form his world?

23. Explain the symbology of the development of the "two great lights."
24. What qualities were developed on the fifth day?
25. What kind of ideas are "creatures" and "sea-monsters"? Compare them with fishes and fowls.
26. What is the sixth step in the creative process of which man is the grand culmination?
27. Explain the cause of which sensation is the result.
28. In what sense is man the "image" of God?
29. When is man the master of ideas and their expression?
30. In what attitude of mind can man truly call his creation "very good?"

Chapter II

Manifest Man

1. What is your conception of Elohim God?
2. Explain the relationship between Jehovah God and Elohim God.
3. What is meant by "I in them, and thou in me, that they may be perfected into one"?
4. What is the true body of Christ?
5. How is the temple or body of Spirit formed?
6. How do we "keep" the Sabbath?
7. Explain something of the Jesus Christ man.
8. Is there a difference between "creating" and "forming"? If so, what is it?
9. How was the breath of life "breathed into" man's nostrils?
10. Was the giving of life a single, complete act, or is it a continuous process?
11. Metaphysically what does the Garden of Eden represent?
12. Symbolically what does "eastward" mean?
13. What is the "tree of life . . . in the midst of the garden"?

14. What is the "tree of the knowledge of good and evil"?
15. Give the metaphysical interpretation of "river."
16. Give the source and course of the river Pishon.
17. The river Pishon is described as encompassing "the whole land of Havilah." Explain.
18. What is the office of the river Gihon?
19. The river Gihon "compasseth the whole land of Cush." Explain.
20. What is the function of the river Hiddekel in man's being?
21. The river Hiddekel "goeth in front of Assyria." Explain.
22. Explain how the Euphrates keeps the garden fruitful.
23. Explain the relationship between the Garden of Eden and the human body.
24. How may one "dress" and "keep" the Garden of Eden?
25. In what way does man "eat" of the substance of ideas?
26. How was materiality as the obverse of spirituality set up?
27. How are soul and body the "help meet" of man?
28. How does man "name" "every living creature"?
29. How does man attain consciousness in mind and body?

Chapter III

The Fall of Man

1. From what estate and into what condition did man fall?
2. Does time or states of mind bring about events?
3. Give the symbology of the man and woman and the serpent in the Garden of Eden.
4. What three fundamental factors are the basis of all manifestation?
5. What does the serpent represent?
6. What is the result if man fails to exercise mastery and dominion over the forces of his being?

7. What is the remedy for this condition?

8. Is it necessary for man to experience "evil" in order to understand life and appreciate the good?

9. Metaphysically what does woman symbolize?

10. What is represented by the "nakedness" of Adam?

11. Jehovah spoke to Adam and Eve in the garden "in the cool of the day." What does this mean?

12. How is the "holy marriage" consummated, and what are its fruits?

13. When and how may sensation be pronounced "good"?

14. Explain the meaning of Jehovah God's curse on the serpent.

15. What do the "seed" of the woman and the "seed" of the serpent represent?

16. What is the "promise" of redemption? How is it fulfilled?

17. In what sense is Eve the "mother of all living"?

18. What is the "coat of skins," and by what is it supplanted?

19. Explain "good and evil" as opposite poles of being.

20. How does man unite with the inner word or sacred life?

21. What in consciousness is represented by Abel? By Cain?

22. How do we offer up sacrifices?

23. What action is indicated by Cain's slaying of Abel?

24. How may every man be said to be his brother's keeper?

25. What action is represented by Cain's going out from the presence of Jehovah and dwelling in the land of Nod?

26. What does the birth of Seth denote?

27. What state of consciousness is represented by Enosh?

28. When does man begin to "call upon Jehovah?"

29. What was the original state of Adam? How did he "fall" from this estate?

30. How does man form an Adamic consciousness?

31. Give the method used to lift up the Adam man.

Chapter IV

The Reaction to Sense Living

1. Explain the reaction called "chemicalization."
2. In what mental attitude should one receive the new ideas of Spirit?
3. What is the real cause of trials and reverses in the life of the individual?
4. Is there any good to be found in such conditions? If so, what is it?
5. How do the "sons of God" wed the "daughters of men," and what is the fruit of such a union?
6. What is the reaction to living in sense consciousness?
7. What is represented by Lamech and by Noah, and what is their metaphysical relationship?
8. What are the causes and results of crosscurrents in the body consciousness?
9. How is a balance maintained between the positive and negative conditions in the body? ·
10. Discuss experimentation versus spiritual revelation.
11. What and where in consciousness is the "ark" of Jehovah?
12. What is the significance of the dimensions of the ark?
13. What are the animals, why "two of every sort," and how are they fed?
14. Discuss the symbolism of Noah and the Flood in relation to the unfoldment of a certain faculty of being.
15. What do "day" and "night" and the number 40 in the 7th chapter represent?
16. What is the general theme of Genesis 8:1-3?
17. What does Mount Ararat symbolize?
18. Noah first sent out the raven, then the dove, in search of dry land. Explain.
19. What is the metaphysical significance of the altar as used by Noah in Genesis 8:20? What and how do we sacrifice?

20. Of what does "the flood" cleanse man?
21. Explain the statement "Flesh with the life thereof, *which is* the blood thereof, shall ye not eat."
22. Once the consciousness has been cleansed and man has awakened to his spiritual nature how is he saved?
23. Of what is the rainbow a symbol?
24. What do the three sons of Noah represent?
25. What does the drunkenness of Noah symbolize?
26. What state is denoted by the nakedness of Noah?
27. What is meant by the "curse of Canaan"?
28. How do we get the most from physical man?
29. To what is the 10th chapter of Genesis devoted?
30. What does the building of the tower of Babel and the scattering of its people symbolize?

Chapter V

The Initial Step toward Redemption

1. What do we mean by going into a new "country"? What is the first step in this process?
2. Why is the call of Abraham significant for us today?
3. Why is Abraham taken as a symbol of faith?
4. What is meant by a plane of consciousness?
5. Describe three planes of consciousness.
6. By what was Abraham characterized before he was "called," and how did he resemble the individual today?
7. What place does the state of consciousness represented by Terah occupy in man's unfoldment?
8. How does the Lord "call" the various faculties into activity?
9. What is the result of this "call"?
10. What quality does Lot represent?
11. What does Canaan symbolize?
12. What is the inner meaning of Abraham's journey down into Egypt?
13. What causes the plagues of bodily disorder and death?

14. Explain the relationship of Abraham and Lot metaphysically.
15. Symbolically what relationship does Beth-el bear to Ai?
16. Of what is the return from Egypt representative?
17. Why must we separate Lot from Abraham in our consciousness?
18. In what way does the inner meaning of the name *Canaan* suggest the immortality of the body?
19. Explain the statement "Lot chose him all the Plain of the Jordan"?
20. Is it necessary to change one's residence in order to enter a new country? To what does the "land which thou seest" refer?
21. What is signified by Lot's captivity?
22. When may Lot and his possessions be said to be carried away by Chedorlaomer and the other kings?
23. Abraham and his confederates rescued Lot. Explain.
24. What is the error belief that man must put aside before he can overcome sensuality?
25. How do we sow "according to belief in the flesh" or "according to Spirit?" What is the harvest in each case?
26. What is the result when the Christ consciousness rules in both mind and body?
27. What is the lesson taught by Abraham's refusal to accept the gifts of the king of Sodom?
28. How may we fully realize our sonship?
29. Does God ever grant man a degree of immunity from the effects of his transgression of the divine law?

Chapter VI

The Promise of Salvation

1. For whom is the promise of salvation?
2. What avenues does Spirit use in imparting real understanding?
3. When and how do we attain the kingdom of the heavens?

4. Why is the history of Abraham and his experiences significant for us?

5. What is symbolized by the nomadic life of Abraham's time?

6. What is the deeper import of God's promise of a son to Abraham?

7. How is Christ, the Son, formed in the individual?

8. How is the seemingly barren soul (Sarah) made to bring forth fruit?

9. What is the one sure method of protection?

10. What causes delay in the manifestation of desire?

11. How may one bring about fulfillment of one's faith?

12. What is man's greatest desire?

13. Why do God's promises sometimes seem vague to us?

14. In what way can we co-operate with God in bringing about their fulfillment?

15. Why is the power of the will important in the management of one's body?

16. Give a brief interpretation of Abraham's vision when he fell into "a deep sleep."

17. What does Hagar represent in man?

18. What is the significance of the contention between Sarah and Hagar?

19. Why was Ishmael not recognized by Jehovah as an heir of the promise?

20. What does Beer-lahai-roi represent?

21. Explain God as El Shaddai.

22. What new name is given to one who overcomes sense consciousness; that is, what name is on your "white stone"?

23. Does the second appearance of Jehovah to Abraham have any spiritual import for us? The third appearance?

24. What does the Promised Land symbolize?

25. Metaphysically explain circumcision. Toward what is it the first step?

26. What does Sarah represent?
27. Does God hear the outer man of flesh as well as the inner man of Spirit? Explain.
28. In what way is our religion based on practical principles?
29. When did God's triune nature become known to Abraham?
30. How is a new state of consciousness produced?
31. Why does the Abraham of our consciousness plead for Sodom and Gomorrah?
32. What do the incidents, men, and places in Abraham's life represent?

Chapter VII

The Fruits of Faith

1. Why did Jehovah appear to Lot as two angels instead of three, as He had appeared to Abraham?
2. Lot escaped to the little city of Zoar. What does this mean?
3. Metaphysically how do you account for the destruction of Sodom and Gomorrah?
4. Is anything ever really destroyed? What is the change that takes place in it?
5. What states of consciousness are represented by Moab and Ben-ammi?
6. How is faith developed in the spiritually awakening individual?
7. When faith makes union with the unregenerate will what is the result?
8. How is one to avoid plagues during the process of transmutation?
9. Why was the birth of Isaac delayed so long?
10. How is Christ "formed" in the individual?
11. In what way are joy and laughter helpful in soul unfoldment?

12. How is the conviction established of the presence of divine substance within?

13. In what way are Ishmael and Isaac opposed to each other?

14. How are these two phases of mind harmonized?

15. What is the result of disregard of divine law?

16. What is denoted by the banishment of Hagar and her son?

17. Explain the relationship between faith and will as illustrated by Abraham and Abimelech.

18. Abimelech's servants had taken Abraham's well by force. How does this apply metaphysically to soul unfoldment?

19. Must there eventually be agreement in consciousness between the spiritual and the so-called material?

20. What do we really lose and what do we gain when we give up sense pleasures?

21. What in consciousness is represented by the "land of Moriah," and how may it be productive of good?

22. What is the fruit of faith and obedience to divine law?

23. What or who is the real source of prosperity?

24. What state of mind results in a demonstration of prosperity?

25. What characterizes the soul of man on its feminine side?

26. What attitude of mind is productive of a new line of thought?

Chapter VIII

The Mental Supplants the Physical

1. Do the higher activities of the soul ever die?

2. What is denoted by Sarah's death at Kiriath-arba?

3. What do we mean by saying that our spiritual ideals are "buried" in the cave of Macpelah?

4. What is the reaction of the human mind to the letting go of states of consciousness that have fulfilled their usefulness?

5. What attitude of mind is helpful in overcoming this tendency?

6. Is is wise to insist on giving value received for everything?

7. Explain the symbology of putting the hand "under my thigh" and swearing.

8. Spiritually interpreted, why did Abraham want Isaac to marry a daughter of his own people?

9. Is a declaration of Truth always demonstrated? What quality of mind serves as a complement to this demonstration?

10. Is there any inner significance in the state of consciousness represented by Mesopotamia?

11. What soul phase does Rebekah symbolize?

12. What is represented by Rebekah's journey to the house of Abraham and her union with Isaac?

13. "Let thy seed possess the gate of those that hate them." Explain.

14. Explain the Scripture "And Isaac went out to meditate . . . and he lifted up his eyes, and saw . . . And Rebekah lifted up her eyes . . . and he loved her."

15. Why did Isaac take precedence over the sons of Abraham's concubines?

16. How does the individual lay the foundation for the manifestation of life throughout mind, soul, and body?

17. What phases of life are symbolized by Jacob and Esau?

18. Was the union of mind and body perfectly expressed in Jacob and Esau?

19. Is age a just claim to superiority?

20. Why did Isaac love Esau more than he loved Jacob?

21. Why did Rebekah love Jacob more than she loved Esau?

22. What is the order of development in the natural world?

23. How does the intellect gain precedence over the body?
24. What is represented by the mess of "pottage"?
25. What is meant by the birthright that Esau bartered away?
26. Why did Jacob take advantage of Esau?
27. How does man become a citizen of the inner kingdom?
28. What is the result when personal will rules? How is such a condition corrected?
29. In what way do the "Philistines" of one's consciousness strive for Abraham's "wells"?
30. Must one be willing to give up the lower for the higher? Explain.
31. What is the predominant impulse of the will as represented by Abimelech?
32. What does the opening up of the seven wells symbolize?
33. Why is it necessary to regard Scripture as the history of soul unfoldment?
34. Why must spiritual understanding determine whether we should follow our dreams and visions or not?
35. Does the physical body have equal rights with the intellect to the benefits of Spirit?
36. Against whom or what were the denunciations of the prophets directed?
37. Can Jacob be said to represent the spiritual man? Explain.
38. What is signified, in the realm of individual unfoldment, by Isaac's blessing upon Jacob?
39. Explain metaphysically the meaning of Esau's threat against the life of Jacob.
40. Compare the results of Jacob's marriage to Rebekah and of Esau's union with the daughter of Ishmael.
41. What does Jacob's experience at Beth-el denote?
42. Explain God as omnipresence.
43. How can common things and the hardness of one's experience be made to bless?
44. Explain God as the all-providing One.
45. How does one begin the ascent from self to selflessness?

Chapter IX

Man Develops Spiritual Faculties

1. Metaphysically what does Jacob's journeying toward the east represent? How do we "put the stone again upon the well's mouth"?

2. What effect does unselfish love have on soul unfoldment?

3. What relationship among certain phases of the soul is symbolized by Jacob's love for Rachel and Leah?

4. What is the first faculty brought forth in man's spiritual development?

5. What must be our attitude of mind before our good can come to us?

6. What office does the love faculty perform?

7. Why do we regard praise as an "increasing" faculty?

8. Explain the relationship between Rachel and Bilhah. What is the fruit of receptivity?

9. What plane of mental evolution is especially portrayed by Jacob's sons?

10. On what planes do the faculties of man evolve? How is the divine man developed?

11. How does man attain power over his thoughts and ideas?

12. Explain the difference between knowledge and wisdom.

13. To what faculty is zeal most closely related?

14. What phases of soul do Leah and Rachel represent?

15. Why is it profitable to cultivate the faculty of order?

16. Is the state of consciousness represented by Haran one to be desired? If so, why?

17. To what quality do we attribute Jacob's rapid increase in possessions? How can we use this quality in our own unfoldment?

18. Under what circumstances does the law of equilibrium adjust all conditions?

19. In what way was Jacob superior to others of the same stock, and what effect did this superiority have on his associates?

20. Jehovah appeared to Jacob in a dream and told him to leave Haran. What does this reveal when considered in relation to spiritual growth?

21. Explain the statement "I am the God of Beth-el, where thou anointedst a pillar, where thou vowedst a vow unto me."

22. When permitted, what effect does Spirit have on one's power of judgment?

23. Is there a higher source of supply than that symbolized by the teraphim? Explain.

24. What is the true bread of life?

25. Give the meaning of the name *Mizpah* and its metaphysical interpretation.

26. What does the name *Galeed* mean, and what does it signify?

Chapter X

The Spiritual Gains Precedence of the Mental

1. What was the "host" after which Jacob named the place called Mahanaim?

2. Does the river Jordan perform an important work in consciousness?

3. Explain something of the equalizing process that takes place between soul and body. Why is such a process necessary?

4. What is symbolized by Jacob's fear of meeting Esau?

5. What is the "strong man" with which the intellect must struggle for control of the body?

6. Through what physical avenue does the mind control the body?

7. Explain the reaction that is indicated by Jacob's thigh being out of joint.

8. Why was Jacob's name changed to Israel?
9. Under what circumstances is the intellect willing to make amends to the body?
10. How can one change the body? Explain.
11. Explain the statement "I have seen God face to face."
12. In what order does the mind project its thoughts toward the body?
13. Why must man give his body place as a, divine creation?
14. What benefit does man derive when mind and body work in unison? What are the children of the mind?
15. Why must the mind penetrate into body consciousness?
16. What do booths or tents represent as compared with permanent houses? When will the abiding spiritual body come into manifestation?
17. Explain the effect of the power of love on the overcoming of self.
18. Is the "battle" of Jehovah a war? Does the Lord fight ignorance or evil?
19. When the "mind of the flesh" is given up what replaces it?
20. Is the intuition of the natural man a true guide to spirituality? Why?
21. What is the purpose of the illumined intellect's penetrating into materiality?
22. What is the result when intuitional natural judgment is united with sense?
23. How can the individual erase thoughts of revenge from his consciousness? What state of mind supersedes it?
24. God commanded Jacob to arise and go unto Beth-el. What does this mean?
25. Why did Jacob change the name of Beth-el to El-beth-el?
26. What does the death of Deborah represent?
27. What state of consciousness does Ephrath symbolize?
28. Explain metaphysically the death of Rachel and the birth of Benjamin.
29. What soul activity is indicated by Jacob's spreading his tent "beyond . . . Eder"?
30. What does Reuben's union with Bilhah denote?

Chapter XI

Joseph a Type of the Christ

1. Explain the part imagination plays in manifestation.
2. Compare Joseph's coat with the seamless garment of Jesus.
3. Where is the home of the imagination?
4. Should one take one's dreams literally? Explain.
5. What may result from uncontrolled activity of the imagination? How is control obtained?
6. Why did Jacob send Joseph down into Shechem?
7. What is represented by Gilead? By the Ishmaelites? By the Midianites?
8. What is symbolized by Joseph's being sold as a slave down in Egypt by his brothers?
9. How can such a situation be made to bless one?
10. What is the secret of Joseph's success even in slavery?
11. Can the imagination ever be wholly overcome by error if one is faithful to high ideals?
12. What is the status of the imagination on the intellectual plane?
13. Has modern civilization profited by the imagination?
14. What is the significance of the dipping of Joseph's coat in blood?
15. Why is an attitude of praise helpful?
16. Through what part of the physical organism is praise expressed?
17. Explain some of the phases through which man passes on his journey from sense to Spirit.
18. How does one come into the estate of the Jesus Christ man?
19. What pattern does the imagination follow in forming substance?
20. What is the first duty of the imagination?
21. Why is it so important to realize and be always conscious of the unity of spirit, soul, and body?

22. What is the true nature and function of the solar plexus?
23. How does Joseph's experience and conduct reveal a sure way to success?
24. Explain the statement "Joseph was comely, and well favored."
25. What is the symbology of Joseph's imprisonment?
26. What is the fruit of faithfulness?
27. What subconscious activities are represented by the chief baker and chief butler?
28. Explain the influence imagination has upon life and substance.
29. Why is Truth revealed in dreams and visions?
30. How does one "unclothe" dreams of their forms?
31. What lies back of the forms in visions and dreams?
32. What is one sure proof that one is receptive to Spirit?
33. Explain what "things" are.
34. Why must will and understanding be dominant factors in soul development?
35. In what way was Asenath a complement to Joseph?
36. Why is Manasseh said to represent the faculty of understanding?
37. Why is Ephraim said to represent the will?
38. Describe the benefits derived from the use of denial and affirmation.
39. When does the spiritually awakening man experience an increase of physical vitality?
40. Explain the seven fat and seven lean years in terms of the increase and decrease in physical vitality.
41. How can the life energy be conserved?

Chapter XII

The I AM and Its Faculties in the Body

1. How does one effect a reunion of mind and body with the faculties?
2. Where does one find the substance required to sustain the whole man?

3. Explain substance as symbolized by Canaan and Egypt.
4. How does the mind form soul and body?
5. What causes "famine" in the body consciousness?
6. Why is the way of the transgressor hard?
7. What is meant by the Israelites being the chosen of God?
8. Why did the Israelites prosper in Egyptian slavery?
9. What is symbolized by Joseph's concern as to whether his father still lived?
10. Joseph could not save his people unless Benjamin was brought down into Egypt. Explain.
11. What other faculty is a necessary adjunct to the imagination?
12. Explain the command "Give, and it shall be given unto you."
13. Why are the other faculties treated as "spies"?
14. What does Jacob's grieving at the loss of his sons represent?
15. Explain the statement "If harm befall him . . . then will ye bring down my gray hairs with sorrow to Sheol."
16. What is the key that opens the door to the storehouse of substance?
17. What is meant by "The blessing of Jehovah, it maketh rich"?
18. Should Joseph's reunion with Benjamin be regarded as purely historical? Explain.
19. What significance do we attribute to the movements of mind described in Genesis 43:16-34?
20. What is the significance of Joseph's having his cup put into Benjamin's sack?
21. What is true repentance, and what follows it?
22. Do all things work together for good to them that love God? Explain.
23. Joseph's people dwelt in the land of Goshen. What does this mean?
24. What change must take place before we can truly unify ourselves with Truth?

25. Pharaoh joyfully welcomed Joseph's kindred. Interpret.
26. What activity is represented by Jacob's journey to Beer-sheba?
27. What is symbolized by the wives, children, goods, and flocks of the Israelites, and by their descending in a body into Egypt?

Chapter XIII

The Blessing of the Faculties

1. Explain some of the duties of our mind faculties toward our vital forces.
2. How are these duties fulfilled?
3. Why is Jacob's blessing on Pharaoh significant?
4. How does the Joseph of our consciousness nourish the other faculties?
5. What is the next step after the developing soul has exhausted its resources?
6. What is the routine followed when man taps the inner reservoir of stored-up substance?
7. What is the central thought in Genesis 47:27-31?
8. Metaphysically interpreted, what does Jacob's desire at this time represent?
9. Explain the statement "And Israel bowed himself upon the bed's head."
10. Describe the yes and no powers of the mind.
11. What is implied by Jacob's action in claiming Joseph's two sons as his own?
12. Why are denial and affirmation so important in our choice of thoughts to entertain?
13. Explain the transition of love from a lower to a higher plane.
14. In what way are understanding and will useful when weakness appears?

15. Under divine law what is the order of development of understanding and will?

16. What is the order of development under natural law? Explain.

17. Unless man accepts divine guidance in unfolding his faculties what is the result?

18. How does understanding as represented by Manasseh come into its rightful heritage?

19. What is the final blessing of the I AM upon the imagination?

20. In what way does the Lord reward a person for exercising his faculties to the best of his ability?

21. What does a blessing signify?

22. Does the blessing by Jacob of his twelve sons have any significance for our own unfoldment?

23. Why did Jacob give his highest blessing to Judah?

24. How can we retain our identity as children of God?

25. Through what means does one put one's latent spiritual powers into action?

26. Does loss occur to the individual when his thought forces are said to "die"?

27. What causes man to grieve at giving up his personal hold on old ideas and objects?

28. Explain how one sifts ideas and thoughts.

29. In what way is the descent of imagination into the subconscious helpful to the illumined ego? Is the physical man also blessed?

30. Explain the promise "Fear ye not: I will nourish you, and your little ones."

31. What is meant by Joseph's seeing Ephraim's children of the third generation?

32. What does the removal of the patriarch's bones from Egypt to Canaan represent?

INDEX

INDEX

About the Author

Charles Fillmore was an innovative thinker, a pioneer in metaphysical thought at a time when most religious thought in America was entirely orthodox. He was a lifelong advocate of the open, inquiring mind, and he took pride in keeping abreast of the latest scientific and educational discoveries and theories. Many years ago he wrote, "What you think today may not be the measure for your thought tomorrow"; and it seems likely that were he to compile this book today, he might use different metaphors, different scientific references, and so on.

Truth is changeless. Those who knew Charles Fillmore best believe that he would like to be able to rephrase some of his observations for today's readers, thus giving them the added effectiveness of contemporary thought. But the ideas themselves—the core of Charles Fillmore's writings—are as timeless now (and will be tomorrow) as when they were first published.

Charles Fillmore was born on an Indian reservation just outside the town of St. Cloud, Minnesota, on August 22, 1854. He made his transition on July 5, 1948, at Unity Village, Missouri, at the age of 93. To get a sense of history, when Charles was eleven, Abraham Lincoln was assassinated; when Charles died, Harry Truman was President.

With his wife Myrtle, Charles Fillmore founded the Unity movement and Silent Unity, the international prayer ministry that publishes *Daily Word*. Charles and Myrtle built the worldwide organization that continues their work today, Unity School of Christianity. Through

Unity School's ministries of prayer, education, and publishing, millions of people around the world are finding the teachings of Truth discovered and practiced by Charles and Myrtle Fillmore.

Charles Fillmore was a spiritual pioneer whose impact has yet to be assessed. No lesser leaders than Dr. Norman Vincent Peale and Dr. Emmet Fox were profoundly influenced by him. Dr. Peale borrowed his catchphrase of *positive thinking* from Charles Fillmore. Emmet Fox was so affected by Fillmore's ideas that he changed his profession. From an engineer, he became the well-known writer and speaker.

Charles Fillmore—author, teacher, metaphysician, practical mystic, husband, father, spiritual leader, visionary—has left a legacy that continues to impact the lives of millions of people. By his fruits, he is continuously known.